BASIC FOR THE APPLE II®

JERALD R. BROWN
LEROY FINKEL
ROBERT L. ALBRECHT

Dymax Corporation
Menlo Park, California

John Wiley & Sons, Inc.
New York • Chichester • Brisbane • Toronto • Singapore

Publisher: Judy V. Wilson
Editor: Dianne Littwin
Composition & Make-up: Cobb/Dunlop, Inc.

Revised and adapted by Jerald R. Brown for Applesoft BASIC from BASIC FOR HOME COMPUTERS by Albrecht, Finkel, and Brown, at Rainbow's End Farm, Sebastopol, California, and at Mr. F. Giovanni Smith's Nibble and Co., and Corol and George Bevier's Rum Point Inn, in Belize, Central America. Programs were checked by Paul Armitige.

Copyright © 1982, by John Wiley & Sons, Inc.

All rights reserved. Published simultaneously in Canada.

Reproduction or translation of any part of this work beyond that permitted by Section 107 or 108 of the 1976 United States Copyright Act without the permission of the copyright owner is unlawful. Requests for permission or further information should be addressed to the Permissions Department, John Wiley & Sons, Inc.

Library of Congress Cataloging in Publication Data

Brown, Jerald, 1940-
   BASIC for the APPLE II.

   (Wiley self-teaching guide)
   Includes index.
   1. Apple II (Computer)—Programming.   2. Basic (Computer program language)   I. Finkel, Leroy.   II. Albrecht, Bob, 1930-   III. Title.
QA76.8.A662B76 1982   001.64'2   82-10962
ISBN 0-471-86596-6

Printed in the United States of America

83 84 10 9 8 7 6 5 4 3

Contents

	To the Reader	iv
	How to Use This Book	v
Chapter 1	Introduction	1
Chapter 2	Getting Started	9
Chapter 3	Assignment Statements, Stored Programs, and Branching	41
Chapter 4	Decisions Using IF-THEN Statements	97
Chapter 5	READ and DATA Work Together	141
Chapter 6	FOR-NEXT Loops	183
Chapter 7	Low-Resolution Graphics	213
Chapter 8	String Variables and String Functions	239
Chapter 9	Subscripted Variables	265
Chapter 10	Double Subscripts	309
Chapter 11	Subroutines	357
	Final Self-Test	383
	BASIC Functions	397
Appendix	ASCII Character Codes	401
	Personal Computing Periodicals	403
	Program Index	405
	Index	407

To the Reader

With the advent of integrated circuits and miniaturization in electronics, suddenly a complete computer, with all the peripherals or attachments needed to use it, can be purchased for as little as $600. Now a computer for your business, home, club, or school is in the same price range as the less expensive stereo component systems! Many of these inexpensive computers, including the Apple®,* use the computer language BASIC.

BASIC was developed at Dartmouth College by John Kemeny and Thomas Kurtz, who recognized the need for an all-purpose computer lanuage that would be suitable for beginning programmers whose educational backgrounds would be varied and diverse. Beginners All-purpose Symbolic Instruction Code (BASIC) was originally designed as a simple language which could be learned in a few short hours. With improvements over the years, the language now may take a few days to learn, but you will find that you can do nearly anything you want in BASIC.

The BASIC you learn in this book will apply to any computer that "understands" a similar version of BASIC. To show you how to converse with a computer using BASIC programs, we have used the particular version of BASIC called Applesoft®* BASIC, developed by the Microsoft Corporation for the Apple computer. (Interestingly, some of the most advanced and versatile versons of BASIC are those developed by various manufacturers of personal computers.) Most versions of BASIC are similar, the more so because Microsoft has been developing similar forms of BASIC for many recent computer models.

Apple computers have been supplied with two versions of BASIC: Integer BASIC, and Applesoft (also called Floating Point) BASIC. This book teaches Applesoft BASIC, the more versatile and advanced version of the two. In particular, the example programs and activities were developed, adapted, and tested on an Apple II Plus, with 48K of memory and one disk drive. However, the minimum system with Applesoft BASIC, 16K and no disk drive or cassette tape machine, is quite sufficient for the programs and activities in this Self-Teaching Guide.

If you have an Apple computer, be certain that Applesoft BASIC is available to use, so that the computer will understand the instructions you will be learning to give it in Applesoft BASIC.

---

*Apple® and Applesoft® are registered trademarks of Apple Computer, Inc.

How to Use This Book

Instructors will find this book to be excellent for courses in BASIC programming at the high school and college levels, as well as for computer center classes, university extension workshops, and in-house instructional settings.

With this book's self-instructional format, you'll be actively involved in learning BASIC. The material is presented in short numbered sections called frames, each of which teaches you something new about BASIC and gives you a question or asks you to write a program. Correct answers are given following the dashed line. For the most effective learning we urge you to use a thick paper to keep the answers out of sight until you have written your answer.

You will learn best if you take pen or pencil in hand and actually write out the answers or programs. The questions are carefully designed to call your attention to important points in the examples and explanations, and to help you learn to apply what is being explained or demonstrated.

Each chapter begins with a list of objectives—what you will be able to do after completing that chapter. If you have had some previous experience using BASIC and the objectives for that chapter look familiar, take the Self-Test at the end of that chapter first to see where you should start your close reading of the book. If you do well, study only the frames indicated for the questions you missed. If you miss many questions, start work at the beginning of that chapter.

The Self-Test can also be used as a review of the material covered in the chapter. You may test yourself immediately after reading the chapter. Or you may wish to read a chapter, take a break, and save the Self-Test as a review before you begin the next chapter. At the end of the book is a Final Self-Test which will allow you to test your overall understanding of BASIC.

This is a self-contained book for learning the computer language called BASIC. You do not need access to a computer to learn BASIC. However, what you learn will be theoretical until you actually sit down at a computer and apply your knowledge of the computer language and programming techniques. So we strongly recommend that you and this book get together with a computer. BASIC will be easier and clearer if you have even occasional access to a computer so that you can try the examples and exercises, make your own modifications, and invent your own programs for your own purposes. You are now ready to teach yourself how to use BASIC.

CHAPTER ONE

Introduction

This chapter will introduce you to some of the vocabulary you will encounter in the world of small computers, whether they are used in business, home, school, or club. You will *not* need access to a computer to complete this chapter. When you complete this chapter, you will know more about such computers. You will also be able to use the following words and phrases from the language of the computer world:

>   Computer language
>   BASIC and, specifically Applesoft™ BASIC
>   Keyboard
>   Printer
>   Disk drive
>   Video monitor or display screen
>   Program and programming
>   BASIC statements
>   Line numbers

1. We will start slowly and simply, easing you gently into the world of Apple computers and BASIC. Just keep in mind that this is intended to be a friendly book about personal computing and an easy-to-learn, easy-to-use computer language called BASIC. We will do our best to teach you how to read and understand computer programs written in BASIC and to help you get started writing original, never-before-seen-on-earth programs, *your* programs. The Apple computer uses a version of BASIC called Applesoft BASIC, which was produced by MICROSOFT, a company that has provided similar versions of BASIC for Radio Shack, IBM, recently for Atari, and versions of BASIC that can be implemented (used) on a wide variety of brands of computers. Apple is the brand name of a microcomputer manufactured by Apple Computer, Inc.

   For this book to be useful to you, only one thing is essential: your computer must speak Applesoft, a version of the computer language called _____ _____ .

_ _ _ _ _ _ _ _ _ _ _

BASIC

2. The personal computer we use speaks a version called Applesoft BASIC. Most BASICs used on personal computers are very similar to MICROSOFT BASIC. The differences that exist are minor; even though this book emphasizes Applesoft BASIC, you should find it useful no matter what particular BASIC you are using. (The reference manual for your version of BASIC will come in handy.)

Our Apple computer looks like the one shown below.

Photo: David Burns

Our Apple computer system consists of an Apple II PLUS computer connected to a television set. The Apple includes a built-in keyboard similar to an electric typewriter keyboard. We use the keyboard to type information into the computer. The "computer" itself is the electronics inside the Apple's case, in back of the keyboard. The computer, with its keyboard, video display screen, and any other attachments, including printer, disk drive, or cassette recorder, is referred to as a computer system. The attachments are often called peripherals, since the computer itself is the core or center of the system.

As we type characters, the information we type is sent to the computer and also is displayed on the screen, for our reference. Information originated by the computer is also displayed on the screen, whether the display is a video monitor or a standard television equipped with an adaptor for connection to the computer. Thus, the combination of keyboard and display screen provides (one-way or two-way—choose the correct answer)_____ communication with the computer.

— — — — — — — —

two-way

3. Below is a sketch of a computer system based around the Apple computer.

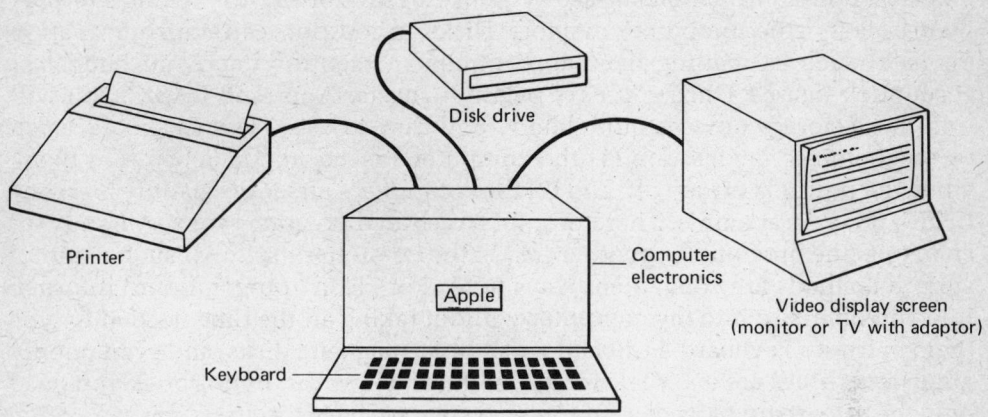

(a) We use the keyboard to type information into the computer. What happens to the information that we type?_____

(b) How does the computer communicate with us, the users?_____

— — — — — — — — —

(a) It is sent to the computer and is also displayed on the screen.
(b) It displays information on the video display screen (TV or monitor).

4. The cassette recorder and the more popular (and expensive) disk drive provide memory storage which is separate from the computer's own electronic memory. Both information storage systems can save or record programs or play them back into the computer's memory. Disks, in addition, can store information (or data) such as mailing lists, appointments, scientific data, and budget or accounting figures. Once you have begun to master Applesoft BASIC, you will find these storage devices quite handy and easy to use. Two reasons for such external storage devices are (1) the computer's electronic memory goes blank when the power is turned off; and (2) the computer's memory can only hold one BASIC program at a time. Therefore, such recorded programs are very handy for changing one program for another inside the computer itself. All such *external* storage methods are convenient ways to feed or "load" programs and information you often use into the computer without taking all the time needed to type them in from a keyboard. Punched paper tape, magnetic disks, and even phonograph recordings are external storage methods. However, in this book you need only the three main parts of a computer system we have discussed earlier, which

are _____

_____ .

a computer, a keyboard, and a display device (printer or video screen)

5. In this book, we will show you many *programs* in Applesoft BASIC, and will help you learn to read, understand, and use these programs for your own enjoyment. We will concentrate on applications that we think will be of interest to users of home/school/personal computers. And so . . . for our appetizer, a computer game.

This program may be "Greek" to you now, but by the time you finish Chapter 4, you will not only be able to read this program, but be able to write a program at least as complex as this one. For now, however, we just want to familiarize you with the *form* of a computer program and the names of its parts. An understanding of the actual instructions to the computer contained in the program will come later.

These lines, down to the word RUN, are a computer program.

```
100 REM *** THIS IS A SIMPLE COMPUTER GAME
110 LET X = INT(100*RND(1))+1
120 PRINT
130 PRINT "I'M THINKING OF A NUMBER FROM 1 TO 100."
140 PRINT "GUESS MY NUMBER!!!"
150 PRINT : INPUT "YOUR GUESS?"; G
160 IF G<X THEN PRINT "TRY A BIGGER NUMBER." : GOTO 150
170 IF G>X THEN PRINT "TRY A SMALLER NUMBER." : GOTO 150
180 IF G=X THEN PRINT "THAT'S IT!!! YOU GUESSED MY NUMBER." : GOTO 110

RUN
```

```
I'M THINKING OF A NUMBER FROM 1 TO 100.
GUESS MY NUMBER!!!

YOUR GUESS? 50
TRY A BIGGER NUMBER.

YOUR GUESS? 90
TRY A SMALLER NUMBER.

YOUR GUESS? 75
TRY A SMALLER NUMBER.

YOUR GUESS? 65
TRY A SMALLER NUMBER.

YOUR GUESS? 58
TRY A BIGGER NUMBER.

YOUR GUESS? 62
TRY A SMALLER NUMBER.

YOUR GUESS? 60
TRY A BIGGER NUMBER.

YOUR GUESS? 61
THAT'S IT!!! YOU GUESSED MY NUMBER.

I'M THINKING OF A NUMBER FROM 1 TO 100.
GUESS MY NUMBER!!!

YOUR GUESS?
```

And this is what the computer does that appears on the display screen.

The guesses are typed by the computer user.

This part, from the word RUN on down, is called the RUN of the program. Following the instructions in the program, the computer generates a random number from 1 to 100. The player types in guesses. After each guess, the computer types a clue to help the player make a better guess.

And so on. The game continues. Chances are that the computer will have a different number this time.

If this sounds confusing, read on! All will be revealed. And it won't be long before you can read and write programs like this in BASIC.

6 BASIC FOR THE APPLE II

Look again at the program shown in our computer game. The program consists of nine (9) *lines*, each containing one or more BASIC *statements*. Each line begins with a *line number*.

This is a line number.
130 PRINT "I'M THINKING OF A NUMBER FROM 1 TO 100."
This is a statement.

In our program, each numbered line contains one or more BASIC _____ _____ . The numbers 100 through 180 are called _____ _____ .

_____

statements; line numbers

6. The program in frame 5 was typed one line at a time on the keyboard. As we typed it, the program was stored in the computer and also displayed on the screen.
   On a video display, as we type the program, it will be stored in the computer and also will appear on the _____ .

_____

screen

Note: The Apple video screen displays 24 lines. So, if the screen is filled (all 24 lines used), new information typed in will cause old information to be "pushed off" the top of the screen, but *not* out of the computer's memory.

7. First, we typed in the entire program (lines 100 through 180). This process is called "entering the program." This stored the program in the computer's memory. Then we typed RUN. This tells the computer to RUN, or carry out, the program. Computer people also say "to *execute* the program." In other words, after storing the program, we then told the computer to follow the instructions (statements) of the program, or execute the program.
   If there is a program in the computer's memory, then typing RUN tells the computer to _____ .

_____

carry out or execute the instructions in the program

8. During the RUN, the computer obeyed the instructions (statements) in the program, as follows: First, the computer generated a random number from 1 to 100, inclusive (line 110). This number is an integer—a "whole" number with no fractional part.

```
110 LET X = INT(100*RND(1))+1
```

In the chapters to come, you will learn how this curious combination of letters, numbers, and symbols tells the computer to "think up" (generate) a random number.

Next, the computer typed instructions to the player (lines 120, 130, and 140).

```
120 PRINT
130 PRINT "I'M THINKING OF A NUMBER FROM 1 TO 100."
140 PRINT "GUESS MY NUMBER!!!"
```

Compare these statements with what the computer causes to be displayed immediately under the word RUN.

Then, the computer asked for a guess (line 150).

```
150 PRINT : INPUT "YOUR GUESS?"; G
```

After the player typed a guess, the computer compared the guess with its secret number and gave the player the appropriate response (lines 160, 170, and 180).

```
160 IF G<X THEN PRINT "TRY A BIGGER NUMBER." : GOTO 150
170 IF G>X THEN PRINT "TRY A SMALLER NUMBER." : GOTO 150
180 IF G=X THEN PRINT "THAT'S IT!!! YOU GUESSED MY NUMBER." : GOTO 110
```

If the player did *not* guess the computer's number, the computer went back to line 150 and asked for another guess. But if the lucky player *did* guess the secret number, the computer acknowledged the correct guess and went back to line 110 to "think" of another number.

```
100 REM *** THIS IS A SIMPLE COMPUTER GAME
```

Oh, yes, line 100 is a REM (REMark) statement. It doesn't tell the computer to *do* anything. It is simply included to tell something *about* the program to us humans who may read the program itself.

What do we type to instruct the computer to execute or carry out a program?

_____

— — — — — — — — —

RUN

Now, to see how much you've learned from this first chapter, try the Self-Test. Then on to Chapter 2, where you'll start to learn how to actually use the computer.

Self-Test

Try this Self-Test, so you can evaluate how much you have learned so far.

1. If your computer does not have a printer in addition to the keyboard for communicating with the computer, what other kind of display device would you expect it to have?_____
2. If another computer "speaks" a different BASIC than your computer does, would you expect your computer to "understand" the terminology taught in this book?_____
3. Since a computer doesn't have legs, what do we want a computer to do when we tell it to RUN?_____
4. What do we call the number that begins a statement in a program?
   _____

Answers to Self-Test

The frame numbers in parentheses refer to the frames in the chapter where the topic is discussed. You may wish to refer to these for quick review.

1. A video display (TV or monitor). (frames 2–4, 6)
2. Yes, because most versions of BASIC for personal computers are like the one we use, with only minor differences which will quickly become obvious. (frame 2)
3. Execute the program (follow the instructions we give it). (frames 5–9)
4. Line number. (frame 5)

CHAPTER TWO

Getting Started

To get you started in computer programming in BASIC, we will now introduce you to some of the statements used to instruct the computer, that is, to tell it what you want accomplished. In this chapter, you will use the *direct*, or immediate, mode of operation. Using direct mode, you tell the computer something to do, and it does it immediately. When you complete this chapter, you will be able to:

- Use direct statements to instruct the computer.
- Recognize error messages from the computer.
- Use the PRINT statement with quotation marks to print strings (messages).
- Correct typing errors or delete a statement with errors.
- Use direct statements to do arithmetic.
- Compute values of simple mathematical expressions using the symbols and rules of BASIC for arithmetic.
- Use the short form for PRINT statements—a question mark (? = PRINT).
- Recognize and convert floating-point or E notation to ordinary numbers.

1. Now we can begin "talking" to the computer. The computer is plugged in, the video display is connected to the computer and turned on, and the computer itself is turned on.

If a bracket like this] appears on the display screen, with the cursor (a little square of light) flashing next to the bracket, then your Apple is ready to serve you with the facilities of Applesoft BASIC.

The reference materials from Apple Computer, Inc. include the *BASIC Programming Reference Manual for Applesoft BASIC, The Applesoft Tutorial,* and the *DOS (Disk Operating System) Manual.* The *Tutorial* provides an introduction to using the Apple keyboard to good effect and may be helpful if you haven't been shown how to get your particular Apple system started. This is especially true if Applesoft BASIC doesn't appear automatically when you turn on the power switch. *The Applesoft Tutorial* tends to emphasize many features unique to the Apple at the expense of providing a thorough background in the fundamentals of BASIC programming. The *Self-Teaching Guide* you are reading provides a systematic approach to aquiring these fundamentals, oriented toward the beginner. Instead of presenting a lot of definitions and then expecting you to use a batch of these concepts together, we present one thing at a time and carefully build up your knowledge of programming by adding to previous concepts. Ideas are introduced one at a time, followed by examples of useful ways to combine them with other BASIC instructions. Both the *Tutorial* and *Reference Manual* provide supplementary and advanced information of value to those using and completing this *Self-Teaching Guide*.

We will start by assuming that we are using a keyboard and video display to communicate with the computer. Here is a diagram of the Apple keyboard.

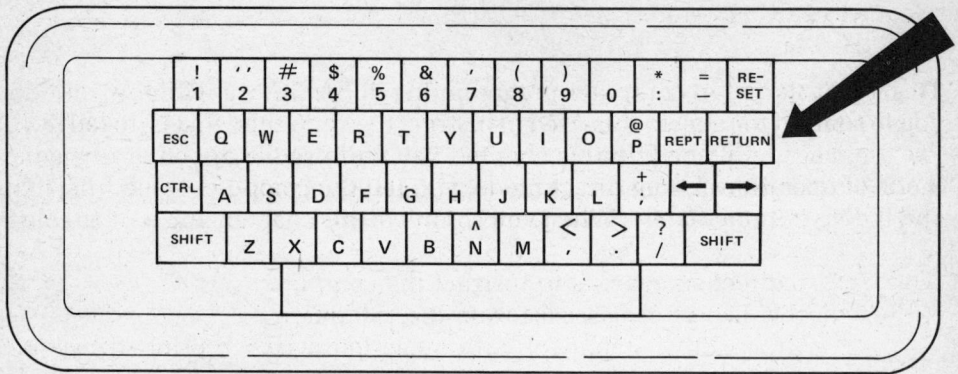

In the diagram, there is a large black arrow pointing to the key labeled _____.

_____

RETURN

2. If you press RETURN (without typing anything else), you will see the cursor (that little block of light) jump down one line on the display screen, and sit there flashing next to the bracket (]). On a printer, the paper will space up one line, performing what is called a *line feed*. If you have an Apple computer at hand, you could try this: Type your name and press RETURN. The computer will probably print an *error message* on the printer.

You type: BOB, LEROY, AND JERRY
It types: ?SYNTAX ERROR

By "it" we mean the computer. Saves space in writing this book!

Hmmmm . . . we know what ERROR means, but what about SYNTAX? You see, the computer is of quite limited intelligence. It simply did not understand us.

BASIC can be thought of as a very simple-minded foreign language, similar to English but with a very small, limited vocabulary. However, there are very exact and strict rules as to the arrangement, or format, or *syntax* of its "sentences," that is, the instructions we call program *statements*. So a SYNTAX ERROR may be an incorrectly spelled word that BASIC would normally understand, or the placing of a word or symbol in the wrong place, or the omission of some word or symbol necessary for BASIC to "understand" or interpret the statement or instruction. The SYNTAX ERROR message will alert you to typing errors, for one thing.

(a) If you type something, then press RETURN, and the computer types ?SYN-
TAX ERROR, what is the computer trying to tell you?_____

_____

(b) After typing ?SYNTAX ERROR, what did the computer type?_____

— — — — — — — — — —

(a) It does not understand you.
(b)] (the bracket indicating Applesoft BASIC is standing by for your next keyboard entry)

3. Despite the error message, no damage has been done. The computer is very patient and forgiving. It will let you make as many mistakes as you wish. Whenever you see] you know it is *your* turn to type.

To avoid misunderstandings with a computer, we must learn its language. We will start with some simple, one-line statements that the computer *does* understand.

In this chapter we will use direct statements. Direct statements do not have line numbers. When you type a direct statement and press RETURN, the computer executes the statement immediately, then forgets the statement. We call this BASIC's *direct* mode of operation. Here is an example of a statement that is "executed in direct mode."

You type: PRINT "MY HUMAN UNDERSTANDS ME"   Then press RETURN.
It types: MY HUMAN UNDERSTANDS ME
             ]

Now you complete the following. If you make a typing error, press RETURN and start again. Other ways of correcting errors will be shown shortly.

You type: PRINT "WAKE UP! BURGLARS ARE IN THE HOUSE."   Then press
                                                            RETURN.
It types: _____

— — — — — — — — — —

     WAKE UP! BURGLARS ARE IN THE HOUSE.
     ]

Along with the wake-up message, we could also arrange (as we'll see later) to have the computer sound a beep several times or to sound some other audible alarm (with appropriate electronic connections).

4. The statement PRINT "MY HUMAN UNDERSTANDS ME" is called a PRINT statement. It tells the computer to print something on the screen or on the printer if you are using a printer. In this case, the computer prints the verbal message following the word PRINT. Note that the message is enclosed in quotation marks. This message, enclosed in quotation marks, is called a *string*.

```
PRINT "MY HUMAN UNDERSTANDS ME"
```

This is a string. It is enclosed in quotation marks. The quotation marks enclose the string, but are not part of the string.

A *string* may include:

    Numerals (0, 1, 2, . . .)
    Letters (A, B, C, . . .)
    Special characters (+, −, *, /, comma, period, etc.)

Since quotation marks define the beginning and the end of a string, do you think they can be used as a character in the string? _____
_ _ _ _ _ _ _ _ _ _ _

No, they cannot. (That would *really* confuse the computer!) However, single quotes ('), also used as apostrophe, can be used in a string as a substitute for quotation marks. For example:

```
You type:  PRINT "THEY SAID, 'ALL RIGHT.' "
It types:  THEY SAID, 'ALL RIGHT.'
           ]
```

5. Complete the statement so that the computer types what we say it types.

```
You type:  PRINT_____
It types:  THE ROAST IS DONE.   TURN OFF THE OVEN.
           ]
```
_ _ _ _ _ _ _ _ _ _ _

    "THE ROAST IS DONE. TURN OFF THE OVEN."

Did you remember the quotation marks? Someday, of course, your computer could actually turn off the oven! Almost anything electric can be controlled by the computer, with the proper electronic connections *and* program, of course.

Note: From now on, we will often omit the] typed by the computer: Doing this saves space and paper and, especially, wear and tear on the authors.

6. Have you made any typing mistakes yet? In case you should make a typing error, BASIC has a dandy way of fixing it. Watch while we make a typing error.

You type: PTINT "DENTIST APPOINTMENT TODAY"
It types: ?SYNTAX ERROR

We misspelled PRINT, so the computer doesn't know what we want. However, if we had noticed that we hit T when we meant to hit R, we could have corrected our mistake by using the *left-arrow* key. This is how we indicate on paper one press of the left-arrow key: ←. On the display screen, the cursor actually "backs up" one space over the mistake.

You type: PT←RINT "DENTIST APPOINTMENT TODAY"
It types: DENTIST APPOINTMENT TODAY

With each press of the left-arrow key, the cursor moves one position to the left and erases or *deletes,* from the computer's memory, each character or space that it "backs up" over. The characters erased remain on the screen until you type new characters over them or until you press RETURN.

In the above example, the left arrow deleted the letter _____ .
Complete the following so that the computer prints what we want it to print.

You type: PRIMR _____ "TOMORROW IS YOUR MOTHER'S BIRTHDAY!!!"

It types: TOMORROW IS YOUR MOTHER'S BIRTHDAY!!!
_____

T
←←NT (The two left arrows delete the M and R, then we type N and T to complete the word PRINT.)

7. But suppose we make a mistake within a string? Watch.

You type: PRINT "MY HUMAN UNNERSTANS ME"
 It types: MY HUMAN UNNERSTANS ME

Well, a string is a string and the computer will type it *exactly* as you typed it, misspellings and all. However, if you notice a mistake, you can correct it by using the left arrow.

One press of the left-arrow key deletes (takes out or erases) one character. Two strikes of the left-arrow key delete the two preceding characters; three left arrows will delete three characters; and so on. Then you type the corrections right over the errors.

Note that you cannot use the left-arrow method to correct a mistake *after* you hit RETURN. You just have to type the statement again, being a little more careful. Later you may wish to use the Apple's special program-editing facilities to make corrections, but wait until the next chapter before that undertaking.

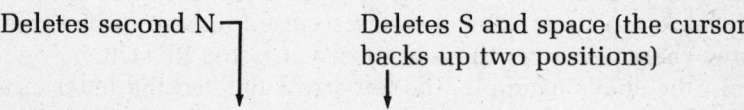

We type: PRINT "MY HUMAN UNN←DERSTANS ←←DS ME"
 It types: MY HUMAN UNDERSTANDS ME

Notice that the computer considers a space as a character, just like a number, letter, or symbol. Remember, to delete the last character typed, type a left arrow. To delete the last two characters, type two left arrows, and so on. To delete the last three characters, type _____ left arrows.

----

three

Remember, a space is a character. You can delete spaces by using the left-arrow key.

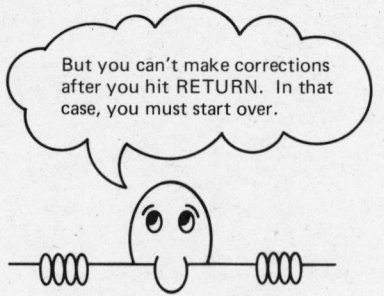

GETTING STARTED 15

8. Look at our next attempt to enter or type a one-line direct statement.

    PRINT "BASIK IS←←←←C IS EASY"

(a) What four characters are deleted in this direct statement?_____
(b) When we finished typing in the statement and pressed RETURN, what did the computer print?_____

— — — — — — — — — —

(a) K, space, I, S
(b) BASIC IS EASY

9. The left-arrow key is great for deleting errors that you have just made. But suppose you are typing a long line and are almost to the end when, alas, out of the left corner of your left eye, you spot a mistake way back at the beginning. If you complete the line and press RETURN, you will probably get an error message. You would *like* to just abort the line—that is, erase it from the beginning. Well, you can. Simply hold down the CTRL (stands for Control) key and then type X. This is called CTRL/X, and the technique is really more important when you start using line-numbered programs. We mention it here so that various correction techniques are grouped together.

   Example:

                                                                       We used CTRL/X.

You type: PRIMT "ONCE UPON A TIME THERE WAS A \
It types:]

When we perform the CTRL/X operation, the computer types a backslash at the end of the deleted or aborted line. Notice that it also responds with the Applesoft bracket instead of an error message, demonstrating that the computer did not try to execute the statement.

   Whenever you see the bracket] and the flashing cursor, what is the computer telling you?_____

— — — — — — — — — —

It is ok to type (the computer is waiting for a keyboard entry).

10. We can also tell the computer to do arithmetic and print the answer. In other words, we can use the computer as a calculator.

You type: PRINT 7 + 5
It types: 12

The statement PRINT 7 + 5 tells the computer to compute the value of 7 + 5 (do the arithmetic) and then print the answer.

Note that actual calculations are indicated to the computer by *not* using quotation marks in the PRINT statement. Compare the formats below.

You type: PRINT "13 + 6"   You type: PRINT 13 + 6
It types: 13 + 6   It types: 19

Your turn. Complete the following, showing what the computer typed.

You type: PRINT 23 + 45

It types: _____

You type: PRINT 1 + 2 + 3 + 4 + 5

It types: _____

You type: PRINT 6.98 + 12.49

It types: _____

— — — — — — — — — —

  .68
  15
  19.47

11. Subtraction? Of course.

You type: PRINT 7 − 5
It types: 2

You type: PRINT 25.68 − 37.95
It types: −12.27

Complete the following, showing what the computer typed.

You type: PRINT 29 − 13
  It types: _____

You type: PRINT 1500 − 2000
  It types: _____

You type: PRINT 5.678 − 1.234
  It types: _____

— — — — — — — — —

    16
  −500
    4.444

12. BASIC uses + for addition and − for subtraction, just as we do with paper and pencil. However, for multiplication, BASIC uses the asterisk (*).

You type: PRINT 7 * 5
It types: 35

You type: PRINT 1.23 * 4.567
It types: 5.61741

You type: PRINT 9 * 8
  It types: _____

You type: PRINT 3.14 * 20
  It types: _____

— — — — — — — — —

  72
  62.8

13. For division, use the slash (/).
You type: PRINT 7/5
  It types: 1.4

You type: PRINT 13/16
  It types: .8125

You type: PRINT 24/3
  It types: _____

You type: PRINT 3.14/4
  It types: _____

— — — — — — — — —

     8
   .785

14. Applesoft BASIC will display or print up to nine (9) digits plus a decimal point as the result of an arithmetic operation. If the true result would have more than nine digits, the printed result is rounded to nine digits.

You type: PRINT 1.234 * 5.678
  It types: 7.006652

You type: PRINT 1/3
  It types: .333333333 ◄─────── The complete answer cannot be given with a finite number of digits. It goes on forever as a repeating decimal.

You type: PRINT 2/3
  It types: .666666667 ◄─────── Rounded at the ninth digit

Calculating by hand, we found that 895.441 times 123.221 equals 110337.135461.

You type: PRINT 895.441 * 123.221
  It types: _____

— — — — — — —

    110337.135 (rounded in the ninth digit from 110337.135461)

15. Write PRINT statements to tell the computer to evaluate each of the following numerical expressions. Also show the result printed by the computer.

Numerical expression	PRINT statement and result
(a) 10 + 6	
(b) 15 − 8	
(c) 23 ÷ 5	
(d) 3 × 13	
(e) 7 ÷ 3	
(f) 120 ÷ 7	

(a) PRINT 10 + 6
    16

(b) PRINT 15 − 8
    7

(c) PRINT 23/5
    4.6

(d) PRINT 3*13
    39

(e) PRINT 7/3
    2.33333333 ◄──────── Rounded to nine significant digits

(f) PRINT 120/7
    17.1428571 ◄──────── Rounded to nine significant digits

16. The computer does arithmetic in *left-to-right* order, with all multiplications (*) and/or divisions (/) performed *before* additions (+) and/or subtractions (−).

$$\left.\begin{array}{c} * \\ / \end{array}\right\} \text{ before } \left\{\begin{array}{c} + \\ - \end{array}\right.$$

Following are some BASIC expressions in which two or more operations are used. For some of these expressions, we have shown the value computed by the computer after it does the indicated arithmetic. You complete the rest.

Expression	Value computed by computer	How it did the arithmetic
2*3−4	2	2*3−4 = 6 − 4 = 2
2+3*4	14	2+3*4 = 2 + 12 = 14
2*3+4*5	___	_____
2+3*4−5	___	_____
2*3+4*5−6*7	___	_____

— — — — — — — — —

26	2 * 3 + 4 * 5 = 6 + 20 = 26	
9	2 + 3 * 4 − 5 = 2 + 12 − 5 = 9	
−16	2 * 3 + 4 * 5 − 6 * 7 = 6 + 20 − 42 = −16	

17. Here are more examples and exercises, using division (/). Study the examples and then complete the exercises. Be sure to follow the computer's order described in frame 16.

Expression	Value computed by computer	How it did the arithmetic
3/4+5	5.75	3/4+5 = .75 + 5 = 5.75
2−3/4	1.25	2−3/4 = 2 − .75 = 1.25
2*3+4/5	6.8	2*3+4/5 = 6 + .8 = 6.8
3/4+5*6	___	_____
2−3/4+5	___	_____

— — — — — — — — —

30.75	3/4 + 5 * 6 = .75 + 30 = 30.75
6.25	2 − 3/4 + 5 = 2 − .75 + 5 = 6.25

18. Following the computer's rules, give the computed value for each of the expressions below. (Remember, do arithmetic in left-to-right order.)

Expression   Value computed by computer

2*3/4   _____

3/4*5   _____

3/4/5   _____

2*3/4+3/4*5   _____

- - - - - - - - - -

1.5   Multiply 2 by 3, then divide result by 4.
3.75 Divide 3 by 4, then multiply result by 5.
.15   Divide 3 by 4, then divide result by 5.
5.25 First compute 2*3/4, then compute 3/4*5, then add the two results.

19. For each of the following numerical expressions, show the order in which the computer does the arithmetic by putting numbers 1, 2, or 3 in the circles above the operation symbols. We have completed the first three for you.

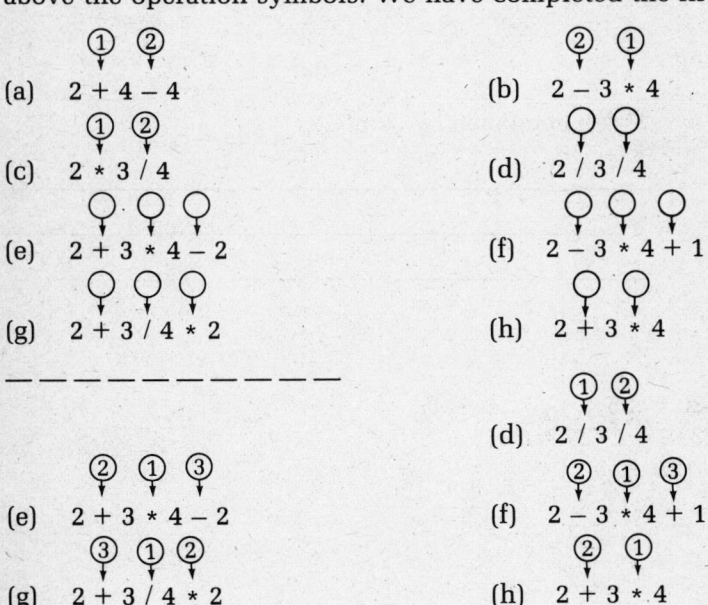

22 BASIC FOR THE APPLE II

20. If you want to change the order in which operations are done by the computer, use parenthesis. Operations in parentheses are done *first*.

Starting with the leftmost inner set of parentheses, the computer does arithmetic within each set of parentheses in *left-to-right* order, with all multiplications (*) and/or divisions (/) performed *before* additions (+) and/or subtractions (−).

$$\left.\begin{matrix}*\\/\end{matrix}\right\} \text{ before } \left\{\begin{matrix}+\\-\end{matrix}\right.$$

Look at these examples of how the order of operations can give different results.

$$2*3+4 = 10$$

but $2*(3+4) = 14$ Compute $3 + 4$ first because it is inside the parentheses, then multiply the result by 2.

$$2+3*4+5 = 19$$

but $(2+3)*(4+5) = 45$ Compute $2 + 3$, then compute $4 + 5$, and then multiply these two results.

Complete the following.

Expression	Value computed by computer
(2+3)/(4*5)	_____
2+3*(4+5)	_____
1/(3+5)	_____

— — — — — — — —

.25   (2+3)/(4*5) = 5/20 = .25
29   2+3*(4+5) = 2+3*9 = 2+27 = 29
.125 1/(3+5) = 1/8 = .125

GETTING STARTED

21. Let's take another look at the order in which arithmetic is done. In the expressions below, the numbers in the circles show the order in which the operations are carried out. Write the final value for each expression. The operations are always done in the innermost set of parentheses first.

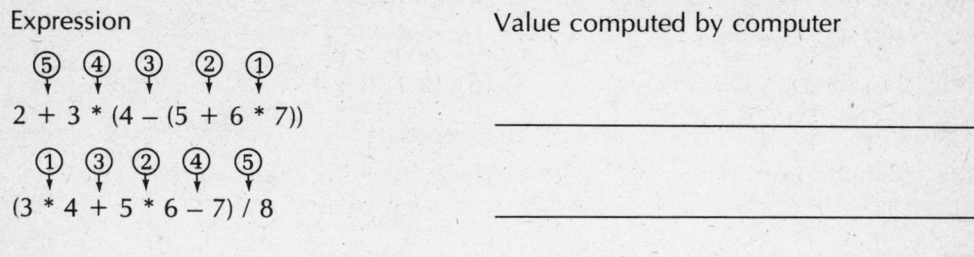

Expression | Value computed by computer

2 + 3 * (4 − (5 + 6 * 7))   _____

(3 * 4 + 5 * 6 − 7) / 8   _____

−127
4.375

22. Your next task is to write a proper PRINT statement to tell the computer to compute and print the value of each expression listed below. We have shown the actual value printed by the computer. Remember to indicate all multiplication and division operations with the proper BASIC symbol.

Expression	PRINT statement	Result
2 × 3 + 6 ÷ 7	_____	6.85714286
16(33 − 21)	_____	192
3.14 × 2 × 2	_____	12.56
$\frac{88-52}{18+47}$	_____	.553846154

```
PRINT 2*3+6/7
PRINT 16*(33−21)    (Did you remember the asterisk?)
PRINT 3.14*2*2
PRINT (88−52)/(18+47)
```

24 BASIC FOR THE APPLE II

23. For each numerical expression, show the order of operations by putting numbers 1, 2, 3, and so on in the circles above the operation.

(a) 2 +○ (3 −○ 4)

(b) 2 /○ (3 /○ 4) *○ (2 +○ 3)

(c) 2 /○ (3 *○ 4)

(d) (2 +○ 3) *○ 4

(e) (2 +○ 3) /○ (4 +○ 1)

(f) 2 /○ (3 +○ 4)

(g) 2 +○ ((3 +○ 4) +○ 8)

(h) 1 +○ 1 /○ (2 +○ 1 /○ (3 +○ 1 /○ 4))

————————————

(a) 2 +② (3 −① 4)

(b) 2 /③ (3 /① 4) *④ (2 +② 3)

(c) 2 /② (3 *① 4)

(d) (2 +① 3) *② 4

(e) (2 +① 3) /③ (4 +② 1)

(f) 2 /② (3 +① 4)

(g) 2 +③ ((3 +① 4) +② 8)

(h) 1 +⑥ 1 /⑤ (2 +④ 1 /③ (3 +② 1 /① 4))

24. There is a fifth arithmetic symbol in BASIC, which indicates raising a number to a power. This operation is called *exponentiation*. The exponent tells how many times the number is to be multiplied by itself. In BASIC, the symbol ∧ means "raise to a power."

The volume of a cube is a good example of how exponential numbers are used. The formula for calculating the volume (V) of a cube is:

$V = S^3$, where S is the length of a side

If $S = 5$, then $V = 5^3 = 5 \times 5 \times 5 = 125$.

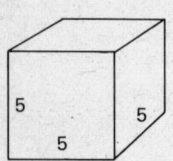

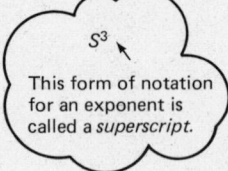

S^3 This form of notation for an exponent is called a *superscript*.

Since the computer can't display superscripts, the symbol ∧ indicates that the value *following* the ∧ is a superscript, that is, exponent, and that the number *preceding* the ∧ is to be multiplied by itself the number of times indicated by the exponent. You tell the computer to raise a number to a power by using the symbol ∧. On the keyboard, depress the SHIFT key and hold it down while you type N, where the ∧ is also located:

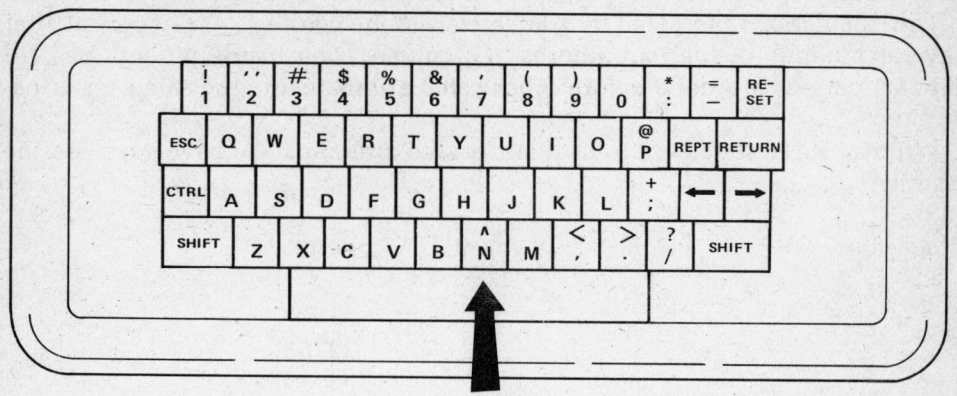

You type: PRINT 5∧3   (5∧3 means 5^3 or 5 × 5 × 5)
It types: 125

Now, complete the following.

You type: PRINT 2∧3
It types: _____

You type: PRINT 2∧4
It types: _____

You type: PRINT 2∧5
It types: _____

You type: PRINT 7∧2
It types: _____

— — — — — — — —

    8   (2∧3 = 2^3 = 2×2×2 = 8)
  16   (2∧4 = 2^4 = 2×2×2×2 = 16)
  32   (2∧5 = 2^5 = 2×2×2×2×2 = 32)
  49   (7∧2 = 7^2 = 7×7 = 49)

25. Because of the way the computer does arithmetic (not like you or I, for sure), very small inaccuracies sometimes result from its calculations. This is especially true for calculations involving exponentiation or division. Thus the computer says that 7∧2 equals 49.0000001, whereas the true result is 49 even. It's not your programming, it's the peculiar way the electronics of the machine perform calculations. And here you thought the computer was as accurate as it is fast! However, its errors are very, very small.

The calculations indicated by ∧ are always done before +, −, *, ,or /, but after any calculations inside parentheses. (Of course, even inside parentheses, all exponentiations are done before other calculations inside the same set of parentheses.)

Write a PRINT statement to evaluate each expression. We have supplied the results.

Expression	PRINT statement	Result
3^7	_____	2187
8 × 8 × 8 × 8 × 8	_____	32768 (Use ∧, not *.)
1.06^{10}	_____	1.79085
$3^2 + 4^2$	_____	25

```
PRINT 3∧7
PRINT 8∧5   (PRINT 8*8*8*8*8 will also produce the desired result.)
PRINT 1.06∧10   (We will see this type of expression later, in compound interest problems.)
PRINT 3∧2+4∧2
```

26. Suppose we put $123 into a savings account that pays 6% interest per year, compounded yearly. The amount of money in the account after N years can be computed using the following compound interest formula:

$$A = P(1 + R/100)^N$$

where

  P = Principal, or original amount put into the account
  R = Rate of interest per year, in percent
  N = Number of years
  A = Amount in account at the end of N years

In our problem, $P = \$123$, $R = 6\%$, and we want to know the value of A for $N = 2$, $N = 5$, and $N = 12$ years.

You type: PRINT 123*(1+6/100)^2 ←——— Compare the BASIC expression
It types: 138.2028 ←   with the formula given above.
                                                  After 2 years

You type: PRINT 123*(1+6/100)^5
It types: 164.601747 ←————————— After 5 years

Your turn. Write the PRINT statement for $N = 12$. We have supplied the result printed by the computer.

You type: _____
It types: 247.500168 ←————————— After 12 years our money
                                                  doubled.

— — — — — — — — —

        PRINT 123*(1+6/100)^12

27. Now here's a timesaver. Watch.

You type: ? 7+5
It types: 12

You type: ? "MY HUMAN UNDERSTANDS ME"
It types: MY HUMAN UNDERSTANDS ME

That's right. To save time, you can use a question mark (?) instead of the word PRINT in Applesoft BASIC and some other versions of BASIC.

For each expression or string below, write a PRINT statement to tell the computer to evaluate the expression and print the result, or to print the string. Use ? instead of PRINT. In each case, we have shown what we want the computer to type.

(a)   Expression: 37 − 50

You type: _____
It types: −13

(b)   String: "WANT TO PLAY?"

You type: _____
It types: WANT TO PLAY?

(c)   String: "2*3+4"

You type: _____
It types: 2*3+4

(a) ? 37 - 50
(b) ? "WANT TO PLAY?"
(c) ? "2*3+4"

28. Computers use a special notation to indicate very large numbers or very small decimal fractions. This method of representing numbers is called *floating-point notation*. You decipher it in the same way you do the *scientific notation* commonly used in mathematics and science textbooks.

For example, the population of the earth is about 4 billion people.

    4 billion = 4,000,000,000

Now let's ask the computer to print the population of the earth.

You type: PRINT 4000000000 ←— No commas. See note below.
It types: 4E+09 ←————— What's this?

Our computer printed the population of the earth as a *floating-point number*. Read it as follows.

    4E+09 = 4 times 10 to the 9th power, or
    4E+09 = 4 × 10^9

Floating-point notation is simply a shorthand way of expressing very large or very small numbers. In floating-point notation, a number is represented by a *mantissa* and an *exponent*.

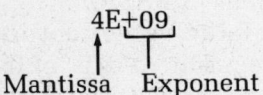
    Mantissa Exponent

The mantissa and the exponent are separated by the letter _____.

— — — — — — — —

E

Note: In typing numbers into the computer, we may *not* use commas as we normally do when writing numerals. Commas have a special use in BASIC PRINT statements. Please be patient. We will get to it soon.

29. Here are some examples showing numbers in good old everyday notation and again in floating-point notation.

One trillion

> Ordinary notation: 1,000,000,000,000
> Floating-point notation: 1E+12

Volume of the earth in bushels

> Ordinary notation: 31,708,000,000,000,000,000,000
> Floating-point notation: 3.1708E+22

Speed of a snail in miles per second

> Ordinary notation: .0000079
> Floating-point notation: 7.9E–06   (The exponent is *negative*.)

In each floating-point number above, underline the mantissa and circle the exponent.

——————————

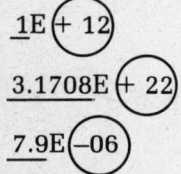

30. Here are more examples, showing how Applesoft BASIC prints and rounds off floating-point numbers. (Remember, you can use ? for PRINT.)

```
You type:   PRINT 1234567890
 It types:  1.23456789E+08

You type:   PRINT 1234567894
 It types:  1.23456789E+08

You type:   PRINT 1234567895
 It types:  1.2345679E+07

You type:   PRINT 1234567899
 It types:  1.2345679E+07
```

Our computer prints at most nine digits for the mantissa and rounds the mantissa at the ninth digit. The mantissa is printed as a nonzero digit to the left of the decimal point and up to eight digits to the right of the decimal point.

You type: PRINT 3333333333
It types: _____

You type: PRINT 6666666666
It types: _____

— — — — — — — — —

    3.33333333E+09
    6.66666667E+09

31. It works the same way with very small numbers expressed as decimal fractions:

You type: ? .0000001234567890
It types: 1.23456789E–08   ———— Negative exponent

You type: ? .0000001234567894
It types: 1.23456789E–08   ———— Negative exponent

You type: ? .0000001234567895
It types: 1.23456789E–08   ———— Negative exponent

You type: ? .0000001234567896
It types: 1.2345679E–08   ———— Negative exponent

You type: ? .0000001234567899
It types: 1.2345679E–08   ———— Negative exponent

The mantissa is printed with how many digits to the *left* of the decimal points? _____ Up to how many digits to the *right* of the decimal points? _____

— — — — — — — —

one; eight (See frames 28 and 29 for examples of mantissas with fewer than eight digits to the right of the decimal point.)

32. Numbers printed in floating-point notation can be converted to ordinary notation as follows. When the exponent is positive, we do the following.

    (a) Write the mantissa separately.
    (b) Move the decimal point of the mantissa to the *right* the number of places specified by the exponent. If necessary, add zeros.

Example: 6.12345E+05
(a)   6.12345 (b) 6.12345. 5 places

Therefore, 6.12345E+05 = 612,345.

Example: 4E+09
(a)   4. (b) 4.000000000. 9 places (add 9 zeros)

Therefore, 4E+09 = 4,000,000,000.

Now you try it: 1.23456E+13

(a) _____ (b) _____

Therefore, 1.23456E+13 = _____.

— — — — — — — — —

(a) 1.23456
(b) 1.2345600000000. 13 places (add 8 zeros)

12,345,600,000,000

33. When the exponent is negative, we simply change the direction that the decimal point moves.

    (a) Write the mantissa separately.
    (b) Move the decimal point of the mantissa to the *left* the number of places specified by the exponent. If necessary, add zeros.

Example: 7.9E–06
(a)   7.9 (b) .000007.9 6 places (add 5 zeros)

Therefore, 7.9E–06 = .0000079

Your turn. 1.23456E–08

(a) _____ (b) _____

Therefore, 1.23456E–08 = _____

(a) 1.23456
(b) .00000001.23456

.0000000123456

34. Write each of the following floating-point numbers in ordinary notation.

Floating-point notation   Ordinary notation

(a) 1.23456E+06   _____

(b) 1.23456E–06   _____

(c) 1.23456E+07   _____

(d) 1.23456E–09   _____

(e) 1E+11   _____

(f) 1E–11   _____

(a) 1234560 or 1,234,560
(b) .00000123456
(c) 12345600 or 12,345,600
(d) .00000000123456
(e) 100000000000 or 100,000,000,000
(f) .00000000001

35. Write each "ordinary" number in floating-point notation.

Ordinary notation   Floating-point notation

(a) 1,234,560   _____

(b) .000000123456   _____

(c) 10,000,000   _____

(d) .000000001   _____

(e) 1234567890   _____

(f) .0000012345678   _____

(g) 6.02×10^{21} (see note)   _____

(h) 1.67×10^{-11} (see note) _____

Note: the numbers in (g) and (h) are written in scientific notation commonly used in mathematics and science.

(a) 1.23456E+06
(b) 1.23456E–07
(c) 1E+07
(d) 1E–09
(e) 1.23456789E+09
(f) 1.23457E–06
(g) 6.02E+21
(h) 1.67E–11

36. Perhaps you have heard of the ancient story of the wise person who did a great service for a wealthy king. The king asked this person what reward would be appropriate. The person's request was simple. She asked only for grains of wheat, computed as follows. For the first square on a chess board, one grain of wheat; for the second square, 2 grains of wheat; for the third square, 4 grains of wheat; and so on, doubling at each square. It goes on as shown below.

Square number	Grains of wheat
1	1
2	2
3	4
4	8
5	16
6	32
7	64

And so on. For square N, there will be 2^{N-1} grains. Let's find out how many grains on square 16. Since $N = 16$, $N - 1 = 15$.
You type: ? 2^15
It types: 32768

You could also do it this way.

You type: ? 2^(16–1)
It types: 32768

Your turn. Write a PRINT statement to find out how many grains of wheat for square number 64. Follow the logic for square 16 as shown above.

You type: _____
It types: 9.22337204E+18   (That's a lot of wheat!)

PRINT 2^63, or ?2 ^63 or PRINT 2^(64–1)

Self-Test

Try this Self-Test, so you can evaluate how much you've learned so far.

1. In this chapter, we used direct statements. Direct statements do not have line numbers. When we type a direct statement and press RETURN, what does the computer do?_____

   _____

2. Assume that you are at a computer keyboard, typing a statement into the computer, and you make a typing error. How would you correct the error?_____

   _____

3. Write the symbols used in Applesoft BASIC for the following arithmetic operations.

   addition _____

   subtraction _____

   multiplication _____

   division _____
   exponentiation
   (raising a number to a power) _____

4. Complete the following.
   You type: PLEASE DO THE HOMEWORK ON PAGE 157

   It types:_____

5. Complete the following.
   You type: PRINT "PLEASE DO THE HOMEWORK ON PAGE 157"

   It types:_____

6. Complete the following.
   You type: PRINT 9*37/5+32

   It types:_____

7. The formula to convert temperature from degrees Fahrenheit (°F) to degrees Celsius (°C) is shown below.

   $$°C = 5/9(°F - 32)$$
       ↑   ↑
   Degrees Celsius   Degrees Fahrenheit

   Write a PRINT statement to tell the computer to compute and print the degrees Celsius (°C) if °F = 72. (Start by substituting 72 for °F in the right side of the formula.)_____

8. After typing in the following, you type CTRL/X instead of RETURN.

   PRINY "THE QUICK RED FOX JUMED OVE

   What happens?_____

9. What does the following statement tell the computer to do?

   PRINT 23+45 _____

10. Indicate which of the following numerical expressions are valid, *as written*, in BASIC.
    ____(a) 2*3*4*5
    ____(b) 7(8+9)
    ____(c) 1.23 ÷ 4.567
    ____(d) 5∧2+12∧2
    ____(e) $\frac{1}{37-29}$
    ____(f) $(1 + 7/100)^3$
    ____(g) 2∧2∧2

11. For each invalid numerical expression in problem 10, write a valid BASIC numerical expression._____

12. For each of the following numerical expressions, show the order in which the computer does the arithmetic by putting numbers 1, 2, 3, and so on in the circles above the operation symbols.

    (a) 2 + 4 − 4   (b) 2 * 3 * 4
    (c) 2 * 3 / 4   (d) 2 / 3 / 4
    (e) 2 / 3 * 4   (f) 2 − 3 * 4
    (g) 2 + 3 / 4   (h) 2 ∧ 3 * 4
    (i) 2 * 3 ∧ 4   (j) 2 ∧ 3 / 4
    (k) 2 / 3 ∧ 4   (l) 2 ∧ 3 ∧ 4
    (m) 1 + 2 * 3 ∧ 4 (n) 2 * 3 − 4 ∧ 3 + 5 ∧ 2

13. For each numerical expression, show the order of operations by putting numbers 1, 2, 3, and so on in the circles above the operation.

(a) 2 + (3 − 4) (b) 2 / (3 / 4)

(c) 2 / (3 * 4) (d) (2 − 3) * 4

(e) (2 + 3) / 4 (f) 2 ^ (3 * 4)

(g) 2 ^ (3 ^ 4) (h) 1 + 1 / (2 + 1 / (3 + 1 / 4))

14. Write each of the following floating-point numbers in ordinary notation.

Floating-point notation	Ordinary notation
(a) 1.23456E+05	
(b) 1.23456E−05	
(c) 1.23456E+08	
(d) 1.23456E−08	
(e) 1E+12	
(f) 1E−12	

15. Write each "ordinary" number in Applesoft notation, including floating-point notation where appropriate.

Ordinary notation	Applesoft notation, including floating-point notation
(a) 1,234,560,000	
(b) .00000000123456	
(c) 10,000,000,000	
(d) .0000000001	
(e) 123456789	
(f) .00000123456789	
(g) 6.02×10^{23} (See note.)	
(h) 1.67×10^{-21} (See note.)	

Note: The numbers in (g) and (h) are written in scientific notation commonly used in mathematics and science.

Answers to Self-Test

The frame numbers in parentheses refer to the frames in the chapter where the topic is discussed. You may wish to refer to these for quick review.

1. Executes the statement, then "forgets" it. (frame 3)
2. Use the left-arrow key to delete the mistake, then type the correct character. (frames 6–9)
3. Addition   +
   Subtraction   −
   Multiplication   *
   Division   /
   Exponentiation   ^
   (frames 16–20, 24)
4. ?SYNTAX ERROR (The computer does not understand what we want). (frame 2)
5. PLEASE DO THE HOMEWORK ON PAGE 157 (frames 3–5)
6. 98.6 (frames 20–23)
7. PRINT 5/9*(F−32) or PRINT (5/9)*(F−32)
   Did you remember the asterisk? By the way, we will also accept PRINT 5*(F−32)/9 (frames 20–23)
8. Computer types a backslash at the end of the line, then deletes the line without an error message. (frame 9)
9. Evaluate the numerical expression 23 + 45 and print the result. The computer will add 23 and 45, getting 68, and print 68. (frame 10)
10. Expressions (a), (d), and (g) are valid. In (g), the computer will evaluate 2^2^2, as follows: 2^2^2 = 4^2 = 16. In other words, the computer will do it left to right, as if it were written (2^2)^2. (frames 16–25)
11. (b)   7*(8 + 9)
    (c)   1.23/4.567
    (e)   1/(37 − 29)
    (f)   (1 + 7/100)^3

    (frames 16–25)

12.

(a) 2 ①+ ②4 − 4   (b) 2 ①* ②3 * 4

(c) 2 ①* ②3 / 4   (d) 2 ①/ ②3 / 4

(e) 2 ①/ ②3 * 4   (f) 2 ②− ①3 * 4

(g) 2 ②+ ①3 / 4   (h) 2 ①∧ ②3 * 4

(i) 2 ②* ①3 ∧ 4   (j) 2 ①∧ ②3 / 4

(k) 2 ②/ ①3 ∧ 4   (l) 2 ①∧ ②3 ∧ 4

(m) 1 ③+ ②2 * ①3 ∧ 4   (n) 2 ③* ④3 − ①4 ∧ ⑤3 + ②5 ∧ 2

(frames 16–25)

13.

(a) 2 ②+ ①(3 − 4)   (b) 2 ②/ ①(3 / 4)

(c) 2 ②/ ①(3 * 4)   (d) ①(2 − 3) ②* 4

(e) ①(2 + 3) ②/ 4   (f) 2 ②∧ ①(3 * 4)

(g) 2 ②∧ ①(3 ∧ 4)   (h) 1 ⑥+ ⑤1 / ④(2 + ③1 / ②(3 + ①1 / 4))

(frames 16–25)

14. (a) 123,456
    (b) .0000123456
    (c) 123,456,000
    (d) .0000000123456
    (e) 1,000,000,000,000
    (f) .000000000001

(frames 29–36)

15. (a) 1.23456E+09
    (b) 1.23456E−09
    (c) 1E+10
    (d) 1E−10
    (e) 123456789
    (f) 1.23456789E−06
    (g) 6.02E+23
    (h) 1.67E−21

(frames 29−36)

CHAPTER THREE

Assignment Statements, Stored Programs, and Branching

This chapter introduces some of the most useful BASIC statements. From here on, we can work with more interesting programs to illustrate a variety of applications of computers.

In this chapter, you will learn the function and format for the statements and commands listed below.

    Statements: LET, INPUT, GOTO, PRINT, REMARK
    Commands: NEW, RUN, LIST

You will learn how you can store programs for automatic and repetitive execution. You will also learn about *variables* and be able to supply values for variables used in BASIC programs. When you have finished this chapter, you will be able to:

- Write programs in which values are assigned to variables by means of direct assignment or LET statements or INPUT statements
- Distinguish between and use numeric variables and string variables
- Write programs in which a value calculated by a BASIC expression is assigned to a numerical variable in a direct assignment statement
- Store a BASIC program in the computer's memory
- Erase an unwanted program from the computer's memory, LIST a program currently in the computer, and RUN (execute) a program
- Edit, correct, and delete statements in a stored program
- Write INPUT statements with messages identifying the INPUT needed
- Write programs that use the GOTO statement to repeat a portion of a program or to skip over a portion of a program
- Use REMark statements to make programs more readable and understandable by *humans*
- Write PRINT statements which identify printed results with descriptive messages
- Use INPUT to control the display from a program loop

1. To illustrate the concept of *variable* and the function of the LET statement in BASIC, imagine that there are 26 little boxes inside the computer. Each box can contain one number at any one time.

A	7	I		Q		V	
B	5	J	4	R		W	
C		K		S	−6	X	2.5
D		L		T		Y	
E		M		U		Z	
F	2	N					
G		O					
H		P	4E + 09				

We have already stored numbers in some of the boxes. For example, 7 is in box A and 5 is in box B.

(a) What number is in box F? _____

(b) In J? _____

(c) −6 is in box _____.

(d) 2.5 is in box _____.

(e) What box contains a floating-point number? _____

(f) What is that floating-point number? _____

— — — — — — — —

(a)2; (b)4; (c)S; (d)X; (e)P; (f)4E+09

2. Boxes C and N are shown again here. Use a *pencil* to do the following.
(a) Put 8 into box C. In other words, write the numeral "8" in the box labeled "C." Do this before you go on to (b).
(b) Put 12 into N. Do this before you go on to (c).
(c) Put 27 into N. But wait! A box can hold only one number at a time. Before you can enter 27 into N, you must first erase the 12 that you previously entered.

C [8]
N [27]

Fill in the boxes before you look at the answer.

— — — — — — — —

C [8]
N [27]

ASSIGNMENT STATEMENTS, STORED PROGRAMS, AND BRANCHING   43

3. When the computer puts a number into a box, it *automatically* erases the previous content of the box, just as you did. In order to put 27 into box N, you first erased the previous content, 12.

We call A, B, C, ..., Z *variables*. The number in box A is the *value of* A; the number in box B is the *value of* B; the number in box C is the *value of* C, and so on.

We use the LET statement to instruct the computer to "put a number in a box." To say it more technically, we are assigning a numerical *value* to a *variable*. Therefore, the LET statement is referred to as a *direct assignment statement*.

```
You type:    LET A = 7           Put  7  into box A.
Then
    type:    PRINT A             Print the content of box A.
    It types:    7
```

In this program, the *variable* is _____ and the *value* assigned to it by the LET statement is _____.

— — — — — — — — —

A; 7

4. Complete the following. You can use ? for PRINT.

(a) You type: LET X = 23
              PRINT X
    It types: _____

(b) You type: LET Z = −1
              PRINT Z
    It types: _____

(c) You type: LET A = 1
              LET A = 2
              PRINT A
    It types: _____

(d) You type: LET D = 7
              LET W = D
              PRINT W
    It types: _____

(e) You type: LET A = 1
              PRINT A
    It types: _____

    You type: LET A = 2
              PRINT A
    It types: _____

(f) You type: LET N = 1
              PRINT N + 1
    It types: _____

    You type: PRINT N + 2
    It types: _____

— — — — — — — — —

(a) 23
(b) −1
(c) 2 (The statement LET A = 2 *replaced* the value previously assigned by LET A = 1.)
(d) 7 (LET W = D copies the value in D into W. The same value is still in D, also.)
(e) 1
    2
(f) 2 (Since N = 1, N + 1 = 2.)
    3 (Since N = 1, N + 2 = 3.)

5. Write a LET statement to assign the value 3.14 to P and a PRINT statement to print the value of P.

You type: _____

           _____

It types: _____

```
    LET P = 3.14
    PRINT P
    3.14
```

6. In most versions of BASIC, including Applesoft, the word LET can be omitted. For example:

You type: P = 3.14
            PRINT P
It types: 3.14

The statement P = 3.14 is called an implied LET statement. Try it on your computer. You can save time and space by omitting the word LET from a direct assignment statement.

Once we have assigned a value to a variable, that variable can be used in mathematical expressions.

You type: LET A = 7
            LET B = 5

We now have 7 in box A and 5 in box B.

    A [7]

    B [5]

ASSIGNMENT STATEMENTS, STORED PROGRAMS, AND BRANCHING   45

You type: PRINT A + B
It types: 12 ←——————— Since A = 7 and B = 5, A + B = 7 + 5 = 12.

You type: PRINT A − B
It types: 2 ←——————— Since A = 7 and B = 5, A − B = 7 − 5 = 2.

Your turn. Complete the following.

You type: PRINT A∗B
It types: _____

You type: PRINT A/B
It types: _____

— — — — — — — — —

   35
   1.4

In a direct assignment statement using the implied LET, you can do the above, as follows.

You type: A = 7
            B = 5
            PRINT A + B

It types: 12   (Remember, you can use ? for PRINT.)

7. The variables that we have used so far are called *numeric* variables. The value assigned to a numeric variable must be a number.

BASIC has another type of variable, called a *string* variable. The value assigned to a string variable must be a string. A string variable is indicated by a letter followed by a dollar sign ($).

You type: LET N$ = "JERRY"

This assigns the value JERRY to the string variable N$.

   N$ | JERRY |

Now, let's print the value of N$.

You type: PRINT N$
It types: JERRY

Complete the following.

You type: LET Z$ = "MY HUMAN UNDERSTANDS ME"
               PRINT Z$
It types: _____

— — — — — — — — —

      MY HUMAN UNDERSTANDS ME

8. Complete the direct assignment statement so that the computer types what we say it typed.

You type: LET C$ = _____
               PRINT C$
It types: SAN FRANCISCO, CALIFORNIA

— — — — — — — — —

      "SAN FRANCISCO, CALIFORNIA" (Did you remember the quotation marks?)

In this chapter and the next few chapters, we will make occasional use of string variables. Chapter 8 will describe string variables in detail.

9. Let's look at a problem. We have three bicycles with wheels of 16-, 24-, and 26-in. diameters. For each bike, we want to know how far the bike travels during one revolution of the wheel. This distance, of course, is the *circumference* of the wheel. Let's use D to represent the diameter of the wheel and C to represent the circumference.

$$C = \pi D$$

where $\pi = 3.14159\ldots$

We will use 3.14 as a crude approximation to π. We could do this problem as follows.

You type: PRINT 3.14 * 16   (for a 16-in.-diameter wheel)
It types: 50.24

You type: PRINT 3.14 * 24   (for a 24-in.-diameter wheel)
It types: 75.36

You type: PRINT 3.14 * 26   (for a 26-in.-diameter wheel)
It types: 81.64

ASSIGNMENT STATEMENTS, STORED PROGRAMS, AND BRANCHING 47

Here is another way to do it. Complete the parts we have omitted.

```
You type:   LET D = 16
            PRINT 3.14 * D
It types:   50.24

You type:   LET D = 24
            PRINT 3.14 * D

It types:   _____

You type:   LET_____
            
            _____
It types:   81.64
```

— — — — — — — — —

```
    75.36
    D = 26
    PRINT 3.14 * D
```

10. Now we are ready to take the big step from one-at-a-time *direct* statements to a *stored program*. We will store this program in the memory of the computer. (Just look at it, then read on.)

```
    10 LET D = 16
    20 PRINT 3.14 * D
```

The above program has two statements, each on a single line. Each statement begins with a *line number* (in this case, the 10 and 20). A line number can be an integer from 1 to 63999 in Applesoft BASIC.

When we type statements with line numbers, the statements are *not* executed when you press RETURN. Instead, the statements are stored in the computer's memory for later execution.

As you learned in Chapter 2, statements without line numbers are called *direct statements*. The computer executes a direct statement immediately and then forgets it. However, this does not happen when we type a statement *with* a line number. Instead, what does happen?

_____

_____

— — — — — — — — —

The statement is stored in the computer's memory for later execution. That is, the computer remembers the statement.

11. The line numbers tell the computer the order in which it is to follow statements in the program. It is not necessary for line numbers to be consecutive integers (e.g., 1, 2, 3, 4, 5, ...). It is common practice to number by tens, as we do in the following program. Then, if we wish, we can easily insert or add more statements into the program between existing statements.

```
10 LET D = 16
20 PRINT 3.14 * D
```

How many additional statements could be added between line 10 and line 20?
_____

— — — — — — — —

9 (lines 11, 12, 13, 14, 15, 16, 17, 18, 19)

Of course, you don't *have* to number by tens. If you prefer numbering by thirteens or fives or jumping around, help yourself!

12. Before we store a program, we must first remove or erase any old program that may already be stored in the computer's memory.

You type: NEW ⟵——————————— And, of course, press RETURN.
It types:]

The computer has erased the portion of its memory that stores BASIC programs. It is now ready to accept a new program.

How do we erase, remove, or delete an old program from the computer's memory? _____

— — — — — — — —

type NEW and press the RETURN key.

Note: If we misspell NEW, we may get an error message. For example:

You type: GNU
It types: ?SYNTAX ERROR

Our computer doesn't appreciate puns, but if we type NEW correctly and press RETURN, all is well.

ASSIGNMENT STATEMENTS, STORED PROGRAMS, AND BRANCHING   49

13. Now we are ready to store our two-line program from frames 10 and 11. First, we must erase any old program by typing _____ and pressing the RETURN key. To store the program, we type the first line or statement and press the RETURN key, then type the second line and _____.

— — — — — — — — — —

NEW; press the RETURN key

14. Let's do it.

```
You type:   NEW
 It types:  ]

You type:   10 LET D = 16
            20 PRINT 3.14 * D
```

If you make a typing error, use the left-arrow key for corrections. The program is now stored. The computer is waiting patiently for our next statement or command.

Hmmmm . . . we wonder if the program really *is* stored in the computer's memory. We can find out by typing LIST and pressing the RETURN key.

```
You type:   LIST  ←——————— And press RETURN.
 It types:  10 LET D = 16
            20 PRINT 3.14*D
            ]
```

The command LIST tells the computer to display or list all of the program statements that are currently stored in its memory. After listing the program, the computer types] to let us know it is our turn again. If there is *no* program stored, then none will be displayed, of course.

How do we tell the computer to type out the program that is currently stored in its memory? _____

— — — — — — — — — —

Type LIST and press the RETURN key.

15. Listing a BASIC program lets us know whether or not a program is stored in the computer's memory. We may want to add more statements to the program. Or we may wish to see if we have typed the statements correctly. If we want the computer to tell us if there is a program stored in its memory, and to display the program for us, we type _____.

— — — — — — — — — —

LIST

16. After you type RUN to tell the computer to execute a program, or after you type LIST to command the computer to tell us "what's on its mind" (that is, what is stored in its memory), what else do you have to do before the computer will respond? _____

— — — — — — — — — —

press the RETURN key

17. Type our little program into the computer if you haven't already done so.

```
10 LET D = 16
20 PRINT 3.14 * D
```

The program is stored in the computer's memory. Now you want the computer to execute (carry out) the program. Type RUN and press the RETURN key.

You type: RUN ⟵──────────   And press RETURN.
It types: 50.24

The computer has RUN the program. That is, it has executed the statements of the program in line number order. First, the computer was told to assign a value to a variable with this statement: 10 LET D = 16. That means that the computer placed the value _____ in the box identified by the variable _____.

— — — — — — — — — —

16; D

18. After following the instruction in the statement with line number 10, the computer went on to the next statement in line number order: 20 PRINT 3.14*D. Part of line 20 tells the computer to multiply two numbers. One number is given in the statement. The other number is stored in a place labeled by the variable D.

What are the two values that the computer uses to multiply? _____

— — — — — — — — — —

3.14 and 16

ASSIGNMENT STATEMENTS, STORED PROGRAMS, AND BRANCHING 51

19. In the last frame we saw that part of line 20 tells the computer to multiply two values. What else does line 20 tell the computer to do? _____

— — — — — — — — —

PRINT the results of the multiplication

20. After executing a direct or immediate mode statement, the computer "forgets" the statement. However, stored, line-numbered statements can be executed or RUN time and again. If you type RUN again, what will the computer do? _____

— — — — — — — — —

Same as before: display the results of the multiplication in the line-20 PRINT statement (50.24, the circumference of a 16-in. wheel)

21. Let's review what happens when we use our little program that calculates the circumference of a bicycle wheel.

NEW	First, we erase any old program.
10 LET D = 16 20 PRINT 3.14 * D	Then, we type in this program, which consists of two statements.
LIST	Next, we tell the computer to LIST the program.
10 LET D = 16 20 PRINT 3.14*D	The computer LISTs (types) the program, and stops.
RUN	Finally, we tell the computer to RUN the program.
50.24	It executes the program, and stops, displaying the bracket and flashing cursor.

What will happen if we now type RUN? _____

— — — — — — — — —

The computer will execute the program again. Since nothing in the program has changed, the same result (50.24) will be printed.

52 BASIC FOR THE APPLE II

22. What happens if we make a typing mistake in entering a program?

You type: 10 LER D = 16 ←───── We misspell LET.
              20 PRINT 3.14 * D
You type: RUN
It types: 0 ←───────────── Oops! Something is wrong here. The computer does not know how to run the program.

You type: LIST
It types: 10 LERD=16 ←───── Sure enough, we notice that LET is misspelled.
              20 PRINT 3.14*D

You type: 10 LET D=16 ←──── We retype line 10, correctly. This replaces the old line 10.

You type: LIST
It types: 10 LET D=16
              20 PRINT 3.14*D   To make sure the new line 10 replaced the old line 10, we LIST the corrected program (and also check to make sure we typed it right this time!).

You type: RUN
It types: 50.24

Suppose we had seen the mistake immediately after we had typed it. How could we have corrected it? _____

_____

— — — — — — — — —

We could have used the left-arrow key, then typed the correct letter. (See frame 6, Chapter 2.)

23. We assume that our circumference program is still stored in memory. Now we want to change the value assigned to D. To do this, we *replace* line 10 with a different line 10. After making this change, we will LIST the modified program.

You type: 10 LET D = 24
              LIST
It types: 10 LET D = 24   Here is the new line 10, and
              20 PRINT 3.14*D   the old line 20.

How do we *replace* a line in a stored program? _____

_____

ASSIGNMENT STATEMENTS, STORED PROGRAMS, AND BRANCHING   53

― ― ― ― ― ― ― ― ― ―

We type a new line with the same line number as the line we wish to replace.

Note: We do *not* type NEW because we want line 20 to remain in the computer while we change *only* line 10. Typing NEW would erase *both* statements from the computer's memory.

24.   Now RUN the modified program of frame 23.

You type: RUN
  It types: 75.36

Complete the following.

You type: 10 LET D = 26
You type: LIST
  It types: _____

              _____

You type: RUN

  It types: _____

― ― ― ― ― ― ― ― ― ―

```
        10 LET D = 26  ←──────── New line 10
        20 PRINT 3.14*D ←─────── Old line 20
        81.64
```

25. How fast does your money grow?

Problem: We put P dollars in a savings account which pays R percent interest, per year, compounded yearly. How much money will we have in the account at the end of N years?

    P is the original amount (principal).
    R is the interest rate, in percent, per year.
    N is the number of years.
    A is the amount after N years.

$$A = P(1 + R/100)^N$$

where the arrows indicate: % interest per year, number of years, original amount (principal), amount after N years.

Below is a program to compute A for P = $1000, R = 6%, and N = 3 years. Complete line 40 in correct BASIC notation, using the formula above as a guide.

```
10 LET P = 1000
20 LET R = 6
30 LET N = 3

40 LET A = _____
50 PRINT A
```

P*(1+R/100)^N   (Did you remember the asterisk? Did you remember to use ^ to tell the computer to raise to a power?)

26. We will store and RUN the program, then ask you to make some changes.

You type:
```
NEW
10 LET P = 1000
20 LET R = 6
30 LET N = 3
40 LET A = P*(1+R/100)^N
50 PRINT A
RUN
```

Don't forget, we are usually omitting the] typed by the computer. We also will omit reminders to use the RETURN key after entering a statement or a command such as RUN, LIST, or NEW.

It types: 1191.02

ASSIGNMENT STATEMENTS, STORED PROGRAMS, AND BRANCHING   55

Now, show how to change line 30 so that $N = 5$.

You type: _____
     RUN
It types: 1338.23 ⟵——————— Value of A for $P = 1000$, $R = 6$, $N = 5$.

————————

   30 LET N = 5 or 30N = 5

27. Now change the program so that $R = 7\%$ and $N = 8$ years.

You type: _____

     RUN
It types: 1718.18619

————————

   20 LET R = 7
   30 LET N = 8

28. Now show how the computer will respond if we type LIST.

You type: LIST
It types: _____
     _____
     _____
     _____
     _____

————————

```
10 LET P = 1000
20 LET R = 7
30 LET N = 8
40 LET A = P*(1+R/100)^N
50 PRINT A
```

29. Direct assignment statements are all fine and good, but what a hassle to change all those LET statements every time you want to change the values of variables. Ah, but leave it to BASIC to come up with a clever solution—the INPUT statement.

The INPUT statement allows the computer user to assign different values to variables each time a program is RUN *without* modifying the program itself. When the computer comes to an INPUT statement in a program, it types a question mark and waits for the user to enter a value for a variable. Following is an example:

You type:	NEW	First, we erase any old program, then enter this program.
	10 INPUT A	
	20 PRINT A	Then we tell the computer to RUN the program.
	RUN	The computer types a question mark, then waits.
It types:	?	

When we typed RUN, what did the computer do? _____

_____

— — — — — — — — — —

It typed a question mark and waited for us to do something.

Note: The question mark is an example of a *prompt*. The computer types a prompt to tell you it is *your* turn to do something. The bracket] is another example of a prompt.

30. The INPUT statement causes the computer to type a question mark, then stop and wait. It is waiting for a value to assign to the variable which appears in the INPUT statement. Computers are very patient. If we don't cooperate by typing a value, the computer will simply wait, and wait, and wait.

So let's cooperate with our ever-patient computer and type in a value for A. We will enter 3 as the value to be assigned to A, then press RETURN. The computer will put our value into box A, then continue running the program.

The computer types the question mark and waits for a value to be typed in.

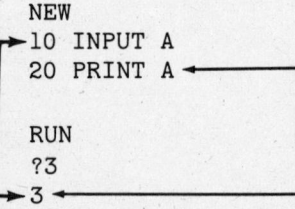

```
NEW
10 INPUT A
20 PRINT A

RUN
?3
 3
```

After we typed 3 as the value for A and then pressed RETURN, the computer went on to line 20 and printed the value we assigned to variable A.

ASSIGNMENT STATEMENTS, STORED PROGRAMS, AND BRANCHING 57

After we typed RUN and pressed the RETURN key, the computer typed a _____. We then typed 3, which is our value for the INPUT variable ____. The computer then executed the PRINT A statement (line 20) and printed the _____ of A.

— — — — — — — — — —

question mark; A; value

31. The program can be RUN again with a different value of A supplied by the user. Pretend you are the computer, and show how a RUN would look if your human computer user typed 23 as the value of A.

    RUN
    _____
    _____

— — — — — — — — — —

    ?23
    23

32. Now let's use an INPUT statement to enter (type in) data for our familiar bicycle wheel problem. *Data* is the name for information used by a computer program.

You type: NEW
               10 INPUT D
               20 PRINT 3.14*D

               RUN
It types: ?

The computer wants a value for D, the diameter of our bicycle wheel. It will then compute the distance traveled in one revolution, and print it. Let's do it for D = 16, D = 24, and D = 26.

```
RUN
```
First, we RUN the program for D = 16.

```
?16
50.24
```
When the computer typed a question mark, we entered 16 as the value of D. The computer computed and printed 3.14*D, then stopped.

```
RUN

?24
75.36
```
We typed RUN again and, when the computer typed a question mark, we supplied 24 as the value of D. The computer zapped out the answer, and stopped.

```
RUN
```
Your turn. Complete the third RUN for a 26" wheel.

_____

_____

- - - - - - - - - - -

```
?26
81.64
```

33. One INPUT statement can be used to assign values to *two or more* variables.

```
10 INPUT A,B  ←── Two variables, A and B.
20 PRINT A+B
RUN
?7,5  ←─────── Two values, 7 and 5, are typed in from the keyboard.
12
```

ASSIGNMENT STATEMENTS, STORED PROGRAMS, AND BRANCHING

When the computer typed a question mark, we typed *two* numbers separated by a comma, then pressed the RETURN key. The computer assigned the first number as the value of A and the second number as the value of B. Note the following.

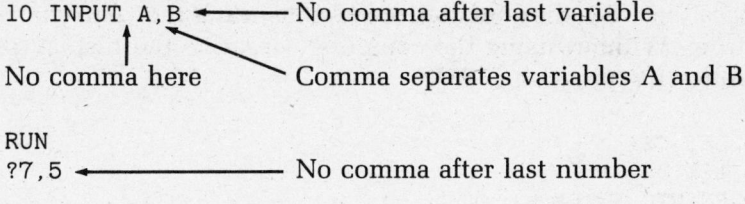

```
RUN
?7,5  ◄─────────── No comma after last number
```

Comma between numbers entered from the keyboard

The value 7 is assigned to the variable A, and the value 5 is assigned to the variable B.

Here is the summary; you fill in the blanks. When a program containing an INPUT statement with multiple variables is RUN, the first value typed in by the user after the INPUT question mark will be assigned to the _____ _____ variable that appears in the INPUT statement; the _____ _____ value typed in by the user will be assigned to the second variable appearing in the INPUT statement; and so on. Both the variables in the INPUT statement in the program, and the values typed in by the user when the program is RUN, must be separated by _____.

— — — — — — — — —

first; second; commas

34. Notice that simply pressing RETURN, without making any other entry on the keyboard, does not cause an error message to be displayed. Instead, what is called a *null string* is assigned to the INPUT string variable. A null string is a special kind of string; it contains no characters. Therefore, a PRINT statement with a variable to which a null string has been assigned will cause no characters to be displayed. The effect is the same as a blank PRINT statement.

We should mention that a direct assignment statement (LET) can also assign a null string to a string variable. An example of such an assignment statement:

```
10 LET A$ = ""
```

The "no space" between the quotation marks constitutes the "zero characters" in the null string. Without using the computer, describe the display produced when the following program is RUN.

```
10 LET C$= ""
20 LET D$= ""
30 PRINT C$, D$
RUN
```

_____

— — — — — — — —

Nothing is displayed. (Asking the computer to display null strings with a PRINT statement results in no characters being displayed.)

35. Here is another RUN of the program in frame 33. We want to enter 73 as the value of A and 59 as the value of B.

```
RUN
? 73   ←———— Oops! We absentmindedly hit the RETURN key.
??
```

The computer typed a double question mark. This means "Didn't you forget something?" We then completed the RUN by entering the *second* number, the value to be assigned to R.

```
RUN
? 73
?? 59
132
```

What happens if we don't enter a numerical value for *every* variable in an INPUT statement? _____

_____

— — — — — — — —

The computer types another question mark.
   Note: If you enter *more* numbers than there are variables, the computer will ignore the extra values, with the message ?EXTRA IGNORED.

ASSIGNMENT STATEMENTS, STORED PROGRAMS, AND BRANCHING   61

36. Suppose you and a bunch of friends, all bicycle aficionados, are gathered about your computer, and they are marveling at your newly acquired computer programming skills. You decide to demonstrate how the computer works by using the program to compute the distance traveled in one turn of the wheel. However, you have to do a separate RUN of the program for each friend. But wait—first add a new statement to the program.

```
10 INPUT D
20 PRINT 3.14*D
30 GOTO 10  ←——————— Something new—a GOTO statement.
```

In BASIC, a GOTO statement tells the computer to jump to or *branch* to the line number following the words GOTO, and then to continue following the instructions in the program in the usual line number order.

In the above program, the GOTO statement tells the computer to jump to line

_____ and start the program over again.

— — — — — — — — — —

line 10

37. Let's see what happens when we RUN this three-line program. (We assume that you, or someone, has typed NEW, then entered the program in frame 36.)

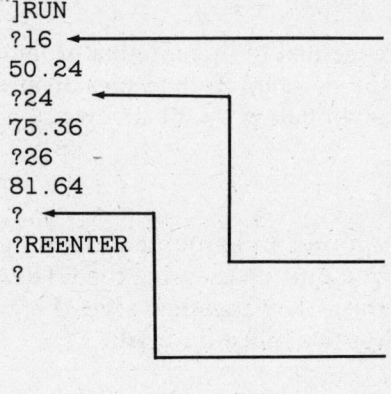

Following the INPUT question mark, we typed a value to be assigned to D. Following the first question mark, we typed 16, then hit RETURN. The computer then computed the value of 3.14*D, displayed the result(50.24), and then displayed another question mark. Next we entered 24. Then, for the third question mark, we typed 26. Entries are always followed by RETURN.

Here we just hit RETURN, *without* typing *any* value to be assigned to D. The computer responds with the message
?REENTER
and displays another question mark, giving us "another chance." (Note that the computer's reaction to nonresponse for a *numeric* INPUT variable is different than for nonresponse to *string* INPUT variables; see frame 34.)

Well, we are finished using this program, but the computer doesn't know we are finished. It is hung up on line 10, waiting for more INPUT data. How do we get out of this situation? Easy! Just press the CTRL (Control) key, and while holding down CTRL, also press the C key; then hit RETURN. Our shorthand notation referring to this sequence of keystrokes is CTRL/C. Notice that the CTRL key is used in a manner similar to the SHIFT key. You will also notice that typing CTRL/C produces no visible character on the display, although it does send a signal to the computer. In the RUN above, we typed the "invisible" CTRL/C, followed by RETURN after the last question mark displayed. The computer gave us the message

```
BREAK IN 10
```

indicating that the computer stopped the RUN while waiting at line 10. The computer will only stop the RUN if CTRL/C is the *first response* typed from the keyboard when the computer is waiting at an INPUT statement. (Shortly you'll see CTRL/C used to stop the RUN of *any* program.) Use the example program to experiment with this method of stopping or ending a RUN of a program waiting at an INPUT statement.

When you press the Control and C keys, *without* typing anything else first, then hit RETURN, what does the computer do? _____

_____

— — — — — — — — — —

It "escapes" from the INPUT statement, and the RUN ends with a message telling us where in the program the computer stopped.

38. Remember: BASIC statements are executed in line number order, unless a GOTO statement changes the order. In the program from frames 36 and 37, the statements are executed in the order shown below by the arrows.

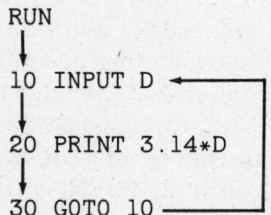

Around and around and around—until you quit by pressing the CTRL key and the C key together after the computer types a question mark.

The above program is an example of a *loop*. The GOTO statement causes the computer to "loop back" to the beginning. In this program, the computer loops back to an INPUT statement and then stops. Watch out! We can write programs with nonstop loops. Here is an example.

```
13 PRINT "TO STOP ME, PRESS 'CTRL' AND 'C' TOGETHER"
27 GOTO 13
```

We have used line numbers 13 and 27 to remind you that you don't have to number by 10, although we usually do.

ASSIGNMENT STATEMENTS, STORED PROGRAMS, AND BRANCHING

Do *not* RUN this program yet! Instead, draw arrows as we did on the previous page to show how the computer executes the program.

```
RUN

13 PRINT "TO STOP ME, PRESS 'CTRL' AND 'C' TOGETHER"

27 GOTO 13
```

— — — — — — — — — —

```
RUN
 ↓
13 PRINT "TO STOP ME, PRESS 'CTRL' AND 'C' TOGETHER" ←┐
 ↓                                                    │
27 GOTO 13 ───────────────────────────────────────────┘
```

39. Now let's enter the program of frame 38 and RUN it. Remember, to stop the computer, press CTRL and C *together*.

```
NEW
13 PRINT "TO STOP ME, PRESS 'CTRL' AND 'C' TOGETHER"
27 GOTO 13

RUN
TO STOP ME, PRESS 'CTRL' AND 'C' TOGETHER
TO STOP ME, PRESS 'CTRL' AND 'C' TOGETHER
TO STOP ME, PRESS 'CTRL' AND 'C' TOGETHER
TO STOP ME, PRESS 'CTRL' AND 'C' TOGETHER
TO STOP ME, PRESS 'CTRL' AND 'C' TOGETHER

BREAK IN 13
            ↑
```

The computer tells us the line number of the next statement that was to be executed when we pressed CTRL and C together. (You only need to press RETURN following the CTRL/C if the computer is waiting at an INPUT statement.)

The computer executed line 13 over and over again, because the GOTO statement in line 27 repeatedly told the computer to go back to line 13. This is a "forever" loop—it just keeps going around and around until someone interrupts it. Sometimes this is referred to as an "infinite" loop, because it does not stop automatically.

How do we interrupt, or stop, the computer when it is running a program?

— — — — — — — — — —

press the CTRL and C keys together (simultaneously)

40. If you should move someday, you may want to write your version of the following program. If you have a printer attached to your computer, try typing

    PR#1

and hit RETURN, before you RUN the program. This has the effect of opening communication between the computer and the printer if the printer has been connected or "interfaced" with your Apple in the usual manner. The program output should be typed by the printer. To return to using only the video display after using the printer, type

    PR#0

then hit RETURN. Now here is the program. (Line 100 is explained in the next frame.)

```
NEW
100 REM ARK   CHANGE OF ADDRESS PROGRAM
110 PRINT
120 PRINT "DEAR FRIENDS, MY NEW ADDRESS IS:"
130 PRINT
140 PRINT "IRENE BROWNSTONE"
150 PRINT "605 PARK AVENUE"
160 PRINT "NEW YORK NY 10016"
170 PRINT
180 GOTO 110
```

You can RUN this program even if you don't have a printer, but the display will go by *very* fast.

To use this program to obtain 10 change of address messages, you type NEW, then enter the program. If using a printer, enter PR#1 before you RUN the program; otherwise, just RUN it.

How do you stop the program after 10 messages?_____

_____

— — — — — — — — — —

Press the CTRL and C keys together.

41. Notice that line 100 in the program in frame 40 begins with a REMARK statement. It is used to tell something about the program to a human who may be reading the program, usually to document what the program does. The computer simply ignores REMARK statements.

Actually, the REMARK statement has a short form that you can use. The short form is simple, the first three letters in REMark. When executing a program, the computer only "looks" at the first three letters, and if those three letters are REM,

ASSIGNMENT STATEMENTS, STORED PROGRAMS, AND BRANCHING   65

then the computer will skip on to the next statement in line number order, without considering anything else on the REM statement line. Therefore, if you think about it, you'll see that you could use the word REMEMBER instead of REMark and the effect would be just the same. Applesoft will always place a space after the M in REMark when you LIST a program, whether you leave one there or not.

Rewrite line 100 from frame 40, using the short form of the REMark statement.

100 _____

— — — — — — — — — —

    100 REM   CHANGE OF ADDRESS PROGRAM

42.   When the computer executes a PRINT statement that has only the word PRINT following the line number and nothing else in the statement, it does the same thing that happens when you press the RETURN key.

    1.   It does a carriage return; and
    2.   It does a line feed (indexes or goes to the next line).

This has the effect of leaving a blank line in the display or printout when the program is RUN. This is very handy for making the display of a program easier to read.

Look at the change of address program in frame 40. Which statements will cause the computer to insert blank lines in the display? _____

_____

— — — — — — — — — —

lines 110, 130, and 170

43.   Here again is the bicycle wheel program from frames 35 and 36.

```
10 INPUT D
20 PRINT 3.14*D
30 GOTO 10

]RUN
?16
50.24
?24
75.36
?26
81.64
?   ←——————————  Remember to use CTRL/C, then RETURN.
```

(Crowded, isn't it?)

We assume that the program is still stored in the computer's memory. (If you are at a computer, check by using LIST, and if not, store the program now.) We will add the statement, then LIST the program.

You type: 25 PRINT   This is an "empty" PRINT statement. The space following PRINT is "empty."

You type: LIST

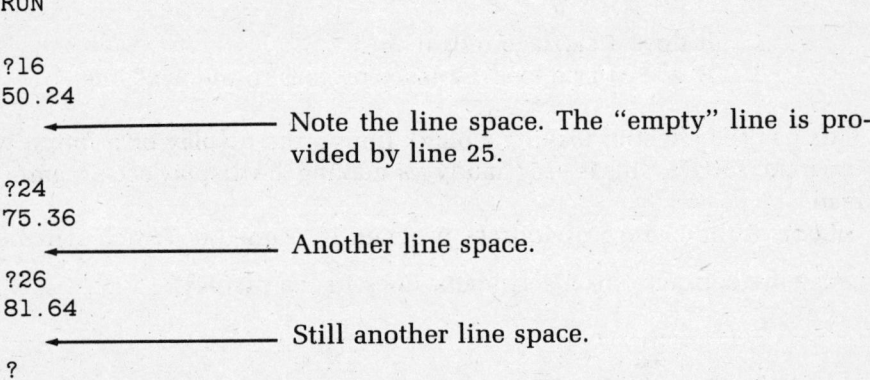

It types: 10 INPUT D
            20 PRINT 3.14*D   The computer has automatically in-
            25 PRINT ←———————— serted our new statement in its
            30 GOTO 10   proper place, *between* line 20 and line 30.

Let's RUN it and see what happens.

```
RUN

?16
50.24
```
———————————— Note the line space. The "empty" line is pro-
vided by line 25.
```
?24
75.36
```
———————————— Another line space.
```
?26
81.64
```
———————————— Still another line space.
```
?
```

To stop the RUN, use CTRL/C followed by RETURN.

Compare the RUN at the bottom of page 65 with the RUN shown above. What does 25 PRINT tell the computer to do?

_____

_____

— — — — — —

It causes the computer to print a line space ("empty" line) after printing the value of 3.14*D. *Note:* This happens *before* the computer executes GOTO 10 and restarts the program.

ASSIGNMENT STATEMENTS, STORED PROGRAMS, AND BRANCHING

44. When a program contains an INPUT statement, we need a way of informing a user of our program what the INPUT statement is asking for. Here is our bike program again, with a more informative INPUT statement containing a *message string* inside quotation marks.

```
10 INPUT "WHEEL DIAMETER? ";D
20 PRINT 3.14*D
25 PRINT
30 GOTO 10

RUN
WHEEL DIAMETER?
```

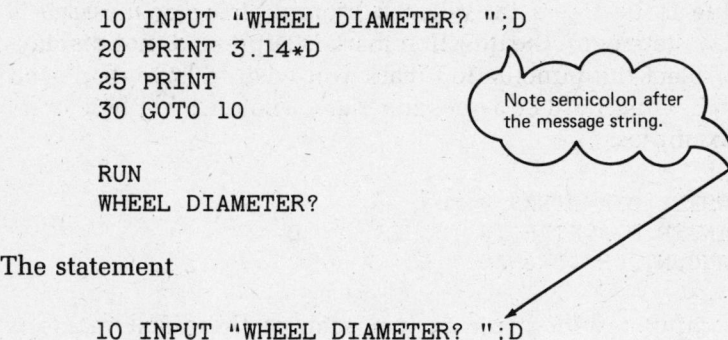

Note semicolon after the message string.

The statement

```
10 INPUT "WHEEL DIAMETER? ";D
```

tells the computer to:

1. Print the string WHEEL DIAMETER?
2. Wait for someone to type a value for D
3. Continue executing the program after someone types a value of D (and presses RETURN)

Suppose we type 16 as the value of D and press RETURN. Show what happens next.

```
WHEEL DIAMETER? 16
_____
_____
_____
```
- - - - - - - - - -
```
50.24

WHEEL DIAMETER?
```

Note: When you use a message string in an INPUT statement, remember to put a semicolon between the string and the variable which follows it. You also must supply the question mark (or other punctuation) inside the INPUT message quotation marks; the computer doesn't supply an INPUT question mark when a message string is included in the INPUT statement.

45. Notice that when a simple INPUT statement, such as

        10 INPUT D

is executed by the computer, the computer stops and displays a question mark, then waits for a value to be typed in. When a prompt string or message is included in the INPUT statement, the question mark is supressed (not displayed), allowing you to select the punctuation mark you wish to have displayed along with the message. This could be a question mark, a colon, a hyphen, or no punctuation at all. Examples:

        10 INPUT "WHEEL DIAMETER? "; D
        10 INPUT "ENTER DIAMETER IN INCHES: "; D
        10 INPUT "AMOUNT OF PURCHASE? $"; A

Show what the computer will display when each of these statements is executed by the computer.

(a) _____

(b) _____

(c) _____

— — — — — — — — — — —

(a) WHEEL DIAMETER?
(b) ENTER DIAMETER IN INCHES:
(c) AMOUNT OF PURCHASE? $

46. Now what the computer wants is clearly identified by the string enclosed in quotation marks in the INPUT statement. We use the same approach in a PRINT statement to identify the calculation performed by the computer for that statement (see line 20).

        10 INPUT "WHEEL DIAMETER? ";D
        20 PRINT "DISTANCE IN ONE TURN IS "; 3.14 * D
        25 PRINT
        30 GOTO 10

In a PRINT statement, this semicolon is optional, but a semicolon is required after an INPUT message string.

ASSIGNMENT STATEMENTS, STORED PROGRAMS, AND BRANCHING

The following statement

        Notice this space.
           ↓
```
20 PRINT "DISTANCE IN ONE TURN IS  "; 3.14 * D
```

tells the computer to:

1. Display the string DISTANCE IN ONE TURN IS (including the space at the end of the string)
2. Compute and print the value of 3.14*D on the same line as, and immediately following, the string.

The extra space at the end of the print statement string is necessary to avoid a display with the calculation jammed up against the word IS at the end of the string. Without the extra space in the string we would get:

```
DISTANCE IN ONE TURN IS50.24
```

If you enter, then LIST the program, it should appear in this form on the video display.

```
]LIST

10 INPUT "WHEEL DIAMETER? ";D
20 PRINT "DISTANCE IN ONE TURN I
   S "; 3.14*D
25 PRINT
30 GOTO 10
```

Notice that line 20 is LISTed on two display lines in the program, even though we typed it in as one program line. This effect of one line-numbered statement using more than one line to complete the display is called wraparound. Any long program line will wraparound as many lines as necessary to completely display the line. For example, a string (in quotes) in a PRINT statement is allowed up to 239 characters in it, and would take several lines to display.

Let's try out this program. Complete the RUN.

```
RUN

WHEEL DIAMETER? 16
DISTANCE IN ONE TURN IS 50.24

WHEEL DIAMETER? 24
DISTANCE IN ONE TURN IS _____

WHEEL DIAMETER? 26
_____

_____

_____
```

— — — — — — — — — —

```
    75.36
DISTANCE IN ONE TURN IS 81.64

WHEEL DIAMETER?
```

Don't forget that the semicolon between "DISTANCE IN ONE TURN IS " and 3.14*D is optional. More features of the PRINT statement will be revealed as we move along.

47. Rewrite the program in frame 44 so that a RUN looks like the one shown below.

```
]RUN
IF YOU ENTER THE DIAMETER OF A BICYCLE
WHEEL, THEN I'LL TELL YOU THE DISTANCE
YOU TRAVEL IN ONE TURN OF THE WHEEL.

WHEEL DIAMETER? 16
DISTANCE IN ONE TURN IS 50.24

WHEEL DIAMETER? 24
DISTANCE IN ONE TURN IS 75.36

WHEEL DIAMETER? 26
DISTANCE IN ONE TURN IS 81.64

WHEEL DIAMETER?    ... and so on. To stop, press CTRL and C together,
                         followed by RETURN.

BREAK IN 60    The computer tells you in what line it stopped the RUN.
```

Write the program below.

_ _ _ _ _ _ _ _ _ _ _ _ _

```
10 REM ARKABLE BICYCLE WHEEL PROGRAM
20 PRINT "IF YOU ENTER THE DIAMETER OF A BICYCLE"
30 PRINT "WHEEL, THEN I'LL TELL YOU THE DISTANCE"
40 PRINT "YOU TRAVEL IN ONE TURN OF THE WHEEL."
50 PRINT
60 INPUT "WHEEL DIAMETER? ";D
70 PRINT "DISTANCE IN ONE TURN IS ";3.14 * D
80 GOTO 50
```

(Remember, the computer ignores everything following REM. See frame 41.)

48. The INPUT statement, like the LET statement, belongs to the class of BASIC instructions called assignment statements. The value we type in response to a question mark is assigned to the variable in the INPUT statement. If the INPUT variable is a string variable, we can type in a string as the value and it will be assigned to the string variable. Here is a simple example.

```
NEW
10 INPUT "WHAT IS YOU NAME? ";N$
20 PRINT "NAME: ";N$
30 PRINT
40 GOTO 10

]RUN
WHAT IS YOUR NAME? "JERALD R. BROWN"   ←— The computer asks the
NAME: JERALD R. BROWN                      question, you type in
                                           the answer.

WHAT IS YOUR NAME? JERALD R. BROWN    ←— What? No quotation
NAME: JERALD R. BROWN                      marks? See note below
                                           and the next frame.

WHAT IS YOUR NAME? LEROY FINKEL
```

You complete this one. What will the computer display next?

_ _ _ _ _ _ _ _ _ _

NAME: LEROY FINKEL

Note that it is OK to omit the quotation marks enclosing a string during INPUT. However, as you will see in the next frame, sometimes the quotation marks are necessary.

49. Below is another RUN of the program in frame 48.

```
]RUN
WHAT IS YOUR NAME? BROWN, JERALD, R.  ←— Our first response.
?EXTRA IGNORED
NAME: BROWN

WHAT IS YOUR NAME? "BROWN, JERALD R." ←— Our second try.
NAME: BROWN, JERALD R.

WHAT IS YOUR NAME?

BREAK IN 10
]
```

When we typed BROWN, JERALD R. with a comma between BROWN and JERALD R., the computer thought we were entering *two* strings. However, the INPUT statement has only *one* string variable. So, the computer assigned BROWN to the variable N$ and politely informed us ?EXTRA IGNORED. It ignored the comma and also ignored JERALD R. It then, of course, printed the value of N$, which was BROWN.

What happened when we typed "BROWN, JERALD R."? _____

— — — — — — —

The computer typed the complete string BROWN, JERALD R., including the comma.

If you wish to INPUT a string that has a comma in it, you must enclose the entire string in quotation marks.

50. String values can be assigned to two or more string variables with a single INPUT statement.

```
10 INPUT "YOUR NAME AND SUN SIGN? ";N$,S$
20 PRINT
30 PRINT N$
40 PRINT "YOUR SIGN IS"
50 PRINT S$
```
Use a comma between variables.

```
]RUN
YOUR NAME AND SUN SIGN? JERRY,SCORPIO

JERRY
YOUR SIGN IS
SCORPIO
```
Use a comma between the two string entries.

```
]RUN
YOUR NAME AND SUN SIGN? JERRY
??
```
The computer wants a second entry, for S$. We just pressed RETURN, which assigns a *null string* (a string with zero characters) to S$.

```
JERRY
YOUR SIGN IS
```
Null strings look the same as blank PRINT statements.

```
]RUN
YOUR NAME AND SUN SIGN?
??
```
We pressed RETURN twice, with no other entry from the keyboard, thus assigning null strings to *both* N$ and S$.

```
YOUR SIGN IS
```
The "invisible" null strings assigned to N$ and S$

Show how you could complete the RUN from this point. (One string was entered for the INPUT variables before the RETURN key was pressed.)

```
RUN
YOUR NAME AND SUN SIGN? JERRY
?? _____

_____
_____
_____
— — — — — — — —
```

```
??SCORPIO

JERRY
YOUR SIGN IS
SCORPIO
```

51. Now you write a program with three string variables in an INPUT statement. A RUN will look like the following.

```
]RUN
YOUR NAME, CITY, AND STATE YOU LIVE IN: JERRY,SEBASTOPOL,CALIFORNIA

JERRY
YOU LIVE IN
SEBASTOPOL
CALIFORNIA
```

10 _____
20 _____
30 _____
40 _____
50 _____
60 _____

```
10 INPUT "YOUR NAME, CITY, AND STATE YOU LIVE IN: ";N$,C$,S$
20 PRINT
30 PRINT N$
40 PRINT "YOU LIVE IN"
50 PRINT C$
60 PRINT S$
```

Commas must be used to separate variables.

52. Review the change of address program in frame 40. Then complete the following RUN so that the results will be displayed as shown.

```
NEW
100 REM *** CHANGE OF ADDRESS PROGRAM
110 INPUT "YOUR NAME? ";N$
120 INPUT "STREET ADDRESS? ";S$
130 INPUT "CITY, STATE, AND ZIP (WITH NO COMMAS)? ";C$
140 PRINT
150 PRINT "DEAR FRIENDS, MY NEW ADDRESS IS:"
160 PRINT
170 PRINT N$
180 PRINT S$
190 PRINT C$
200 PRINT
210 GOTO 140
```

ASSIGNMENT STATEMENTS, STORED PROGRAMS, AND BRANCHING 75

Fill in the blanks.

```
RUN
YOUR NAME? _____

STREET ADDRESS? _____
CITY, STATE, AND ZIP (WITH NO COMMAS)? _____

DEAR FRIENDS, MY NEW ADDRESS IS:

JERALD R. BROWN
13140 FRATI LANE
SEBASTOPOL CA 95472

DEAR FRIENDS, MY NEW ADDRESS IS:

JERALD R. BROWN
13140 FRATI LANE
SEBASTOPOL CA 95472

DEAR FRIENDS, MY NEW ADDRESS IS:

JERALD R. BROWN
13140 FRATI LANE
SEBASTOPOL CA 95472

BREAK IN 190    ◄──── We pressed CTRL/C to stop the computer.
]
```

_____

```
]RUN
YOUR NAME? JERALD R. BROWN
STREET ADDRESS? 13140 FRATI LANE
CITY, STATE, AND ZIP (WITH NO COMMAS)? SEBASTOPOL CA 95472
```

No quotation marks were required. However, they would be required if any of the lines typed in contained a comma. For example: "NEW YORK, NEW YORK 10016"

53. Here's a program that lets you use the computer as an adding machine, by repeating an "adding routine" with a GOTO loop. A "routine" is one or more statements to complete a computing task.

```
NEW
100 REM    ***WORLD'S MOST EXPENSIVE ADDING MACHINE!!!
110 PRINT "I AM THE WORLD'S MOST EXPENSIVE ADDING MACHINE."
120 PRINT "EACH TIME I TYPE 'X=?' YOU TYPE A NUMBER AND"
130 PRINT "PRESS THE RETURN KEY.  I WILL THEN TYPE THE TOTAL"
140 PRINT "OF ALL THE NUMBERS YOU HAVE ENTERED."
150 LET T = 0
⎡160 PRINT                              ⎤
⎢170 INPUT "X=? "; X                    ⎥  Lines 160 through 200 are a GOTO
⎢180 LET T = T + X                      ⎥  loop. These lines are done for
⎢190 PRINT "TOTAL SO FAR IS "; T        ⎥  each number entered by the user.
⎣200 GOTO 160                           ⎦
```

Notice the LET statements using the variable T in lines 150 and 180. Line 150 is *outside* the GOTO loop. It is executed *once* before the loop begins, setting T equal to zero. This is called *initializing*, giving an initial or starting value to a variable.

Line 180 is *inside* the GOTO loop. Therefore, line 180 will be executed *each time* through the loop. In line 180, a *new* value of T is computed by adding the old value stored in box T to the INPUT value of X entered by the computer user.

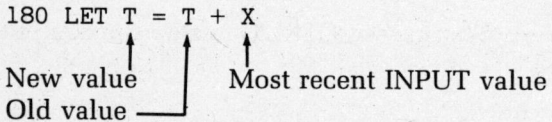

(a) Suppose the *old* value of T is zero and the INPUT value of X is 12.

What is the *new* value of T? _____

(b) Suppose the *old* value of T is 12 and the INPUT value of X is 43. What is the *new* value of T? _____

— — — — — — — —

(a) 12; (b) 55

54. Note how the PRINT statements (lines 110–140) are used to provide the user with an explanation and instructions for using the program. Are the PRINT statements inside or outside the GOTO loop? _____

— — — — — — — —

outside

55. It's RUN time. Let's see how the program works.

```
RUN
I AM THE WORLD'S MOST EXPENSIVE ADDING MACHINE.
EACH TIME I TYPE 'X=?' YOU TYPE A NUMBER AND
PRESS THE RETURN KEY.  I WILL THEN TYPE THE TOTAL
OF ALL THE NUMBERS YOU HAVE ENTERED.

X=? 12
TOTAL SO FAR IS 12

X=? 43
TOTAL SO FAR  IS 55

X=? 33
TOTAL SO FAR IS 88

X=? 92
TOTAL SO FAR IS 180

X=? 76.25
TOTAL SO FAR IS 256.25

X=?
```
←——— Do you remember how to get out of this? If not, check frame 37.

Let's focus on the statement in line 180. For the RUN above, the *first* time through the program the values of the variables to the right of the = symbol in 180 LET T = T + X will be:

Value asigned   Value assigned to X
T by line 150   by INPUT X

So the *new* value for T is 12. The value is printed. Notice that the computer substitutes the current values in the boxes for the variables to the right of = each time it executes line 180.

For the *second* time through the "loop" section of the program show the values:

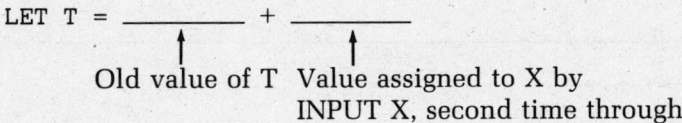

Old value of T   Value assigned to X by
                 INPUT X, second time through

The *new* value of T is _____.
— — — — — — — — — —

```
LET T = 12 + 43
55
```

The following section is for those who have a disk drive connected to the Apple computer. If your system has more than one disk drive, use drive #1. The disk drive provides an extremely handy way to SAVE programs on a diskette, outside the computer. The preparation of new diskettes for use in SAVEing programs is called *initializing*, and is covered in the *DOS (Disk Operating System) Manual* provided by Apple Computer, Inc. with their disk drives.

After you have typed a program into the computer, you can "record" the program (SAVE it) on the diskette, and later "play back" (LOAD) the program back into the computer's memory, without having to retype it from the keyboard. This will save you much time, since you can LIST, RUN, and modify or expand a previously entered (typed in) program without repeating the time-consuming work you have already done. This technique of "building on" to an existing program is common among programmers. In this text we often use this method of LOADing a program into the computer (that we previously SAVEd) to add new features to the program, change existing features, and eventually even combine parts of originally separate programs.

The steps for SAVEing a program are:

1. Pick a name for your program.
    a. The name cannot be more than 30 characters in length, including spaces.
    b. The name cannot contain commas or certain control characters, such as CTRL/C.
    c. Although the name cannot be more than 30 characters in length, including spaces, longer names may be typed in, but the name will be truncated (cut off) after 30 characters, and only those first 30 characters will be used for the program name in the disk's catalog of files.
2. Type the word SAVE, then the name for your program, then hit RETURN. The disk drive will operate, then the bracket and flashing cursor will reappear. The program will still be in the computer's memory as well as recorded on the disk.

Now you SAVE the World's Most Expensive Adding Machine program on the disk, if you have one. Name this program ADDING MACHINE #1, or think up your own name. Show below what you must type into the computer to accomplish this. _____

__ __ __ __ __ __ __ __ __ __

```
SAVE ADDING MACHINE #1 (then hit RETURN)
```

ASSIGNMENT STATEMENTS, STORED PROGRAMS, AND BRANCHING 79

Each disk has an index, directory, or CATALOG that contains the name of everything "filed" or recorded on that disk, including programs you have saved. To see this directory, type the word CATALOG followed by a press of the RETURN key. The disk drive will operate, and the computer will display the disk's "table of contents" or directory, as in the sample shown below. If the directory has a long list of entries, the computer will display one screen-full, then it stops and waits. If the bracket and flashing cursor do not reappear, then another press of the RETURN key will display the next screen-full of catalog entries.

Show what you must type into the computer to cause the directory of whatever disk is in the drive to be displayed. _____

— — — — — — — — —

    CATALOG (followed by RETURN)

Since each program you SAVE uses up space on the disk, you will eventually try to SAVE a program, but instead, the message DISK FULL will appear on the screen. We recommend that you initialize several spare disks in advance to accept programs you wish to SAVE. See the *Apple DOS Manual* for the procedure.

56. Now that you know how to stop a "runaway" computer, try this program, which causes the computer to print counting numbers, 1, 2, 3, 4, 5, and so on, until you press CTRL and C, together.

```
10 LET N=1
20 PRINT N
30 LET N=N+1
40 GOTO 20

RUN

1
2
3
4
5
6
7

BREAK IN 20
```

How does it work? Follow the arrows.

```
10  LET  N=1
     ↓
20  PRINT  N  ←──────┐
     ↓               │
30  LET  N=N+1       │
     ↓               │
40  GOTO  20  ───────┘
```

This program is another example of a *loop*. Line 10 is outside the loop. Lines 20, 30, and 40 comprise the loop; they are repeated over and over and over. Line 10 is done *once*, initializing N equal to 1.

Line 30 is *inside* the loop. It will be done each time through the loop. In line 30, a new value of N is computed by adding 1 to the old value of N.

```
30  LET  N  =  N  +  1
            ↑     ↖
        New value  Old value
```

(a) Suppose the old value of N is 1. What will the new value of N be? _____
(b) Suppose the old value of N is 2. What will the new value of N be? _____

— — — — — — — — —

(a) 2; (b) 3 (Line 20 will print the new value next time around the loop.)

57. With a counting loop and a few other statements, we can write a program to show how our money grows, year by year. Here it is.

```
100 REM***WATCH YOUR MONEY GROW
110 PRINT "IF YOU TYPE THE AMOUNT OF PRINCIPAL AND THE"
120 PRINT "INTEREST RATE PER YEAR, I WILL SHOW YOU HOW"
130 PRINT "YOUR MONEY GROWS, YEAR BY YEAR. TO STOP ME,"
140 PRINT "PRESS THE 'CTRL' AND 'C' KEYS TOGETHER."
150 PRINT
160 INPUT "PRINCIPAL? ";P
170 INPUT "INTEREST RATE? ";R
180 LET N=1           ←——————— Start year (N) at 1.
190 PRINT
200 LET A=P*(1+R/100)^N ⎤
210 PRINT "YEAR = ";N   ⎬  Compute and print results for year N.
220 PRINT "AMOUNT = ";A ⎦
230 LET N=N+1         ←——————— Increase year (N) by 1 and go around
240 GOTO 190                    again.
RUN
IF YOU TYPE THE AMOUNT OF PRINCIPAL AND THE
INTEREST RATE PER YEAR, I WILL SHOW YOU HOW
YOUR MONEY GROWS, YEAR BY YEAR. TO STOP ME,
PRESS THE 'CTRL' AND 'C' KEYS TOGETHER.

PRINCIPAL? 1000
INTEREST RATE? 6

YEAR = 1
AMOUNT = 1060

YEAR = 2
AMOUNT = 1123.6

YEAR = 3
AMOUNT = 1191.02
```

And so on, until someone presses CTRL and C. Which statements are part of the loop? Give the line numbers. _____

_ _ _ _ _ _ _ _ _

190, 200, 210, 220, 230, and 240

We suggest that you also draw a box around the loop with a felt-tip pen. Note that lines 100 through 180 are outside the loop. They are done once during a RUN, while lines 190 through 240 are repeated over and over until you press CTRL and C.

58. As you noticed when the interest-calculating program was RUN, the information was displayed on the screen faster than you could read it. To control the display of information produced by a program loop like this one, use the INPUT statement. We call this the Press RETURN to Continue technique.

Since the computer waits at an INPUT statement for a response from the keyboard, an INPUT statement inserted into the program loop will cause the computer to display one set of information produced in the loop, then, upon executing the INPUT statement, to wait. One approach is shown below. Add the following two statements to the interest calculating program, and RUN it again.

```
231 PRINT
232 INPUT "PRESS 'RETURN' TO CONTINUE"; R$
```

When the computer executes line 232, the INPUT message is displayed, and the computer waits for a response from the keyboard. By pressing RETURN with no other keyboard entry, what is assigned to the INPUT string variable R$?

_____

— — — — — — — — — — —

a null string

59. Since R$ is not used elsewhere in the program, it doesn't matter what is assigned to R$.

An alternative technique is provided by using the following modification for the interest-calculating program, *instead of* the lines 231 and 232 shown in frame 58. First, include the PRESS 'RETURN' instructions (line 141) with the other PRINT statements at the beginning of the program. Then use the tricky form of the INPUT statement shown in line 231.

```
141 PRINT "PRESS 'RETURN' ONLY TO DISPLAY ANOTHER YEAR."
231 INPUT ""; R$
```

Try these modifications to the interest-calculating program, instead of the ones provided earlier. Remember to delete (take out) line 232 by typing *only* the line number, then RETURN.

When the computer executes line 231, it stops and waits. Notice that the INPUT prompt string message is a null string; there are no characters or spaces between the quotation marks. Therefore, no INPUT message is printed, but neither is the question mark normally displayed by a "bare" INPUT statement (one with no prompt string message). Thus we have fooled the computer into supressing (not displaying) the INPUT question mark. The computer just sits and waits for the RETURN key (with or without any other keyboard entry) to be pressed. The continuously repeated PRESS 'RETURN' message caused by the first technique shown is eliminated by this second method. Now you know how to slow down any display where the information displayed is produced in a program loop.

ASSIGNMENT STATEMENTS, STORED PROGRAMS, AND BRANCHING   83

Using this second technique, what is assigned to the INPUT variable?

_____

— — — — — — — —

a null string (same as the first method shown)

60. Yet another way to control the display is by setting the speed at which the Apple sends characters to the display (or printer) during a RUN. The SPEED= command is automatically set at its fastest value, which is 255, when you turn on the computer. With a statement such as

    10 SPEED= 25

at the beginning of the program, you slow things down considerably. You can then reset the speed to normal (that is, fast) with a statement such as

    250 SPEED= 255

at the end of a program. You can also use SPEED= in direct mode to set or reset the display speed. Legal values for SPEED= are from 0 (zero, which is the slowest) to 255 (fastest). Try using the above example statements with the interest calculating program, instead of the Press RETURN to Continue technique.

Which of the following statements will cause the characters to be sent to the display at the slowest speed? Circle your answer.

(a)   100 SPEED= 85
(b)   100 SPEED= 150

— — — — — — — —

(b)

61. In this book, we have used the simplest variables: a letter of the alphabet for numeric variables, and a letter followed by a $ (dollar sign) that tells the computer to expect a string (or $tring, if that helps you remember it). Notice that D and D$ are distinct variables, and refer to different storage areas in the computer's memory, one for a numeric value, the other for a string.

However, longer variables (also referred to in computer jargon as labels, datanames, or identifiers) are permitted in Applesoft, according to the following rules:

    1. A variable (or variable "name") must start with an alphabetic character (A to Z).
    2. After the first letter, a variable name can have either numbers or letters in it.
    3. In Applesoft BASIC, a variable is allowed to have more characters in

it than you would ever use (238 to be exact), but only the first two characters are actually used as variable labels for the "storage boxes"; the rest are essentially ignored. This is true both when the variable is assigned a value and when the variable is used later in a program to "recall" a value or a string.

Examples of legal (permitted, acceptable) variables:

    X   XRAY   X$ XRAY$ B   B$ B1   B1$ B2   B2$ B3   B3$
    PAUL   PREREQUISITE$ AA   BB   AB   BA

Note: For long string variable names such as XRAY$ and PREREQUISITE$, the computer actually uses XR$ and PR$ as the variables. Which of the following are acceptable variable names?

(a)   K9
(b)   MM
(c)   3$
(d)   B35$
(e)   MM$
(f)   EDGAR
(g)   TALLY$

_____

a, b, d, e, f, g

62. There is just one more (very important) catch in using long variable names (other than a letter followed by a number, or a single letter): the variable names cannot contain any of the words or abbreviations that are used in Applesoft BASIC instructions or commands. There is quite a long list of such *reserved words*, including some that are not otherwise mentioned in this book. Three simple ones that cannot be included in a variable name are TO, AT, and OR, so that if these combinations of letters are located anywhere in a variable name, an error will result. Other reserved words are already familiar to you: RUN, LET, LIST, NEW, PRINT. See your Apple reference manuals for complete lists of reserved words. If you decide to use long variable names to help you keep track of what variables stand for, here is a simple test you can use. Suppose you wanted to use the variable SUBTOTAL, but you weren't sure it was free of embedded reserved words. The following is a test.

```
10 LET SUBTOTAL = 35
20 PRINT SUBTOTAL
```

If you RUN this program, the message

    ?SYNTAX ERROR IN 10

will result. If you LIST this program, then Applesoft will separate out the embedded reserved word with spaces, like this:

    LIST
    10 LET SUB TO TAL = 35
    20 PRINT SUB TO TAL

Now follow the rules for variable names to predict the RUN for the following program.

    10 LET JOHN = 5
    20 LET GERTRUDE = 10
    30 PRINT JOHN + GERTRUDE
    40 PRINT JOE + GENE
    RUN

_ _ _ _ _ _ _ _ _ _ _

    RUN
    15
    15

(Both line 30 and line 40 will print the same thing, because only the first two characters in the variables are used to store information, in this case JO and GE.)

Self-Test

Try this Self-Test, so you can evaluate how much you have learned in this chapter.

1. Before entering a program, we usually first type NEW and press RETURN. Why? _____

2. How do we tell the computer to type a complete listing of a program stored in its memory? _____

3. Assume that we have just stored a program in the computer's memory. How do we tell the computer to execute the program?

4. Assume that the following program is stored in the computer's memory.

   ```
   10 PRINT "MY COMPUTER UNDERSTANDS ME"
   20 PRINT "MY COMPUTER CONFUSES ME"
   ```

   Describe how to replace the second statement (line 20) without erasing the entire program. _____

   _____

5. What is the difference between direct or immediate mode statements and statements to be stored in the computer's memory for later execution? _____

   _____

6. We store the following program and RUN it.

   ```
   100 PRINT "I PROMISE NOT TO CHEW BUBBLE GUM IN CLASS"
   200 GO TO 100
   ```

   How do we stop the computer? _____

   _____

7. Each of the following statements contains an error. Mark the error and show the statement in correct BASIC format (syntax, that is).

   (a) 10 INPUT WHEEL DIAMETER;D
   _____

   (b) 20 PRINT DISTANCE IN ONE TURN IS; 3.14*D
   _____

   (c) 20 "DISTANCE IN ONE TURN IS"; 3.14*D
   _____

   (d) 20 LET P*(1 + R/100)^N = A
   _____

   (e) 20 TYPE "X="; X
   _____

8. Describe what is wrong with each statement.

   (a) 99999 LET A = 7 _____

   (b) 30 GOTO 3.14 _____

   (c) 30 GOTO −100 _____

   (d) 10 INPUT,Z _____

   (e) 10 INPUT Z, _____

9. Describe what is wrong with each program.

   (a) 10 INPUT A

       20 INPUT B

       30 PRINT A+B

       40 GOTO 12

   (b) 10 LET A = 7

       20 LET B = 5

       20 PRINT X + Y

10. Complete the RUN on the line provided.

    ```
    10 INPUT "A=? ";A
    20 INPUT "B=? ";B
    30 PRINT "A+B = ";A+B

    RUN
    A=? 7
    B=? 5
    _____
    ```

11. Show the RUN for the following program.

```
10 LET A$="   XXXXX"
20 LET B$=" X       X"
30 LET C$="(X 0 0 X)"
40 LET D$=" X  V  X"
50 LET E$=" X < > X"
60 LET F$=" X     X"
70 LET G$="   XXX"
80 PRINT A$
90 PRINT B$
100 PRINT C$
110 PRINT D$
120 PRINT E$
130 PRINT F$
140 PRINT G$
```

RUN

12. Write a program to convert temperatures given in degrees Celsius (°C) to degrees Fahrenheit (°F) using the following formula.

$$°F = \frac{9}{5} °C + 32$$

A RUN of your program should look like this.

```
RUN
YOU ENTER DEGREES CELSIUS. I WILL TYPE DEGREES FAHRENHEIT.

DEGREES CELSIUS? 0
DEGREES FAHRENHEIT = 32

DEGREES CELSIUS? 100
DEGREES FAHRENHEIT = 212

DEGREES CELSIUS? 37
DEGREES FAHRENHEIT = 98.6

DEGREES CELSIUS?    And so on.
```

13. Congratulations! You are the big winner on a TV show. Your prize is selected as follows.

A number from 1 to 1000 is chosen at random. Call it N. You then select one, and only one, of the following prizes. You have 60 seconds to make your selection.

Prize no. 1: You receive N dollars
Prize no. 2: You receive D dollars, where $D = 1.01^N$

Perhaps you recognize the formula for D. It is the amount you would receive if you invested $1 at 1% interest per day, compounded daily for N days.
The question, of course, is: For a given value of N, which prize do you take prize no. 1 or prize no. 2? Write a program to help you decide. A RUN might look like this.

```
]RUN

N=? 100
PRIZE NO. 1 =100
PRIZE NO. 2 =2.70481405  ←──── Take prize no. 1

N=? 500
PRIZE NO. 1 =500
PRIZE NO. 2 =144.772833  ←──── Take prize no. 1

N=? 1000
PRIZE NO. 1 =1000
PRIZE NO. 2 =20959.173  ←──── Take prize no. 2

N=? ←──────────────── And so on
```

14. Write this program to assist you in performing that tiresome task called "balancing the checkbook." Here is a RUN of our program.

```
RUN
I WILL HELP YOU BALANCE YOUR CHECKBOOK.
ENTER CHECKS AS NEGATIVE NUMBERS AND
DEPOSITS AS POSITIVE NUMBERS.

OLD BALANCE? 123.45

CHECK OR DEPOSIT? -3.95
NEW BALANCE: 119.5
```
← Remember to enter checks as negative numbers.

```
CHECK OR DEPOSIT? -25
NEW BALANCE: 94.5

CHECK OR DEPOSIT? -73.69
NEW BALANCE: 20.81

CHECK OR DEPOSIT? -8.24
NEW BALANCE: 12.57

CHECK OR DEPOSIT? 50
NEW BALANCE: 62.57
```
← At last! A deposit, and just in time!

```
CHECK OR DEPOSIT?
```
← And so on. Do you remember how to get out of this? If not, see frame 37.

ASSIGNMENT STATEMENTS, STORED PROGRAMS, AND BRANCHING   91

15. Suppose we enter this program and then type RUN. Show the first seven numbers printed by the computer.

```
10 LET N = 1
20 PRINT N
30 LET N = N + 1
50 GOTO 20
```

RUN

_____

_____

_____

_____

_____

_____

_____

How do we stop the computer from continuing to print numbers?
_____

16. The United States is going metric, so here is a metric problem. Write a program to convert feet and inches to centimeters, as indicated by the following RUN.

```
RUN

FEET    = ? 5   ⟵──────  We enter, as requested, the number of
INCHES  = ? 11  ⟵         feet and the number of inches.
CENTIMETERS =180.34 ⟵─ The computer computes and prints the
                          number of centimeters.

FEET   =? 3
INCHES =? 0
CENTIMETERS =91.44

FEET   =? ⟵──────────── And so on.
```

Answers to Self-Test

The frame numbers in parentheses refer to the frames in the chapter where the topic is discussed. You may wish to refer to these for quick review.

1. This erases, or removes, any old program that might be in the computer's memory. If we *don't* do this, statements of an old program might be intermingled with statements of the new program, thus causing mysterious and unpredictable behavior when we try to RUN the new program. (frames 12, 13)
2. Type LIST and press the RETURN key. (frames 14, 15)
3. Type RUN and press the RETURN key. (frames 15, 17)
4. Type a new line numbered 20 and press the RETURN key. The old statement 20 is automatically erased and we may now replace it. If we type the line number (and only the line number) of a statement and press RETURN, the computer deletes from its memory the statement (if any) with that line number. (frames 22, 23)
5. Direct statements do *not* have line numbers and are executed immediately after we press RETURN. A statement to be stored must have a line number; the computer "remembers" it for later execution (at "RUN time" as we sometimes say). (frame 10).
6. Press the CTRL key and the C key at the same time. (frames 37, 38)
7. (a)   10 INPUT▼WHEEL DIAMETER▼ ;D   Quotation marks missing
   #   10 INPUT "WHEEL DIAMETER";D   (frame 44)

   (b)   20 PRINT▼DISTANCE IN ONE TURN IS▼ ;3.14*D   Quotation marks missing
   20 PRINT"DISTANCE IN ONE TURN IS ";3.14*D   (frame 46)

   (c)   20 "DISTANCE IN ONE TURN IS ";3.14*D
   PRINT or ? is missing.
   20 ? "DISTANCE IN ONE TURN IS ";3.14*D   (frame 46)

   (d)   20 LET P*(1 + R/100^N = A
   Left side of = must be *only* a variable.
   20 LET A = P*(1 + R/100)^N   (frames 1–4)

   (e)   20 TYPE "X= ";X
   Computer doesn't know what TYPE means.
   20 PRINT "X=";X
   20?"X=";X ◄——— Either is OK. (Chapter 2)

8. (a) The line number is too big. (frame 10)
   (b) The 3.14 is not a valid line number because it is not an *integer* in the range 1 to 63999. (frame 10)
   (c) −100 is not a valid line number. (frame 10)
   (d) There should not be a comma following the word INPUT. (frame 34)
   (e) There should not be a comma at the end of the INPUT statement (INPUT statements with two or more variables have commas *between* variables). (frame 34)

9. (a) The program does not have a line number 12. Therefore, the computer cannot execute the statement 40 GOTO 12. Instead, it will display ?UNDEF'D STATEMENT ERROR IN 40 (which means Undefined Statement reference in line 40). (frames 35, 37, 38)
   (b) The PRINT statement does not use the same variables assigned values in the first two statements. (In MICROSOFT BASIC, the computer would print a 0 (zero) for the PRINT statement.) We probably should have done one of the following.

   ```
   10 LET A = 7        10 LET X = 7
   20 LET B = 5        20 LET Y = 5
   30 PRINT A + B      30 PRINT X + Y    (frames 1-8)
   ```

10. Here is the complete RUN.

    ```
    RUN
    A=? 7
    B=? 5
    A+B = 12
    ```

    This statement: 30 PRINT"A+B = ";A+B
    Causes this: A+B = 12

    (frame 47)

11.   XXXXX
      X   X
     (X O O X)
      X V X
      X < > X
       X   X
        XXX

    (Chapter 2 and frame 47)

12. ```
    100 REM **PROGRAM TO CONVERT CELSIUS TO FAHRENHEIT
    110 PRINT "YOU ENTER DEGREES CELSIUS.
        I WILL TYPE DEGREES FAHRENHEIT."
    120 PRINT
    130 INPUT "DEGREES CELSIUS? ";C
    140 PRINT "DEGREES FAHRENHEIT = "; (9/5)*C+32
    150 GOTO 120
    ```

    (frames 47, 48)

13. ```
    100 REM **TV SHOW PRIZE PROBLEM
    110 PRINT
    120 INPUT "N=? ";N
    130 PRINT "PRIZE NO. 1 =";N
    140 PRINT "PRIZE NO. 2 =";1.01^N
    150 GOTO 110
    ```

    (frames 47, 48)

14. ```
    100 REM **CHECKBOOK BALANCING PROGRAM
    110 PRINT "I WILL HELP YOU BALANCE YOUR CHECKBOOK."
    120 PRINT "ENTER CHECKS AS NEGATIVE NUMBERS AND"
    130 PRINT "DEPOSITS AS POSITIVE NUMBERS."
    140 PRINT
    150 INPUT "OLD BALANCE? ";B
    160 PRINT
    170 INPUT "CHECK OR DEPOSIT? ";X
    180 LET B=B+X  ───────────── Compute new balance as
                                 shown below.
    190 PRINT "NEW BALANCE: ";B
    200 GOTO 160
    ```

    180 LET B = B + X
    - check or deposit
    - old balance
    - new balance

    (frames 52–57)

15. RUN
    1
    2
    3
    4
    5
    6
    7   And so on.

    This program illustrates a *counting loop*. Once you type RUN, the computer will begin counting. It will count and count and count and keep on counting until the power fails or the computer breaks down or you press CTRL and C together to stop the computer. (frames 51–54)
    ```

16.
```
100 REM **CONVERT FEET AND INCHES TO CENTIMETERS
110 PRINT
120 INPUT "FEET =? ";F
130 INPUT "INCHES =? ";I
140 LET T = 12*F+I          T is total number
150 LET C = 2.54*T          of inches in F feet plus I inches
160 PRINT "CENTIMETERS =";C  C is number
170 GOTO 110                of centimeters in T inches.
```

(frame 47)

CHAPTER FOUR

Decisions Using IF-THEN Statements

By now you have proabably gotten the idea that a computer only does what you very specifically tell it to do. So how can a computer ever decide anything on its own? Well, it can't decide "on its own," but it can make certain comparisons that you instruct it to make, and then either execute or skip other statements in the program according to whether the comparison you specified is true or false. The statement that you use to set up such comparisons is the IF-THEN statement. (As you will see, IF-THEN is actually a whole family of statements.) When you finish this chapter, you will be able to:

- Use the IF-THEN statement
- Use the following comparisons in an IF-THEN statement:

Symbol	Meaning
<	Less than
>	Greater than
=	Equal to
<>	Not equal to
=> (or >=)	Greater than or equal to
=< (or <=)	Less than or equal to

- Use the RND function to generate random numbers
- Use the INT function to "drop" the fractional part of a number
- Use the INT and RND functions together to generate random digits
- Use the ON-GOTO statement to selectively branch to various statements in a program
- Use a colon (:) to separate multiple statements in the same line as a means to organize your programs and to save computer memory space
- Use multiple statements per line to increase the usefulness of IF-THEN statements.

1. In this chapter, we present a very important capability of BASIC—the ability to compare and decide. We will begin with the IF-THEN statement, which tells the computer to carry out a specified operation IF a given condition is TRUE. However, if the condition is FALSE (not true), the operation will not be done. An IF-THEN statement is shown below.

```
150 IF X > 0 THEN PRINT "YOUR NUMBER IS POSITIVE"
```

This IF-THEN statement tells the computer: If the value of X is greater than zero, then print the message, YOUR NUMBER IS POSITIVE, and go on to the next statement in line number order. The symbol > means "is greater than."

If the value of X is *less than* zero or *equal to* zero, the computer does *not* print the message. Instead, it simply continues executing the program in the line number order.

Here is another way to look at it. Follow the arrows.

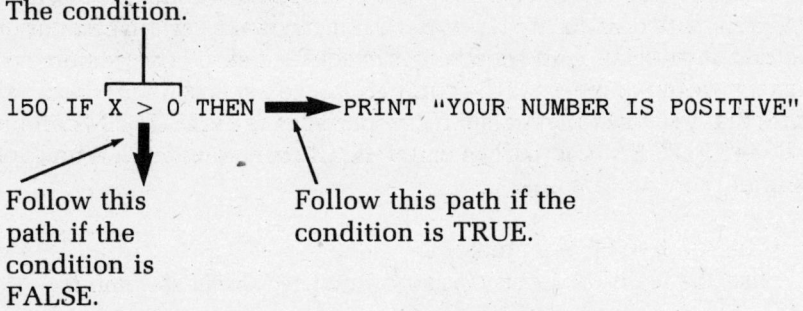

What is the *condition* in the above IF-THEN statement?_____

_____

— — — — — — — — —

$X > 0$ or X is greater than zero.

2. Using our sample statement from frame 1:
(a) Suppose $X = 3$. Is the condition TRUE or FALSE?_____
(b) Suppose $X = -7$. Is the condition TRUE or FALSE?_____
(c) Suppose $X = 0$. Is the condition TRUE or FALSE?_____

— — — — — — — — —

(a) TRUE. The computer *will* print the message: YOUR NUMBER IS POSITIVE.
(b) FALSE. The computer will *not* print the message.
(c) FALSE. The computer will *not* print the message.

DECISIONS USING IF-THEN STATEMENTS

3. The symbol > in an IF-THEN comparison means "is greater than." The symbol = means "is equal to." You can guess that the symbol < used in an IF-THEN comparison means _____

— — — — — — — — —

"is less than"

4. Here is a simple program illustrating the use of the IF-THEN statement. This program has three IF-THEN statements that tell the computer to "compare and decide." Remember, the message in an IF-THEN PRINT statement will be printed only if the comparison is true.

```
NEW
100 REM **DETERMINE IF X IS POSITIVE, NEGATIVE OR ZERO
110 PRINT "WHEN I ASK, YOU ENTER A NUMBER AND I WILL TELL YOU"
120 PRINT "WHETHER YOUR NUMBER IS POSITIVE, NEGATIVE OR ZERO."
130 PRINT
140 INPUT "WHAT IS YOUR NUMBER? ";X
150 IF X>0 THEN PRINT "YOUR NUMBER IS POSITIVE"
160 IF X<0 THEN PRINT "YOUR NUMBER IS NEGATIVE"
170 IF X=0 THEN PRINT "YOUR NUMBER IS ZERO"
180 GOTO 130

RUN
WHEN I ASK, YOU ENTER A NUMBER AND I WILL TELL YOU
WHETHER YOUR NUMBER IS POSITIVE, NEGATIVE OR ZERO

WHAT IS YOUR NUMBER? -7
YOUR NUMBER IS NEGATIVE ←— This message printed by line 160.

WHAT IS YOUR NUMBER? 3
YOUR NUMBER IS POSITIVE ←— This message courtesy of line 150.

WHAT IS YOUR NUMBER? 0
YOUR NUMBER IS ZERO ←——— Thank you, line 170.

                                And so on. (Do you remember how to
WHAT IS YOUR NUMBER? ←——— stop a program waiting at the INPUT
                                question mark?)
```

(a) What is the condition in line 150? _____

(b) What is the condition in line 160? _____

(c) What is the condition in line 170? _____

— — — — — — — — —

(a) X > 0 or X is greater than zero.
(b) X < 0 or X is less than zero.
(c) X = 0 or X is equal to zero.

5. In running the program from frame 4, the computer executes lines 100, 110, and 120 once, since they are "outside the loop." Lines 130 through 180 are included in the loop and are executed for each value of X supplied by the user after an INPUT question. Suppose the user runs the program and types 13 after the INPUT question, then presses RETURN. This assigns the value 13 to the variable X. Now look back at the program. Since X = 13 (13 is the value of X), the condition in line 150 is TRUE and the conditions in lines 160 and 170 are FALSE. So, the computer will print the message in line 150, but will *not* print the messages in lines 160 and 170.

(a) Suppose X = −7. The condition in line 160 is (TRUE or FALSE) _____

_____ and the conditions in lines 150 and 170 are (TRUE or FALSE) _____.

(b) Suppose X = 0. Which condition is TRUE? (Give line number.) _____

_____ Which conditions are FALSE? (Give line numbers.)

_____

— — — — — — — — — —

(a) TRUE; FALSE. The computer will print the message in line 160, but will *not* print the messages in lines 150 and 170.
(b) line 170; lines 150 and 160. The computer will print the message in line 170, but will *not* print the messages in lines 150 and 160.

6. The following program compares two numbers, A and B, and prints an appropriate message. Complete lines 160 and 170 so that the program will RUN as shown.

```
NEW
100 REM **COMPARE TWO NUMBERS, A AND B
110 PRINT "WHEN I ASK, ENTER VALUES FOR A AND B."
120 PRINT
130 INPUT "A =? "; A
140 INPUT "B =? "; B
150 IF A>B THEN PRINT "A IS GREATER THAN B"

160 IF A<B _____

170 _____
180 GOTO 120

RUN
```

```
    WHEN I ASK, ENTER VALUES FOR A AND B.

    A =? 1
    B =? 2
    A IS LESS THAN B

    A =? 7
    B =? 2
    A IS GREATER THAN B

    A =? 55
    B =? 55
    A IS EQUAL TO B

    A =?
```

```
    160 IF A < B THEN PRINT "A IS LESS THAN B"
    170 IF A = B THEN PRINT "A IS EQUAL TO B"
```

7. Let's look at another IF-THEN statement.

This statement:

```
    190 IF X= -1 THEN GOTO 230
```

Tells the computer:

> If the value of X is equal to −1, then go to line 230.
> If the value of X is *not* equal to −1, the computer continues in usual line number order.

In general, the IF-THEN statement has the following form.

> IF *condition* THEN *statement*

The statement could be almost any BASIC statement. The condition is usually a comparison between a variable and a number, between two variables, or between two BASIC expressions. The following table of comparison symbols is handy.

BASIC symbol	Comparison	Math symbol
=	Is equal to	=
<	Is less than	<
>	Is greater than	>
<=(or=<)	Is less than or equal to	≤
>=(or=>)	Is greater than or equal to	≥
<>	Is not equal to	≠

Write each of the following conditions in proper BASIC.

(a) M is greater than 10._____

(b) Z is less than or equal to A squared._____

(c) X is not equal to Y._____

(d) 3 times P is equal to Z times Q._____

— — — — — — — — —

(a) M > 10
(b) Z <= A ∧ 2 or Z <= A * A
(c) X <> Y
(d) 3 * P = Z * Q

8. So far you have seen two members of the IF-THEN family of statements.

    IF-THEN PRINT (message in quotes)
    IF-THEN GOTO (line print)

The second IF-THEN statement shown above tells the computer to branch or GOTO the line number given, if the comparison is true. You may omit the instruction GOTO following THEN, and just specify the line number. Show how you could write the following statement in shorter form.

    190 IF X = −1 THEN GOTO 230

— — — — — — — — —

    190 IF X = −1 THEN 230

9. Remember, the basic form of the IF-THEN statement is as follows.

    IF (condition) THEN (almost any BASIC statement)

Since almost any BASIC statement can follow THEN, we could have the computer assign a value or ask for an INPUT (provided that the condition or comparison is true) in an IF-THEN statement.

    IF Y = 3*Q THEN LET X = 1
    IF 2*Y = 6∧N THEN INPUT "WHAT IS YOUR GUESS? " ; G

It's your turn to practice writing the IF-THEN statements that will assign values if the comparison is true. From the following descriptions, write an IF-THEN statement.

(a) If A does not equal B, then assign the new value 10 to variable B.

(b) If X is equal to or greater than Y, then ask the computer user for another guess and assign the guess to variable G.

— — — — — — — — — —

(a) IF A <> B THEN B = 10 (Remember, you can omit the LET in a direct assignment statement.)
(b) IF X >= Y THEN INPUT "ANOTHER GUESS? "; G or
    IF X => Y THEN INPUT "ANOTHER GUESS? "; G
    (Either >= or => will be understood by the computer.)

10. For each description, write an IF-THEN statement.
(a) If the value of A is less than or equal to 10, go to line 100.

(b) If A is less than 2∗B then increase the old value of T by 1.

(c) If X is greater than 2 times Y, then print the message X IS MORE THAN Y DOUBLED.
(d) If Z does not equal −1, then INPUT a new value for X.

— — — — — — — — — —

(a) IF A <= 10 THEN 100 (GOTO is optional and usually omitted.)
(b) IF A < 2∗B THEN T = T+1 or
    IF A < 2∗B THEN LET T = T+1
    (The LET may be included or omitted.)
(c) IF X > 2∗Y THEN PRINT "X IS MORE THAN Y DOUBLED."
(d) IF Z <> −1 THEN INPUT X

11. One common use of the IF-THEN statement is to recognize a signal called a "flag" that terminates one process and begins another. Here is another version of the "World's Most Expensive Adding Machine" which you first encountered in Chapter 3, frame 53. You may wish to review that frame before plunging onward. Notice that we have used Applesoft BASIC's shortcuts for many of the statements, just to give you practice in recognizing them.

```
100 REM **WORLD'S MOST EXPENSIVE ADDING MACHINE
110 ? "I AM THE WORLD'S MOST EXPENSIVE ADDING MACHINE."
120 ? "EACH TIME I TYPE 'X = ?' YOU TYPE A NUMBER. WHEN"
130 ? "YOU ARE FINISHED ENTERING NUMBERS, TYPE -1 AS YOUR"
140 ? "NUMBER AND I WILL TYPE THE TOTAL OF YOUR PREVIOUS INPUTS."
150 T=0

160 ?
170 INPUT "X =? "; X
180 IF X=-1 THEN 210
190 T=T+X
200 GOTO 160
```
Lines 160 through 200 are a GOTO loop. However, if someone types −1 for the value of X, line 180 will cause the computer to jump out of the loop and go to line 210.

```
210 ?
220 ? "TOTAL = "; T
230 ?
240 GOTO 110
```
This section of the program tells the computer to print a line space, the total of the numbers, and then another line space, then go back to line 110 and start over.

```
RUN
I AM THE WORLD'S MOST EXPENSIVE ADDING MACHINE.
EACH TIME I TYPE 'X = ?' YOU TYPE A NUMBER. WHEN
YOU ARE FINISHED ENTERING NUMBERS, TYPE -1 AS YOUR
NUMBER AND I WILL TYPE THE TOTAL OF YOUR PREVIOUS INPUTS.

X =? 6.95

X =? .47

X =? 1.28

X =? 8.49

X =? 3.06

X =? -1
```
← Aha! Here is our flag saying, "That's all, folks."

```
TOTAL = 20.25

I AM THE WORLD'S MOST EXPENSIVE ADDING MACHINE.    And so on.
```

The flag used in our program is −1; statement 180 checks each and every input value of X and, if it is −1, causes the computer to jump out of the loop to line 210. Lines 210 through 240 print the total (T) and then cause the computer to jump back to line 110 and start over.

Any unusual number that will not be used as a normal INPUT value could be used as a flag.

Modify the program so that, instead of using −1 as the flag, we use 999999 as the flag. You will have to change lines 130 and 180.

130 _____

180 _____

— — — — — — — — — —

```
130 ? "YOU ARE FINISHED ENTERING NUMBERS, TYPE 999999 AS YOUR"
180 IF X=999999 THEN 210
```

12. In our program in frame 11 we first used −1 as the flag. This may not be a good idea if some of the values we wish to use are negative. For example, here are temperatures recorded during one cold week in Minneapolis, Minnesota.

S	M	T	W	T	F	S
10	3	−9	−15	−23	−25	−30

In this case, using 999999 as the flag would prevent confusion between a temperature of −1 and an end-of-data flag of −1.

With a few changes, we can modify the program in frame 11 and obtain a program to compute the mean, or average, of a set of numbers. The formula for determining the mean of a set of N numbers is as follows.

$$\text{Mean} = \frac{\text{sum or total of the numbers}}{\text{number of numbers}} = \frac{T}{N}$$

In the Friendly "Mean" Program, we use the variable T for the total (sum) of the numbers, and N for the number of numbers. That's two different counting (or "tallying") statements in the same program. Complete the program.

```
100 REM **A FRIENDLY 'MEAN' PROGRAM
110 PRINT "I WILL COMPUTE THE MEAN, OR AVERAGE, OF NUMBERS ENTERED."
120 PRINT "WHEN I TYPE 'X =? ' YOU TYPE A NUMBER. WHEN YOU ARE"
130 PRINT "FINISHED ENTERING NUMBERS, TYPE 999999."

140 LET T=0

150 LET N= _____     ←——— We will use N to count the
                                  numbers.

160 PRINT
170 INPUT "X =? " ; X
180 IF X=999999 THEN 220
190 LET T=T+X

200 LET N= _____     ←——— Increase the count by 1.
210 GOTO 160
220 PRINT

230 PRINT "N = " ; _____     ←——— First, print the num-
                                          ber of numbers.

240 PRINT "TOTAL = " ; T

250 PRINT "MEAN = " ; _____  ←——— Compute and
                                          print the
                                          mean.
260 PRINT
270 GOTO 110
```

The RUN is as follows.

```
RUN
I WILL COMPUTE THE MEAN, OR AVERAGE, OF NUMBERS ENTERED.
WHEN I TYPE 'X =? ' YOU TYPE A NUMBER. WHEN YOU ARE
FINISHED ENTERING NUMBERS, TYPE 999999.

X =? 10

X =? 3

X =? -9

X =? -15

X =? -23

X =? -25

X =? -30

X =? 999999            ──── The flag!

N = 7                  ──── N is the number of numbers. One week's
TOTAL = -89                 worth. That was the cold week that was,
MEAN = -12.7142857          or yes, that was a mean week.
```

```
150 LET N=0
200 LET N=N+1
230 PRINT "N = " ; N
250 PRINT "MEAN = " ; T/N
```

13. For temperatures in Minneapolis, 999999 is a good flag. We assume, of course, that the temperature *never* reaches 999999 degrees, even in the summer. For other types of data, 999999 may not be a good flag. One of the most outrageous and least likely BASIC numbers we can think of is the floating-point number, 1E38. For most data, 1E38 would be a good flag. So, modify lines 130 and 180 in the program of frame 12 so that the flag is 1E38.

130 _____

180 _____

```
130 PRINT "FINISHED ENTERING NUMBERS, TYPE 1E38."
180 IF X=1E38 THEN 220
```

14. You have helped us write several computer programs using IF-THEN comparisons. Now it is time for you to do a solo flight and write a program on your own. Think carefully about the use of IF-THEN comparisons, and what the computer will do if the conditions are TRUE or if they are FALSE. Following is a RUN of the program we want you to write.

```
RUN
INPUT A NUMBER AND I WILL TELL YOU IF IT IS
100 OR LESS, OR OVER 100.

YOUR NUMBER? 99
YOUR NUMBER IS 100 OR LESS.

YOUR NUMBER? 101
YOUR NUMBER IS OVER 100.

YOUR NUMBER? 100
YOUR NUMBER IS 100 OR LESS.

YOUR NUMBER?
```

Now you write the program.

```
100 REM **NUMBER SIZE PROGRAM
110 PRINT "INPUT A NUMBER AND I WILL TELL YOU IF IT IS"
120 PRINT "100 OR LESS, OR OVER 100."
130 PRINT
140 INPUT "YOUR NUMBER? " ; N
150 IF N <= 100 THEN PRINT "YOUR NUMBER IS 100 OR LESS."
160 IF N > 100 THEN PRINT "YOUR NUMBER IS OVER 100."
170 GOTO 130
```

15. Soon we will enter the fun-filled realm of computer games. But first, you should learn about random numbers and the unpredictable BASIC function known as RND.

Random numbers are numbers chosen at random from a given set of numbers. Many games come with dice or a spinner or some other device for generating random numbers. Roll the dice; they come up 8. Move 8 spaces.

Functions are automatic features of BASIC that you use to perform special operations. These functions are like built-in programs; most of them could be replaced by a program or segment of a program. However, computers are called upon often enough to do the operations accomplished by these functions that it is worthwhile to "build them in" to the computer language.

BASIC provides a special function, called the RND function, that generates numbers that seem to be chosen at random, like picking numbers out of a hat. The following program shows the use of the RND function. We show you the program (enclosed in a box) and two different runs of that program. We interrupted the first RUN by pressing CONTROL/C, then typed RUN again.

```
10 PRINT RND (1)
20 GOTO 10
```

```
]RUN
.973136996
.103117626
.0177148333
.779343355
.551834438
.617419111
.960296981
.547150891
.802192734
.814107273
.131137465
.80924873
.846447204
.841536558   ←—— We pressed
                 CTRL/C
BREAK IN 10
```

```
]RUN
.591965711
.26800113
.419217095
.878831482
.368373372
.123235316
.280111176
.836328912
.115622079
.815110127
.573253785
.889939655
.427020051
.0226942065
.123590262
.98134051
.128457588   ←—— We pressed
                 CTRL/C
BREAK IN 10
```

(Remember, you can use the techniques shown at the end of Chapter 3 to control the speed of the display.)

Two runs of the program are shown. Are the lists of random numbers in the two runs the same? _____

_ _ _ _ _ _ _ _ _

No. In fact, *don't* expect that by entering our program into your computer and typing RUN, you will get either list. That's the idea of random numbers. They are, well random!

16. The statement 10 PRINT RND(1) causes the computer to produce a *different* list of random numbers each time the program is RUN. The RND function generates numbers that appear to be chosen at random. In our example, the RND function is written RND(1).

We use the number 1 in parentheses. However, *any* positive number is OK, even numbers with decimal fractions! A positive number in parentheses following RND will cause the computer to produce a different list of random numbers each time. This will not be true if zero (0) or a negative number is used. To see how RND works for zero or negative numbers, experiment when you have the opportunity.

Examine the random numbers in frame 15.

(a) Is any number less than zero (negative)? _____

(b) Is any number equal to zero? _____

(c) Is any number greater than one? _____

(d) Is any number equal to one? _____

(e) From the evidence, it appears that random numbers produced by the RND function are _____ zero and _____ one.

— — — — — — — —

(a) no
(b) no
(c) no
(d) no
(e) greater than; less than. However, we haven't shown much evidence—only a few random numbers. When you have a computer to use, we suggest you run off a bunch of random numbers on your computer in order to get more evidence. (But remember, evidence is not proof!)

DECISIONS USING IF-THEN STATEMENTS   111

17. It's true that random numbers produced by the RND function *are* greater than zero and less than one. Another way to say it; random numbers produced by the RND function are *between* 0 and 1. Or, in still another way: 0 < RND(1)< 1.

However, random numbers between 0 and 1 are not always convenient. Sometimes we would like random *digits* (the numbers 0, 1, 2, 3, 4, 5, 6, 7, 8, and 9) or random integers (whole numbers) from 1 to 100. Below is a RUN in which the computer acts as a teaching machine to teach *one-digit* addition to children.

```
RUN

1 + 4 =?5  ←─────────────── Computer typed: 1 + 4 = ?
RIGHT ON...GOOD WORK!!!       Student typed the answer, 5,
                              and pressed RETURN.
9 + 6 =?14 ←─────────────── Student missed this one.
HMMM...I GET A DIFFERENT ANSWER.

9 + 6 =?15 ←─────────────── Computer repeats problem.
RIGHT ON...GOOD WORK!!! ←─── This time student gets it cor-
                              rect.
7 + 2 =?9
RIGHT ON...GOOD WORK!!!

8 + 0 =?  ←──────────────── New problem . . . and so on.
```

Undoubtedly, you are anxious to see the program. Patience! Let's build it, piece by piece. First, how do we generate *random digits*?

The random numbers produced by the RND function are *uniformly distributed* between 0 and 1. That is, they are "spread evenly" between 0 and 1. Each random number is about as likely (or unlikely) to occur as any other random number.

RND(1) is *between* 0 and 1, but is never 0 or 1. Therefore, 10∗RND(1) is between 0 and _____.

── ── ── ── ── ── ── ──

10. But 10∗RND(1) is never *equal to* 0 or 10.

18. Below is a program to print random numbers between 0 and 10. We show you two RUNs to remind you that you get a different list each time.

```
10 PRINT 10*RND(1)
20 GOTO 10
```

]RUN
4.29002079
1.97376049
7.34810327
3.67957921
3.99990709
3.75041519
2.53772171
1.28916366
6.36510833
9.56083769

BREAK IN 10

]RUN
4.97292619
4.81585843
7.3278014
6.75114126
1.8262696
7.82880158
1.75432536
6.34381771
3.74943727
8.122274
.907438741

BREAK IN 10

Each random number in the runs is greater than 0 and less than 10. Each random number can be thought of as having an *integer* part to the left of the decimal point and a fractional part to the right of the decimal point. For example:

The integer part of 8.35007 is 8 and the fractional part is .35007.

Although it is not actually printed, the integer part of .717177 is zero (0). The fractional part is .717177.

(a) What is the integer part of 2.81303? _____ The fractional part? _____

(b) What is the integer part of .0523684? _____ The fractional part? _____

— — — — — — — —

(a) 2; .81303
(b) 0; .0523684

19. Now you write three short programs to print random numbers in the ranges specified.

(a) between 0 and 100
_____
_____

(b) between 0 and 50
_____
_____

(c) between 0 and 6
_____
_____

— — — — — — — — — —

(a) 10 PRINT 100*RND(1)
    20 GOTO 10

    ]RUN
    98.1568261
    70.6743818
    98.4803409
    79.4972044
    28.9463256
    71.4379359
    75.1928718
    9.10165628
    85.5416984
    75.8044101
    6.80029713

    BREAK IN 10

(b) 10 PRINT 50*RND(1)
    20 GOTO 10

    ]RUN
    41.4218715
    44.5642131
    38.0001683
    12.8445135
    25.2467624
    21.6907612
    8.45179742
    6.46988141
    1.88372652

    BREAK IN 10

(c) 10 PRINT 6*RND(1)
    20 GOTO 10

    ]RUN
    2.57401247
    1.18425629
    4.40886196
    5.73650261
    2.98375571
    2.88951506
    4.39668084

    BREAK IN 10

20. For each random number *between* 0 and 10, the integer (whole number) part is a *single digit*. Wouldn't it be nice if we could direct the computer to delete the fractional part and keep the integer part?

Well, as you may suspect, we can. BASIC has another clever and useful function called INT. Here are some examples.

```
INT (3) = 3            INT (7) = 7
INT (3.14159) = 3      INT (7.99999) = 7
INT (1.23456) = 1      INT (.999999) = 0
```

(Say it like this: "The integer part of 3.14159 is 3.")

In general, if X is any positive number, INT(X) is the *integer part* of X. Now, you apply INT to some random numbers.

(a) INT (7.45547) = _____   (b) INT (.333645) = _____
(c) INT (2.57104) = _____   (d) INT (.032279) = _____

— — — — — — — — —

(a) 7
(b) 0 (Think of .333645 as being equal to 0.333645.)
(c) 2
(d) 0 (Think of .032279 as being equal to 0.032279.)

21. *Caution:* INT works as shown in frame 20 only for *positive* numbers or zero. In general, INT(X) computes *the greatest integer less than or equal to X*. For example:

```
INT (3.14) = 3     but     INT (−3.14) = −4
INT (7) = 7        and     INT (−7) = −7
INT (.999) = 0     but     INT (−.999) = −1
```

For positive numbers, or zero, INT(X) computes the integer part of X. In a program, the *value* assigned to X will be substituted for X in the INT parentheses when the program is RUN. The computer then performs the INT function on the numerical value. Of course, any variable could be used instead of the letter X, as long as it has been assigned a value earlier in the program.

You be the computer and show what you will print when your human tells you to RUN the following programs.

(a) 10 X=15.77   (b) 10 A=99.999   (c) 10 F=98.6
     20 ? INT(X)   20 ? INT(A)   20 ? INT(F)
     RUN   RUN   RUN
     _____   _____   _____

— — — — — — — — —

(a) 15; (b) 99; (c) 98

22. Instead of a number, we can write a variable, a function, or any BASIC expression in the parentheses that follow the word INT.

    INT( )
          └── Any BASIC number, variable, function, or expression here

You should be able to distinguish between *values*, *variables*, *expressions*, *functions*, and *strings*. To show that you can, identify each of the following with one of the words given above in italics.

(a) X _____
(b) X*2 _____
(c) RND(1) _____
(d) "A+B IS AN EXPRESSION" _____
(e) 22 _____
(f) 1+1 _____
(g) INT(52.88) _____
(h) "=" _____
(i) 4*(3+X) _____
(j) Which of the above could be used in the parentheses of a function such as INT or RND? _____

— — — — — — — —

(a) variable
(b) expression
(c) function
(d) string
(e) value
(f) expression
(g) function
(h) string
(i) expression
(j) a, b, c, e, f, g, and i

116 BASIC FOR THE APPLE II

23. Remember, the general form for the INT function is as follows.

    INT ( )
         └── Any BASIC number, variable, function, or expression here

So, it is OK to write INT(10*RND(1)). This is an expression containing a function as part of the expression.

    RND(1) is a random number between 0 and 1.
    10*RND(1) is a random number between 0 and 10.
    INT(10*RND(1)) is a *random digit*.

The following program causes the computer to generate and print random digits. Digits are the numbers 0, 1, 2, 3, 4, 5, 6, 7, 8, and 9, or 0 to 9, inclusive. Note that "inclusive" means it includes both 0 and 9, as well as the digits between 0 and 9.

```
10 PRINT INT(10*RND(1))
20 GOTO 10
```

```
]RUN              ]RUN
9                 8
1                 5
0                 2
7                 4
5                 8
6                 3
9                 1
5                 2
8                 8

BREAK IN 10       BREAK IN 10
```

This program prints random digits, which are integers from ___ to ___, inclusive.

————————————

0; 9

DECISIONS USING IF-THEN STATEMENTS

24. Now write a short program to print random integers (whole numbers) from 0 to 19, inclusive. Our RUN looks like this.

```
]RUN
3
10
17
5
9
19
7
2

BREAK IN 10
```

```
10 PRINT INT(20*RND(1))
20 GOTO 10
```

Be sure to match the parentheses. There must be a right, or closing, parenthesis for every left, or opening, parenthesis; if not, the computer will give you an error message when you RUN the program.

25. What if we want random integers from 1 to 20, inclusive, instead of from 0 to 19? Well, that's easy. Simply add a 1 to the random integer. You could do it in two ways.

```
10 PRINT INT (20*RND(1)+1)
20 GOTO 10
```

or

```
10 PRINT INT (20*RND(1))+1
20 GOTO 10

]RUN
14
20
2
1
19
7
20
2
15

BREAK IN 10
```

118 BASIC FOR THE APPLE II

The "+1" can be added to the random number either before or after taking the integer part of 20*RND(1). The resulting random integer will be the same in either case.

Now you write three simple programs to print a list of random integers.

(a) from 1 to 10 inclusive

_____

_____

(b) from 1 to 100, inclusive

_____

_____

(c) from 1 to 12, inclusive

_____

_____

― ― ― ― ― ― ― ― ― ―

(a) 10 PRINT INT(10*RND(1))+1   or   10 PRINT INT (10*RND(1)+1)
     20 GOTO 10   20 GOTO 10
(b) 10 PRINT INT(100*RND(1))+1   or   10 PRINT INT(100*RND(1)+1)
     20 GOTO 10   20 GOTO 10
(c) 10 PRINT INT(12*RND(1))+1   or   10 PRINT INT(12*RND(1)+1)
     20 GOTO 10   20 GOTO 10

26. What if we want random integers from 5 to 10 inclusive? Here is a hint: to get random integers from 1 to 10 instead of 0 to 9, we added a +1. Look at it like this.

          0 to 9
         +1   +1
         ―――――――――
          1 to 10

(a) The function INT(6*RND(1)) will generate what random digits? _____

     _____

(b) What should we add to the expression INT(6*RND(1)) in order to generate integers from 5 to 10 inclusive? _____

(c) What should we add in order to generate integers from 11 to 16 inclusive?

     _____

― ― ― ― ― ― ― ― ― ―

(a) 0 to 5 inclusive, that is, 0, 1, 2, 3, 4, and 5, a total of 6 digits.
(b) +5   0 to 5
                         +5   +5
                         ─────────
                         5   10
(c) +11   0 to   5
                         +11   +11
                         ─────────
                         11   16

27. Look back at the RUN in frame 17 before we continue. Now we are ready to build the addition practice program. Here is the first section of the program that produced the RUN.

```
100 REM **ADDITION PRACTICE PROGRAM
200 REM **GENERATE RANDOM NUMBERS, A AND B
210 LET A =  INT (10 * RND (1))
220 LET B =  INT (10 * RND (1))
```

The values of A and B will be_____

— — — — — — — — — — —

random digits (0, 1, 2, 3, 4, 5, 6, 7, 8, or 9)

28. Ready for the next piece? Here we go.

```
300 REM **DISPLAY PROBLEM AND ASK FOR ANSWER
310 PRINT
320 PRINT A;" + ";B;" =";
330 INPUT C
```

Line 320 is something new. The statement

```
320 PRINT A;" + ";B;" =";
```

tells the computer to print the value assigned to A, then print the symbol +, then print the value of B, then print =. We have separated these print statement items with semicolons, which helps you see the separate items. These semicolons may be omitted, except for the last one, which is doing special duty. A semicolon at the very end of a PRINT statement, like the fourth or last one in line 320 in the program for frame 28, tells the computer to stay where it stopped printing, so that the display of the next characters continues from the place on the same line where the last ones ended. Thus the semicolon keeps the computer from displaying the next output on the next display line down.

Do you remember? The INPUT statement causes the computer to print a *question mark*. This question mark will be printed on the same line as the information from the PRINT statement, because of that semicolon at the end of line 320.

120 BASIC FOR THE APPLE II

For example, if A = 7 and B = 5, then lines 320 and 330 will cause the computer to print the following.

$$7 + 5 = ?$$

from line 320 ⎯⎯⎯⎯⎯⎯⎯⎯   from line 330 (INPUT question mark)

If A = 3 and B = 4, what will be printed by lines 320 and 330? _____

― ― ― ― ― ― ― ―

    3 + 4 =? (This, of course, is the *random problem* which helps the eager young learner practice addition.)

29. After the learner types an answer and presses the RETURN key, the computer assigns the answer value to variable C and continues.

Note how we are using REM statements to tell something about each piece of the program. This doesn't help the computer, but it does help *people* read and understand how the program works.

```
400 REM **IS THE ANSWER CORRECT?
410 IF C = A + B THEN 610
```

If the student's answer (C) is correct, the computer will go to line _____.

― ― ― ― ― ― ― ―

610 (If the answer is not correct, the computer continues in regular line number order.)

30. If the student's answer is not correct, then the IF-THEN condition is false. The computer next does the following as it continues on in the program in line number order.

```
500 REM **ANSWER IS NOT CORRECT
510 PRINT "HMMM...I GET A DIFFERENT ANSWER."
520 GOTO 310
```

Assume an incorrect answer. The computer prints HMMM . . . I GET A DIFFERENT ANSWER, then goes to line 310. From there (check previous frames if necessary), what happens next? _____

― ― ― ― ― ― ― ―

The computer repeats the problem.

Note: In a previous book, we had the computer type YOU GOOFED. TRY AGAIN. Now that we know more about learners, we wish to make the computer seem friendly and compassionate, rather than nasty and authoritarian. Remember that what the computer "says" depends on the person who writes the program, and not the machine itself.

31. Review frame 29, which shows lines 400 and 410 of the program. If the learner's answer is correct, line 410 causes the computer to go to line 610.

```
600 REM **ANSWER IS CORRECT
610 PRINT "RIGHT ON...GOOD WORK!!!"
620 GOTO 210
```

Assume a correct answer. The computer prints RIGHT ON...GOOD WORK!!! and then goes to line 210. What happens next?_____

_____

— — — — — — — — —

The computer generates a new problem (new values for A and B) and prints the new problem.

32. Below is a listing of the complete ADDITION PRACTICE PROGRAM.

```
100 REM **ADDITION PRACTICE PROGRAM
200 REM **GENERATE RANDOM NUMBERS, A AND B
210 LET A = INT (10 * RND (1))
220 LET B = INT (10 * RND (1))
300 REM **DISPLAY PROBLEM AND ASK FOR ANSWER
310 PRINT
320 PRINT A;" + ";B;" =";
330 INPUT C
400 REM **IS THE ANSWER CORRECT?
410 IF C = A + B THEN 610
500 REM **ANSWER IS NOT CORRECT
510 PRINT "HMMM...I GET A DIFFERENT ANSWER."
520 GOTO 310
600 REM **ANSWER IS CORRECT
610 PRINT "RIGHT ON...GOOD WORK!!!"
620 GOTO 210
```

Change line 210 so that the value of A is a random integer from 0 to 19, inclusive, instead of 0 to 9.

    210 LET A =_____

— — — — — — — — —

    210 LET A=INT(20*RND(1))

33. Careful on this one! Change line 220 so that the value of B is a random integer from 10 to 20, inclusive.

    220 LET B =_____

— — — — — — — — —

```
220 LET B = INT (11 * RND (1)) + 10
```

That gives us 10 to 20 inclusive, eleven numbers in all.

```
   0 to  10
 +10    +10
  10 to  20
```

We changed lines 210 and 220 of the program in frame 32 to look like the answer to frame 32, and ran the modified program. Remember, a RUN on your computer will probably show different numbers in the problems. These are random numbers, after all.

```
RUN

16 + 14 =?30
RIGHT ON...GOOD WORK!!!

16 + 15 =?31
RIGHT ON...GOOD WORK!!!

4 + 10 =?15
HMMM...I GET A DIFFERENT ANSWER.

4 + 10 =?14
RIGHT ON...GOOD WORK!!!

6 + 16 =?
```
← And so on as the RUN continues.

34. When the learner's answer is correct, the computer always prints: RIGHT ON . . . GOOD WORK!!! To relieve the monotony, let's modify the program so that the computer selects at random from three possible replies to a correct answer. The changes are in the portion of the program beginning at line 600.

```
600 REM **ANSWER IS CORRECT
610 LET R =  INT (3 * RND (1)) + 1   ← Note the + 1.
620 IF R = 1 THEN 630
621 IF R = 2 THEN 650
622 IF R = 3 THEN 670
630 PRINT "RIGHT ON...GOOD WORK!!!"
640 GOTO 210
650 PRINT "YOU GOT IT! TRY ANOTHER."
660 GOTO 210
670 PRINT "THAT'S GREAT! KEEP IT UP!"
680 GOTO 210
```

The possible values of R are ____, ____, and ____.

1, 2, and 3 (not 0, 1, and 2, because we added +1 at the end of line 610)

35. So, we see, R can be 1 or 2 or 3.
(a) If R = 1, the computer will print_____
(b) If R = 3, the computer will print_____
(c) If R = 2, the computer will print_____

(a) RIGHT ON . . . GOOD WORK!!!
(b) THAT'S GREAT! KEEP IT UP!
(c) YOU GOT IT! TRY ANOTHER.

36. We made the changes in response (frame 34) from the original program (frame 32) and ran the modified program. Here is what happened.

```
RUN

9 + 19 =?28
THAT'S GREAT! KEEP IT UP!

6 + 15 =?21
YOU GOT IT! TRY ANOTHER.

17 + 12 =?29
THAT'S GREAT! KEEP IT UP!

12 +11 =?23
RIGHT ON...GOOD WORK!!!

0 + 19 =?19
RIGHT ON...GOOD WORK!!!

8 + 17 =?22
HMMM...I GET A DIFFERENT ANSWER.

8 + 17 =?
```

If the learner's answer is incorrect, the computer always prints: HMMM . . . I GET A DIFFERENT ANSWER. Modify the program in frame 32 so that, for an incorrect response, the computer selects randomly one of the two following responses.

```
HMMM...I GET A DIFFERENT ANSWER
TRY A DIFFERENT ANSWER. GOOD LUCK!

500 REM***ANSWER IS NOT CORRECT
510 LET R =_____
520 IF_____
530 IF_____
540 PRINT_____
550 GOTO 310_____
560_____
570 GOTO 310_____
```

— — — — — — — —

```
500 REM **ANSWER IS NOT CORRECT
510 LET R =  INT (2 *  RND (1)) +1
520 IF R = 1 THEN 540
530 IF R = 2 THEN 560
540 PRINT "HMMM...I GET A DIFFERENT ANSWER."
550 GOTO 310
560 PRINT "TRY A DIFFERENT ANSWER. GOOD LUCK!"
570 GOTO 310
```

Again, we are trying to make the computer seem friendly and helpful, instead of harsh and unforgiving.

37. The three statements:

```
620 IF R=1 THEN 630
621 IF R=2 THEN 650
622 IF R=3 THEN 670
```

can be replaced by a single statement.

```
620 ON R GOTO 630,650,670
```

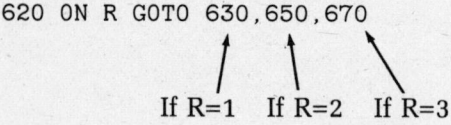

If R=1   If R=2   If R=3

DECISIONS USING IF-THEN STATEMENTS

With this change, the program segment in frame 34 can be rewritten as follows. (Remember to delete (take out) lines 621 and 622 by typing *only* the *line number*, followed by RETURN.)

```
600 REM **ANSWER IS CORRECT
610 LET R =   INT (3 *  RND (1)) + 1
620 ON R GOTO 630,650,670
630 PRINT "RIGHT ON!!!...GOOD WORK!!!"
640 GOTO 210
650 PRINT "YOU GOT IT! TRY ANOTHER."
660 GOTO 210
670 PRINT "THAT'S GREAT! KEEP IT UP!"
680 GOTO 210
```

(a) Look at line 610. What are the *possible* values of R? _____
(b) Suppose, during a RUN, the random number generated by RND(1) in line 610 is .34319. What value will R have? _____
(c) In this case, which line will the ON R GOTO statement send the computer to? _____

──────────

(a) 1, 2, 3
(b) 2. INT(3*.34319)+1 = INT(1.02957)+1 = 1 + 1 = 2
(c) line 650

38. In general, the ON ... GOTO statement has the following form.

   ON e GOTO $l_1, l_2, l_3, \ldots, l_n$

Where e can be any BASIC expression and $l_1, l_2, l_3, \ldots, l_n$ are line numbers. Valid values for e are integers 1, 2, 3, ..., n. If e = 1, the computer goes to line l_1. If e = 2, the computer goes to l_2. And so on. If the value of e, is not an integer from 1 to n, the fraction part is dropped, and the remaining integer part of the number will be used.

Use an ON ... GOTO to replace the two IF statements (lines 520 and 530) in our solution to frame 36. Don't forget to delete line 530.

```
500 REM **ANSWER IS NOT CORRECT
510 LET R =   INT (2 *  RND (1)) + 1
520 ON_____
540 PRINT "HMMM...I GET A DIFFERENT ANSWER."
550 GOTO 310
560 PRINT "TRY A DIFFERENT ANSWER. GOOD LUCK!"
570 GOTO 310
```

──────────

```
520 ON R GOTO 540,560
```

39. And now, a wonderful space-saving method! Here is the first part of our addition practice program, featuring *multiple statements per line*.

```
100 REM **ADDITION PRACTICE PROGRAM
200 REM **GENERATE RANDOM NUMBERS, A AND B
210 LET A =   INT (20 *  RND (1))
220 LET B =   INT (11 *  RND (1)) + 10
300 REM **DISPLAY PROBLEM AND ASK FOR ANSWER
310 PRINT : PRINT A;" + ";B;" =";: INPUT C
400 REM **IS THE ANSWER CORRECT?
410 IF C = A + B THEN 610
500 REM **ANSWER IS NOT CORRECT
510 LET R =   INT (2 *  RND (1)) + 1
520 ON R GOTO 540,560
540 PRINT "HMMM...I GET A DIFFERENT ANSWER.": GOTO 310
560 PRINT "TRY A DIFFERENT ANSWER. GOOD LUCK!": GOTO 310
```

Line 310 has 3 statements.

Lines 540 and 560 each have 2 statements per line.

If you have the earlier version in the computer, remember to delete lines 320, 330, 550, and 570, after combining these lines into multiple statements.

In the program, line 310 contains three statements, and lines 540 and 560 each contain two statements. In a line that contains more than one statement, what symbol, or character is used between statements? _____

_____

a colon (:)

```
                    ┌─ colon ─── colon ─┐
310 PRINT : PRINT A;" + ";B;" =";: INPUT C
```

40. For readability, Applesoft BASIC will insert spaces into a program line and eliminate spaces (outside of strings) that you may have left. In fact, leaving out spaces and unneeded semicolons, we could have entered line 310 as shown below. The only necessary semicolon is the one at the end of the second PRINT statement.

```
310?:?:A" + "B" =";:INPUTC
```

Now, if you LIST line 310, Applesoft inserts spaces to help make the statement easier to read.

```
310 PRINT : PRINT A" + "B" =";: INPUT C
```

DECISIONS USING IF-THEN STATEMENTS

We didn't show you the entire program in the last frame, because we want you to rewrite the part of the program beginning with line 600 as shown in frame 37, using multiple statements in those lines where it makes sense to group statements to work together.

```
600 REM **ANSWER IS CORRECT
610 LET R =  INT (3 *  RND (1)) + 1
620 ON R GOTO 630, 640, 650

630_____

640_____

650_____
```
— — — — — — — — — —

```
630 PRINT "RIGHT ON...GOOD WORK!!!" : GOTO 210
640 PRINT "YOU GOT IT! TRY ANOTHER." : GOTO 210
650 PRINT "THAT'S GREAT! KEEP IT UP!" : GOTO 210
```

(Now lines 660, 670, and 680 in the previous version can be deleted. And don't forget to change line 620 as shown above. RUN and then SAVE your completed program.)

41. Here is the computer game we promised you earlier in the chapter. Note the use of multiple statements per line in lines 150, 160, 170, and 180. If you think this program looks familiar, look back at Chapter 1 and see how far you have come already in learning BASIC!

```
100 REM **GUESS MY NUMBER — A COMPUTER GAME
110 LET X=INT(100*RND(1))+1
120 PRINT
130 PRINT "I'M THINKING OF A NUMBER FROM 1 TO 100."
140 PRINT "GUESS MY NUMBER!"
150 PRINT : INPUT "YOUR GUESS? " ; G
160 IF G < X THEN PRINT "TRY A BIGGER NUMBER." : GOTO 150
170 IF G > X THEN PRINT "TRY A SMALLER NUMBER." : GOTO 150
180 IF G = X THEN PRINT "THAT'S IT! YOU GUESSED MY NUMBER!" : GOTO 110

RUN

I'M THINKING OF A NUMBER FROM 1 TO 100.
GUESS MY NUMBER!

YOUR GUESS? 50
TRY A BIGGER NUMBER.

YOUR GUESS? 75
TRY A SMALLER NUMBER.

YOUR GUESS? 68
TRY A BIGGER NUMBER.

YOUR GUESS? 72
TRY A BIGGER NUMBER.

YOUR GUESS? 73
THAT'S IT! YOU GUESSED MY NUMBER!

I'M THINKING OF A NUMBER FROM 1 TO 100.
GUESS MY NUMBER!

YOUR GUESS?                       And so on.
```

Line 110 tells the computer to generate a random number and store it in variable X. This number will be a(n) _____ from _____ _____ to _____.

__ __ __ __ __ __ __ __ __ __

integer (or whole number); 1; 100

42. Multiple statements per line give us another nice shortcut. You'll recall that if the comparison in an IF-THEN statement is false, the computer skips the rest of the statement and goes on to the next line in the program in line number order. The nice thing is that the computer will also skip any statements that follow a false IF-THEN comparison if they are on the same multiple statement line. The rest of the statements on a line will be executed if the IF-THEN comparison is true. Therefore, in one line, you can have the computer do more than one thing if an IF-THEN comparison is true. Consider line 170 as it is shown here. The computer will both PRINT and GOTO if the condition is true, but it won't do either if the condition is false.

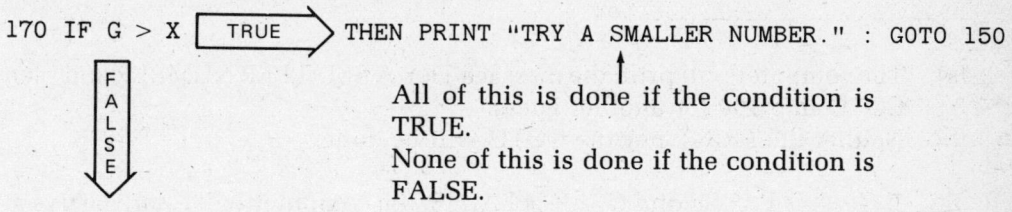

The condition is: $G > X$

(a) Suppose $G = 90$ and $X = 73$. Is the condition TRUE or FALSE? _____

(b) Suppose $G = 70$ and $X = 73$. Is the condition TRUE or FALSE? _____

(c) Suppose $G = 73$ and $X = 73$. Is the condition TRUE or FALSE? _____

— — — — — — — — — —

(a) TRUE; (b) FALSE; (c) FALSE

43. Line 150 causes the computer to print YOUR GUESS? When the player types a guess, the computer stores it in variable G. Lines 160, 170, and 180 compare the guess G with the random number X. Let's look at line 160.

```
160 IF G < X THEN PRINT "TRY A BIGGER NUMBER." : GOTO 150
```

If the guess G is less than the number X, the computer will print the message TRY A BIGGER NUMBER and will then GOTO line 150 to ask for another guess. However, if G is greater than X or equal to X, *neither* the PRINT *nor* the GOTO will be done. Here is another way to "picture" that idea.

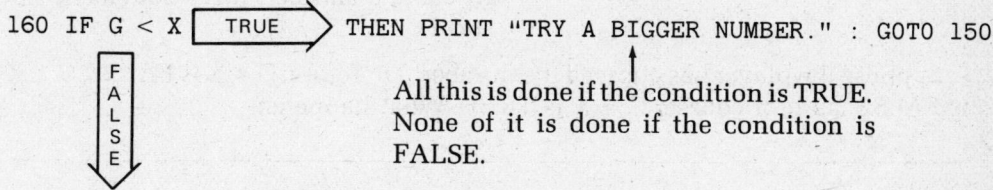

130 BASIC FOR THE APPLE II

So, if G < X is FALSE, the computer goes on to line 170. Describe what happens when the computer executes line 170.

```
170 IF G > X THEN PRINT "TRY A SMALLER NUMBER." : GOTO 150
```

(a) If G is greater than X (G > X is TRUE), then_____
_____.

(b) However, if G is *not* greater than X (G > X is FALSE), then_____
_____.

— — — — — — — — —

(a) The computer will print the message TRY A SMALLER NUMBER and then GOTO line 150 for another guess.
(b) Neither the PRINT nor the GOTO will be done.

44. If G < X is FALSE *and* G > X is FALSE, the computer will finally arrive at line 180. Here is a picture of the entire process of arriving at line 180.

160 IF G < X [TRUE ⇒ THEN PRINT "TRY A BIGGER NUMBER" : GOTO 150

    ↓ FALSE

170 IF G > X [TRUE ⇒ THEN PRINT "TRY A SMALLER NUMBER" : GOTO 150

    ↓ FALSE

180 IF G = X [TRUE ⇒ THEN PRINT "THAT'S IT! YOU GUESSED MY NUMBER"; GOTO 110

    ↓ FALSE

This will never happen because, if G < X is FALSE and G > X is FALSE, then G = X must be TRUE. In fact, we could have written line 180 without the IF G = X, using a simple PRINT statement instead.

Suppose the player has guessed the number. Therefore, G < X is FALSE, G > X is FALSE, and, of course, G = X is TRUE. What happens?

_____
_____
_____

The computer prints the message THAT'S IT! YOU GUESSED MY NUMBER, then goes to line 110, where it is directed to "think of" a new number and start the game again.

45. For very young children, we may wish to reduce the range of integers generated by the statement that uses the RND functions (line 110). For example, instead of generating a number from 1 to 100, we may wish a number from 1 to 25. Conversely, advanced players may prefer a larger range, say 1 to 1000.
(a) Modify lines 110 and 130 so that the range is 1 to 25.

110 _____

130 _____

(b) Modify lines 110 and 130 so that the range is 1 to 1000.

110 _____

130 _____

(a)
```
110 LET X=INT(25*RND(1))+1
130 PRINT "I'M THINKING OF A NUMBER FROM 1 TO 25."
```

(b)
```
110 LET X=INT(1000*RND(1))+1
130 PRINT "I'M THINKING OF A NUMBER FROM 1 TO 1000."
```

46. Here is a convenient way to make it easy to change the range.

```
100 REM **GUESS MY NUMBER — A COMPUTER GAME
105 LET R=100
110 LET X=INT(R*RND(1))+1
120 PRINT
130 PRINT "I'M THINKING OF A NUMBER FROM 1 TO " ; R
```

Now the range is 1 to R, where R is assigned a value in line 105, then used in lines 110 and 130. So, to change the range, you simply change line 105. Suppose you want the range to be 1 to 500. What do you write for line 105?

105 _____

```
105 LET R=500  or simply  105 R=500
```

47. Using IF-THEN statements and multiple statements per line, modify and rewrite your NUMBER SIZE PROGRAM from frame 14 so that it will RUN like the one following.

```
RUN
INPUT A NUMBER AND I WILL TELL YOU IF IT IS
LESS THAN 100, BETWEEN 100 AND 1000, OR OVER 1000.

YOUR NUMBER? 99
YOUR NO. IS LESS THAN 100.

YOUR NUMBER? 100
YOUR NO. IS BETWEEN 100 AND 1000.

YOUR NUMBER? 999
YOUR NO. IS BETWEEN 100 AND 1000.

YOUR NUMBER? 1000
YOUR NO. IS BETWEEN 100 AND 1000.

YOUR NUMBER? 1001
YOUR NO. IS OVER 1000.

YOUR NUMBER?
```

- - - - - - - - - - -

```
100 REM **NEW NUMBER SIZE PROGRAM
110 PRINT "INPUT A NUMBER AND I WILL TELL YOU IF IT IS"
120 PRINT "LESS THAN 100, BETWEEN 100 AND 1000, OR OVER 1000."
130 PRINT : INPUT "YOUR NUMBER? " ; N
140 IF N<100 THEN PRINT "YOUR NO. IS LESS THAN 100." : GOTO 130
150 IF N<=1000 THEN PRINT "YOUR NO. IS BETWEEN 100 and 1000." : GOTO 130
160 IF N >1000 THEN PRINT "YOUR NO. IS OVER 1000." : GOTO 130
```

48. Now we want you to put your accumulated knowledge of BASIC to work and write a program to provide practice for a person learning or reviewing the "times table," that is, multiplication from 1 times 1 to 12 times 12. Of course, we are calling this program COMPASSIONATE MULTIPLICATION PRACTICE. Study the RUN and our notes, then build your program. If you have a computer handy to use, check your own program before looking at our way of doing it.

Generate a problem, using random numbers from 1 to 12. Print the problem and ask for an answer. Compare the player's answer with the correct answer.

> If the answer is smaller than the correct answer, print TRY A BIGGER NUMBER and repeat the problem.
> If the answer is bigger than the correct answer, print TRY A SMALLER NUMBER and repeat the problem.
> If the answer is correct, tell the player that she or he has typed the correct answer.

Our program uses three different replies to a correct answer. These are chosen at random from the following three possibilities.

> THAT'S IT!
> CORRECT ANSWER
> GOOD WORK! KEEP IT UP

A RUN of the program we want you to write is shown on the next page.

```
RUN
2 × 4 =?8
GOOD WORK! KEEP IT UP!

2 × 2 =?4
GOOD WORK! KEEP IT UP!

2 × 8 =?15
TRY A BIGGER NUMBER.

2 × 8 =?16
CORRECT ANSWER!

10 × 1 =?10
CORRECT ANSWER!

10 × 9 =?100
TRY A SMALLER NUMBER.

10 × 9 =?90
GOOD WORK! KEEP IT UP!

11 × 7 =?
```

```
100 REM **COMPASSIONATE MULTIPLICATION PRACTICE
110 LET A=INT(12*RND(1))+1 : LET B=INT(12*RND(1))+1
120 PRINT : PRINT A; " × "; B; " ="; : INPUT C
130 IF C<A*B THEN PRINT "TRY A BIGGER NUMBER." : GOTO 120
140 IF C>A*B THEN PRINT "TRY A SMALLER NUMBER." : GOTO 120
150 LET R=INT(3*RND(1))+1 : ON R GOTO 160,170,180
160 PRINT "THAT'S IT!" : GOTO 110
170 PRINT "CORRECT ANSWER!" : GOTO 110
180 PRINT "GOOD WORK! KEEP IT UP!" : GOTO 110
```

49. Some of the older versions of BASIC required an END statement as the last statement in a program. Most versions of BASIC for home computers do not need this final END. However, the END statement, and its relative, the STOP statement, can be handy for terminating a program in some place other than the last line numbered statement.

It is often handy to be able to end or stop a program as a result of an IF-THEN decision. END or STOP can be the condition to fulfill after THEN if the condition is TRUE. Examples:

```
20 IF X = 10 THEN STOP
20 IF X = 10 THEN END
```

For our version of BASIC, using STOP will cause the computer to type a message, as shown below, giving the line number where the STOP statement was encountered and the RUN ended.

```
BREAK IN 20
```

However, a RUN that ends when an END statement is encountered just gives the standard bracket].

In a multiple-statement line with IF-THEN, END or STOP could be used as below:

```
120 IF Y * Q = 100 THEN PRINT "THAT'S ALL, FOLKS": END
120 IF Y * Q = 100 THEN PRINT "THAT'S ALL, FOLKS": STOP
```

At the end of a math drill or game playing program, you could use the following approach.

```
310 INPUT "ANOTHER GAME (YES OR NO)? "; A$
320 IF A$ = "NO" THEN END
330 GOTO 100
```

In a counting loop program, insert a line to tell the computer to quit counting when F is greater than 6.

```
10 LET F = 1
20 _____
30 PRINT "F ="; F
40 LET F = F + 1
50 GOTO 20
```

```
20 IF F > 6 THEN END
```

or

```
20 IF F > 6 THEN STOP
```

Self-Test

Try this Self-Test, so you can evaluate how much you have learned in Chapter 4.

1. Give the BASIC symbols for each of the following comparisons.

   _____ is equal to

   _____ is less than

   _____ is greater than

   _____ is less than or equal to

   _____ is greater than or equal to

   _____ is not equal to

2. Describe each IF-THEN statement in words. That is, describe what the statement tells the computer to do.

   (a) IF G = X THEN 200_____

   (b) IF X > = 0 THEN C = C+1_____

   (c) IF N <> INT(N) THEN PRINT "N IS NOT AN INTEGER." : GOTO 210_____

   (d) IF A*A+B*B = C*C THEN PRINT "YES, IT IS A RIGHT TRI-ANGLE."_____

3. For each description, write an IF-THEN statement.
   (a) If the value of N is less than or equal to 7, go to line 15.

   (b) If A is less than 2*P, then increase the value of N by 1 and go to line 180.

   (c) If M/N is equal to INT(M/N), then print the message M IS EVENLY DIVISIBLE BY N.

4. Complete the following program to tell how many years are needed to "double your money." Use multiple statements in line 190.

```
100 REM **HOW MANY YEARS TO DOUBLE YOUR MONEY
110 PRINT "IF YOU TYPE THE AMOUNT OF PRINCIPAL AND THE"
120 PRINT "INTEREST RATE PER YEAR, I WILL SHOW YOU HOW"
130 PRINT "MANY YEARS TO DOUBLE YOUR MONEY."
140 PRINT
150 INPUT "PRINCIPAL? " ; P
160 INPUT "INTEREST RATE? " ; R
170 LET N=1
180 LET A=P*(1+R/100)^N
190_____
200 PRINT
210 PRINT "YEARS TO DOUBLE YOUR MONEY: " ; N
220 PRINT "THE ACTUAL AMOUNT WILL BE $" ; A
```

This is a loop — lines 180 and 190.

```
RUN
IF YOU TYPE THE AMOUNT OF PRINCIPAL AND THE
INTEREST RATE PER YEAR, I WILL SHOW YOU HOW
MANY YEARS TO DOUBLE YOUR MONEY.

PRINCIPAL? 1000
INTEREST RATE? 6
```
— 1000 at 6% per year.

```
YEARS TO DOUBLE YOUR MONEY: 12
THE ACTUAL AMOUNT WILL BE $2012.2
```

5. What will be the result of running the following program? Show the RUN.

```
10 LET K=1
20 PRINT K
30 LET K=K+1
40 IF K<=5 THEN 20
RUN
```

6. What will the RUN look like for this program?

```
10 LET K=1
20 IF K<5 THEN K=K+1 : GOTO 20
30 PRINT K
```

7. Describe the random numbers generated by each of the following expressions.

   (a) RND(1) _____

   _____

   (b) 2*RND(1) _____

   _____

   (c) INT(2*RND(1)) _____

   _____

   (d) INT(2*RND(1))+1 _____

   _____

   (e) INT(3*RND(1))−1 _____

   _____

   (f) 3.14159*RND(1) _____

   _____

8. Here is an incomplete program to simulate (imitate) flipping a coin. Please complete the program. (*Hint:* C should be 0 or 1, at random.)

```
100 REM **COIN FLIPPER
110 LET C =_____
120 IF C=0 THEN PRINT "TAILS" : GOTO 110
130 IF C=1 THEN PRINT "HEADS" : GOTO 110

RUN
HEADS
HEADS
TAILS
TAILS
HEADS
HEADS
HEADS
HEADS
TAILS
HEADS
TAILS
TAILS
HEADS
HEADS
```

Answers to Self-Test

The frame numbers in parentheses refer to the frames in the chapter where the topic is discussed. You may wish to refer to these for quick review.

1. =   is equal to
   <   is less than
   >   is greater than
   <=   is less than or equal to (=< is also acceptable)
   >=   is greater than or equal to (=> is also acceptable)
   <>   is not equal to

   (frame 7)

2. (a) If the value of G is equal to the value of X, go to line 200. Otherwise (G = X is FALSE), continue in the usual line number order. (frames 1–8)
   (b) If the value of X is greater than or equal to zero, increase the value of C by 1. Otherwise (X > = 0 is FALSE), do not execute the LET portion. In either case, continue in regular line number order. (frame 10)
   (c) If N < > INT(N) is TRUE, this means that the value of N is not an integer. In this case, print the string N IS NOT AN INTEGER and then go to line 210. However, if N *is* an integer, N <> INT(N) will be FALSE. In this case, neither the PRINT nor the GOTO will be executed and the computer will simply continue in regular line number order. (frames 1–8, 20–23, 42)
   (d) If the value of A squared plus B squared is equal to the value of C squared, print the string YES, IT IS A RIGHT TRIANGLE. Otherwise if A*A+B*B = C*C is FALSE, *don't* print the string. In either case, continue in regular line number order. (frames 1–8)

3. (a) IF N<=7 THEN GOTO 15
   (b) IF A<2*P THEN LET N=N+1 : GOTO 180
   (c) IF M/N = INT(M/N) THEN PRINT "M IS EVENLY DIVISIBLE BY N"

   (frames 1–10)

4. 190 IF A < 2*P THEN LET N = N + 1 : GOTO 180

   In other words, if the newly computed amount A is still less than twice the original principal P, increase the year N by 1, and go back to line 180 to compute a new amount A. (frames 9–10)

5.]RUN   The PRINT statement is *inside* the loop. Therefore,
   1   it is done every time.
   2
   3
   4
   5
   (frame 8)

6.]RUN
   5   This time, the PRINT statement is *outside* the loop. It is done only once, after the loop has been completed. (frame 8)

7. (a) Numbers between 0 and 1. Each random number is greater than zero, but less than one. This answer is also acceptable: $0 < \text{RND}(1) < 1$. (frames 16, 17)
   (b) Numbers between 0 and 2. Each random number will be greater than 0, but less than 2. Also: $0 < 2*\text{RND}(1) < 2$. (frames 17–19)
   (c) 0 or 1 No other values are possible. (frames 20, 23–26)
   (d) 1 or 2 (frames 20, 23–26)
   (e) −1, 0, or 1 (frames 20, 23–26)
   (f) Numbers between 0 and 3.14159. Each random number is greater than 0, but less than 3.14159. Also: $0 < 3.14159*\text{RND}(1) < 3.14159$. Since 3.14159 is an approximation to π, we might also say, although somewhat imprecisely, that these numbers are between 0 and π. (frames 20, 23–26)

8. 110 LET C = INT(2*RND(1)) (frames 26, 27)

CHAPTER FIVE

READ and DATA Work Together

This chapter is designed to give you practice using the BASIC statements and programming skills you have learned so far and to add to your bag of programming tricks. You will be able to extend your understanding of the capabilities of the PRINT statement, in order to better control the output of your programs and write more efficient instructions or programming codes. In addition, you will learn two frequently used statements that always work together to assign values to variables: the READ and DATA statements. When you finish this chapter, you will be able to:

- Use READ statements to assign values or strings to one or more variables at a time, from items in DATA statements
- Control the spacing of output through the use of commas and semicolons separating items in PRINT statements
- Identify the standard print positions in printout and write PRINT statements using comma spacing
- Show the way numbers are printed or displayed as compared to strings

1. You've seen how LET statements and INPUT statements can be used to assign values to variables. (We hope you've been able to use them at a computer, too.) A third method uses two statements in combination, READ and DATA, to assign values to variables.

```
NEW
10 READ X
20 ? "THIS TIME THROUGH THE LOOP, X = "; X
30 GOTO 10
40 DATA 10, 15, 7, 3.25, 11

RUN
THIS TIME THROUGH THE LOOP, X = 10
THIS TIME THROUGH THE LOOP, X = 15
THIS TIME THROUGH THE LOOP, X = 7
THIS TIME THROUGH THE LOOP, X = 3.25
THIS TIME THROUGH THE LOOP, X = 11

?OUT OF DATA ERROR IN 10
```

This statement 10 READ X tells the computer to READ one value from the DATA statement, and assign the value to the variable X. Every time the READ statement is executed (each time through the loop), the computer reads the next value from the DATA statement, and assigns the new value to the variable X. The computer keeps track of each value as it is read out—in effect, moving a pointer across the items in the DATA statement, one notch at a time.

How many values are in the DATA statement? _____

__ __ __ __ __ __ __ __

5

2. As the computer executed the program, each time through the loop it read and printed one value from the DATA statement. Then on the sixth trip through the loop, it tried to find still another number. Since it couldn't find another number to read from the DATA statement, the computer printed OUT OF DATA ERROR IN LINE 10. It isn't really an error. It just informs you that the computer has used up all the available data, tried to find more, but couldn't.

When the program in frame 1 was RUN, how many times was a new value assigned to the READ variable? _____

__ __ __ __ __ __ __

5 values were assigned

3. Look at the format for DATA statements.

    40 DATA 10, 15, 7, 3.25, 11

No comma here   Commas between values   No comma at the end of the DATA line

DATA statements may contain whole numbers, numbers with decimal fractions (such as 3.25 above), numbers in floating-point or "E" notation, or negative numbers.

DATA statements may *not* contain variables, arithmetic operations, other functions, or fractions.

This is OK: 90 DATA 3, 8, 2.5
This is NOT OK: 95 DATA 2+3, 1/4, 2/5, 7*8

Write a DATA statement for these values.

```
342         60.25
1256        -412
205         2.05E +08
```

```
60 DATA 342, 1256, 205, 60.25, -412, 2.05E +08
```

Your line number may be different. And remember, no commas can be used in large numbers, such as 1256 above. However, floating-point or "E" notation may be used.

4. Data statements may be placed anywhere in the program.

```
10 READ N        10 DATA 123
20 PRINT N       20 READ N
30 DATA 123      30 PRINT N
RUN              RUN
123              123
```

Can the DATA statement be placed as shown in the following program?

_____

```
10 READ N
20 DATA 123
30 PRINT N
```

— — — — — — — — —

yes

5. These DATA statements are not written in correct BASIC. Tell what is wrong with each one.

(a)   20 DATA, 15, 32, 85, 66 _____

(b)   30 DATA 22.3; 81.1; 66.66; 43.22 _____

(c)   40 DATA 266, 985, 421, 968, 420, _____

— — — — — — —

(a) should not have comma after DATA
(b) should use commas instead of semicolons to separate values in a DATA statement
(c) should not have comma after last item in DATA statement

6. This program converts inches to centimeters. One inch = 2.54 centimeters. When the program is RUN, the computer prints the value in inches on one line, and the equivalent in centimeters on the next. Fill in the missing statement (line 20).

```
10 REM **CONVERT INCHES TO CENTIMETERS

20 _____
30 PRINT
40 PRINT "INCHES = " ; I
50 PRINT "CENTIMETERS = " ; 2.54*I
60 GOTO 20
90 DATA 1, 8, 12

RUN
```

```
        INCHES = 1
        CENTIMETERS = 2.54

        INCHES = 8
        CENTIMETERS = 20.32

        INCHES = 12
        CENTIMETERS = 30.48

        ?OUT OF DATA ERROR IN 20
```

```
        20 READ I
```

7. Now you write a program to convert ounces to grams. One ounce = 28.35 grams (rounded to two decimal places). Use a DATA statement to hold the values in ounces that you want converted to grams. Here is what your program should print when it is RUN.

```
        RUN

        OUNCES = 1
        GRAMS = 28.35

        OUNCES = 13
        GRAMS = 368.55

        OUNCES = 16
        GRAMS = 453.6

        ?OUT OF DATA ERROR IN 20
```

```
        10 REM **CONVERT OUNCES TO GRAMS
        20 READ Z
        30 PRINT
        40 PRINT "OUNCES = "; Z
        50 PRINT "GRAMS = " ; 28.35*Z
        60 GOTO 20
        90 DATA 1, 13, 16
```

We used Z to represent ounces because O (oh) can be confused with 0 (zero).

8. Write a "World's Most Expensive Adding Machine" program (from Chapter 3, frame 53) using READ and DATA statements instead of an INPUT statement so that a RUN of the program will look like the one below. Examine the RUN to determine the values in the DATA statement.

```
RUN
X = 12
TOTAL SO FAR IS 12

X = 43
TOTAL SO FAR IS 55

X = 33
TOTAL SO FAR IS 88

X = 92
TOTAL SO FAR IS 180

X = 76.25
TOTAL SO FAR IS 256.25

?OUT OF DATA ERROR IN 120
```
⟵ This line number may be different for your program.

- - - - - - - - - - -

```
100 REM **WORLD'S MOST EXPENSIVE ADDING MACHINE
110 LET T=0
120 READ X
130 LET T=T+X
140 PRINT "X = " ; X
150 PRINT "TOTAL SO FAR IS " ; T
160 PRINT
170 GOTO 120
180 DATA 12, 43, 33, 92, 76.25
```

Your line numbers may be different.

9. Do you remember our program to compute the mean, or average, of a group of numbers? If not, review Chapter 4, frame 12. Below is a rewrite of that program, using READ and DATA statements. We use lots of REMs (REMarks) to explain what is happening.

```
NEW
100 REM **A FRIENDLY 'MEAN' PROGRAM
110 REM **INITIALIZE T (FOR TOTAL) AND N (FOR NUMBER OF NUMBERS)
120 T=0 : N=0
130 REM **READ A NUMBER, X. IF IT IS THE FLAG 1E38
140 REM **GOTO PRINTOUT. OTHERWISE, UPDATE T AND X
150 READ X : IF X=1E38 THEN 180
160 T=T+X : N=N+1 : GOTO 150
170 REM **PRINT ANSWERS
180 PRINT "N = " ; N
190 PRINT "TOTAL = " ; T
200 PRINT "MEAN = " ; T/N
900 REM **DATA FOLLOWS
910 DATA 10, 3, -9, -15, -23, -25, -30, 1E38      The flag

RUN
N = 7
TOTAL = -89
MEAN = -12.7143
```

Notice that the use of a flag, and the flag-detecting IF-THEN statement (line 150), keeps the computer from trying to READ past the end of the DATA statement. Therefore, no ?OUT OF DATA error message is produced to end the RUN.

To RUN this program for a different set of data, simply replace line 910 by one or more DATA statements containing the new data and the flag 1E38. (You'll recall from Chapter 3 that to replace a statement, just type the new statement using the old line number.) For example, suppose we wish to use this data: 63, 72, 50, 55, 75, 67, 59, 61, 64. Write the DATA statement.

910 DATA _____

― ― ― ― ― ― ― ―

910 DATA 63, 72, 50, 55, 75, 67, 59, 61, 64, 1E38 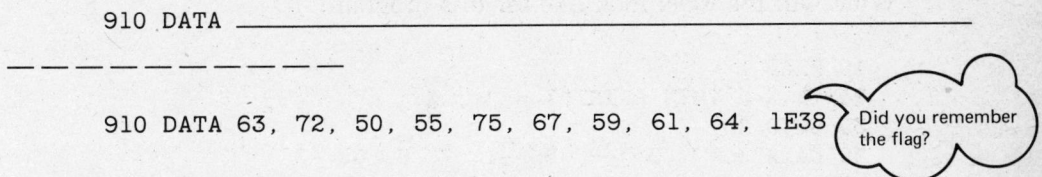 Did you remember the flag?

10. The following program causes the computer to read numbers from a DATA statement and print only the numbers that are *positive* (greater than zero). Numbers that are less than zero or equal to zero are not printed.

```
NEW
10 READ X
20 IF X>0 THEN PRINT "X = " ; X
30 GOTO 10
40 DATA 3, 7, 0, -2, 5, -1, 7, 8, 0, -3
RUN
X = 3
X = 7
X = 5
X = 7
X = 8

?OUT OF DATA ERROR IN 10
```

Note: 7 is printed *twice* because it occurs twice in the DATA statement.

Look at the numbers in the DATA statement.
(a) For which numbers is the condition X > 0 TRUE? _____
(b) When X > 0 is TRUE, what does line 20 cause the computer to do?

_____

(c) For which numbers is the condition X > 0 FALSE? _____
(d) When X > 0 is FALSE, what happens in line 20? _____

— — — — — — — — —

(a) 3, 7, 5, 7, 8
(b) print the message X = followed by the value of X
(c) 0, -2, -1, 0, -3
(d) Nothing. The PRINT portion of line 20 is not executed and the computer goes on to line 30.

11. What will the RUN look like for this program?

```
10 READ X
20 IF X<0 THEN PRINT"X = " ; X
30 GOTO 10
40 DATA 3, 7, 0, -2, 5, -1, 7, 8, 0, -3
RUN
```

```
           RUN
           X = -2
           X = -1
           X = -3

           ?OUT OF DATA ERROR IN 10  ←——— Did you remember this?
```

12. Complete the following program so that the RUN will occur as shown.

    ```
    10 READ X

    20 _____
    30 GOTO 10
    40 DATA 3, 7, 0, -2, 5, -1, 7, 8, 0, -3

    RUN
    X = 0                    Two zeros are printed because there are
    X = 0                    two zeros in the DATA statement.

    ?OUT OF DATA ERROR IN 10
    ```

    ──────────────

    ```
    20 IF X=0 THEN PRINT "X = "; X
    ```

13. For more practice, do each of the following. If possible, try each one on your computer.

    (a) Complete line 20 so that only *nonzero* numbers are printed.

        20 IF _____ THEN PRINT " = "; X

    (b) Complete line 20 so that the computer prints numbers that are greater than or equal to zero.

        20 IF _____ THEN PRINT "X = "; X

    (c) Complete line 20 so that the computer prints numbers that are less than or equal to 3.

        20 IF _____ THEN PRINT "X = "; X

──────────────

(a) X <> 0 (The computer will print 3, 7, -2, 5, -1, 7, 8, and -3.)
(b) X >=0 or X=> 0 (The computer will print 3, 7, 0, 5, 7, 8, and 0.)
(c) X <=3 or X =< 3 (The computer will print 3, 0, -2, -1, 0, and -3.)

If you need review, see Chapter 4, frame 7.

150 BASIC FOR THE APPLE II

14. In BASIC you may have more than one variable following a READ instruction. The following is an example. Use commas to separate the variables.

No comma here   No comma here

This will cause the computer to take three values from the DATA statement and assign them in order to the three READ variables.
Complete the RUN of this program (fill in blanks).

```
10 READ X, Y, Z
20 PRINT X, Y, Z
30 GOTO 10
40 DATA 10, 20, 30, 40, 50, 60
RUN
10              20              30
___             ___             ___


?OUT OF DATA ERROR IN 10
```
— — — — — — — —

      40, 50, 60

The second time through the loop, these values were assigned to X, Y, and Z, and printed by line 20. (We'll discuss the spacing of items in PRINT statements later on.)

15. Fill in the blank spaces in the program and in the RUN.

```
10 _____
20 PRINT A + B
30 GOTO 10
40 DATA 3, 5, 6, 4, 7, 9, 2, 1

RUN
8
___
___
___

?OUT OF DATA ERROR IN 10
```

```
       10 READ A,B
       RUN
       8
       10
       16
       3
```

16.   You may have more than one READ statement in a program. However, all READ statements assign values to their variable(s) from the same DATA statement. An item from DATA is assigned to a READ variable in the order that the computer comes to READ statements when the program is RUN.

```
       10 READ P
       20 READ Q
       30 PRINT P
       40 PRINT Q
       50 GOTO 10
       60 DATA 3, 5, 6, 4, 7, 9
       RUN
       3      First data item assigned to P, second assigned to Q
       5
       6      Second trip through the loop: third data item is assigned to P,
       4      fourth to Q
       7
       9

       ?OUT OF DATA ERROR IN 10
```

For the third trip through the loop, what value is assigned to P? _____
What value is assigned to Q? _____

7; 9

17. Write a program that:

> Uses three READ statements to assign values to three different READ variables X, Y, and Z
> Then prints the sum of X + Y + Z
> Then loops back to repeat the process until the data are all used up

Show what the computer will print when your program is RUN. Here are the data for the DATA statement: 3, 5, 6, 4, 7, 9, 2, 5, 2.

```
10 READ X
20 READ Y
30 READ Z
40 PRINT X + Y + Z
50 GOTO 10
60 DATA 3, 5, 6, 4, 7, 9, 2, 5, 2
]RUN
14
20
9

?OUT OF DATA ERROR IN 10
```

18. Here is a questionnaire we gave to 50 people.

> Does your computer understand you?
>   1. Yes
>   2. No

Each of the 50 responses was either 1 (YES) or 2 (NO). The responses are shown below in five DATA statements. The last response is followed by –1, the flag signaling end of data.

```
900 REM **DATA* 1=YES, 2=NO, -1=END OF DATA
910 DATA 1, 2, 2, 2, 1, 2, 1, 2, 1, 2
920 DATA 2, 1, 1, 1, 2, 1, 2, 2, 2, 1
930 DATA 2, 2, 2, 1, 2, 1, 2, 2, 1, 2
940 DATA 1, 1, 1, 1, 2, 1, 2, 2, 1, 1
950 DATA 2, 2, 2, 2, 1, 1, 1, 2, 1, 2, -1
```

READ AND DATA WORK TOGETHER   **153**

How many YES answers? _____
How many NO answers? _____

Write the number of YES answers in the box labeled "Y" and the number of NO answers in the box labeled "N."

Y [   ]

N [   ]

- - - - - - - - - -

Y [23]

N [27]

19. Here is a program to read the answers from the DATA statements and count the numbers of YES answers and NO answers. The variable Y is used to count YES answers. The variable N is used to count NO answers.

```
100 REM **QUESTIONNAIRE ANALYSIS PROGRAM
110 REM **INITIALIZE:  SET COUNTING VARIABLES TO ZERO
120 Y=0 : N=0
200 REM **READ AND COUNT VOTES
210 READ A : IF A=-1 THEN 410
220 IF A=1 THEN LET Y=Y+1 : GOTO 210
230 IF A=2 THEN LET N=N+1 : GOTO 210
400 REM **PRINT THE RESULTS
410 PRINT
420 PRINT "YES: " ; Y
430 PRINT " NO: " ; N
900 REM **DATA* 1=YES, 2=NO, -1=END OF DATA
910 DATA 1, 2, 2, 2, 1, 2, 1, 2, 1, 2
920 DATA 2, 1, 1, 1, 2, 1, 2, 2, 2, 1
930 DATA 2, 2, 2, 1, 2, 1, 2, 2, 1, 2
940 DATA 1, 1, 1, 1, 2, 1, 2, 2, 1, 1
950 DATA 2, 2, 2, 2, 1, 1, 1, 2, 1, 2, -1

RUN
YES: 23
 NO: 27
```

Note the multiple statements in lines 120, 210, 220, and 230.

(a) Which section of the program is a loop that is repeated for each value in the DATA statements? Lines _____ to _____.
(b) Which statement reads a value corresponding to one vote and puts it into box A? _____
(c) Which line determines whether a vote is YES and, if it is, increases the YES count by one? _____
(d) Which line determines whether a vote is No and, if it is, increases the NO count by one? _____

— — — — — — — — — —

(a) lines 210 to 230; (b) line 210; (c) line 220; (d) line 230

20. Now look at this new questionnaire.

> Does your computer understand you?
>   1. Yes
>   2. No
>   3. Sometimes

Modify the program in frame 19 so that the computer counts the YES, NO, and SOMETIMES answers. Use the variable Y to count YES answers. Use the variable N to count NO answers. Use the variable S to count SOMETIMES answers. Use the following data.

   2, 1, 3, 2, 3, 3, 1, 3, 3, 2, 1, 2, 1, 2, 1, 1, 3, 3, −1

Using these data, the results when the program is RUN should be printed as follows.

```
YES: 6
 NO: 5
SOMETIMES: 7
```

Here are our changes.

```
120 Y=0 : N=0 : S=0
240 IF A=3 THEN LET S=S+1 : GOTO 210
440 PRINT "SOMETIMES: " ; S
900 REM **DATA: 1=YES, 2=NO, 3=SOMETIMES, -1=END OF DATA
910 DATA 2, 1, 3, 2, 3, 3, 1, 3, 3, 2, 1, 2, 1, 2, 1, 1, 3, 3, -1
920
930
940
950
```

We deleted lines 920, 930, 940, and 950 from the program of frame 19. If the program is in the computer, we can do this by typing the line number and pressing RETURN. If you have a computer handy, LIST the program to show the modifications and to prove that the deleted lines have disappeared from the computer's memory. The following is our listing.

```
LIST

100 REM **QUESTIONNAIRE ANALYSIS PROGRAM
110 REM **INITIALIZE: SET COUNTING VARIABLES TO ZERO
120 Y=0 : N=0 : S=0
200 REM **READ AND COUNT VOTES
210 READ A : IF A= -1 THEN 410
220 IF A=1 THEN LET Y=Y+1 : GOTO 210
230 IF A=2 THEN LET N=N+1 : GOTO 210
240 IF A=3 THEN LET S=S+1 : GOTO 210
400 REM **PRINT THE RESULTS
410 PRINT
420 PRINT "YES: " ; Y
430 PRINT " NO: " ; N
440 PRINT "SOMETIMES: " ; S
900 REM **DATA: 1=YES, 2=NO, 3=SOMETIMES, -1=END OF DATA
910 DATA 2, 1, 3, 2, 3, 3, 1, 3, 3, 2, 1, 2, 1, 2, 1, 1, 3, 3, -1
```

21. Back in Chapter 2, we used PRINT statements in the following form.

    PRINT e

where e is a numerical expression. For example:

    PRINT 7 + 5
           └──┬──┘
    numerical expression

A PRINT statement of this form tells the computer to compute and evaluate (do the arithmetic of) the numerical expression and then print the result.

The following PRINT statement tells the computer to evaluate *four* numerical expressions and print the four results.

You type.   PRINT 7 + 5, 7 − 5, 7 * 5, 7 / 5

It types: 12   2   35
            1.4

In the above, draw arrows connecting each numerical expression with its computed and printed value. We have drawn the first arrow, connecting the expression, 7 + 5, with its printed result, 12.

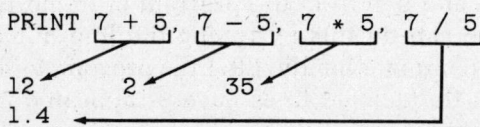

22. If a PRINT statement has more than one expression, then the expressions are separated by commas.

```
PRINT 7 + 5, 7 − 5, 7 * 5, 7/5
            ↑       ↑      ↑
          comma   comma  comma
```

The following PRINT statement directs the computer to compute and print the values of 2 + 3, 2 − 3, 2 * 3, and 2/3. However, we forgot to put in commas. Please insert commas in the correct BASIC form.

PRINT 2 + 3 2 − 3 2 * 3 2/3

PRINT 2 + 3, 2 − 3, 2 *33, 2/3

Note: No comma following PRINT and no comma following 2/3. A comma following 2/3 (at the very end of the PRINT statement) has a special purpose which we will discuss later.

23. Complete the following. (Remember, for direct statements, you do not need a line number and you only have to press RETURN to have the computer execute the statement.)

You type: PRINT 3*3, 5*5, 7*7
It types: _____   _____   _____

You type: PRINT 2*3+4*5, (2+3)*(4+5)
It types: _____   _____

— — — — — — — — — —

9   25   49
26   45

24. Your turn. Let's go back to our three bicycles, with wheels of 20-, 24-, and 26-in. diameters. You want to find out, for each bike, how far it travels during one turn of the wheel. In other words, you want to evaluate the following three expressions.

       20-in. wheel: 3.14*20   First expression
       24-in. wheel: 3.14*24   Second expression
       26-in. wheel: 3.14*26   Third expression

Write a PRINT statement to tell the computer to evaluate the three expressions and PRINT the results, all in one statement.

You type: _____
It types: 62.8   75.36   81.64

— — — — — — — — — —

    PRINT 3.14*20, 3.14*24, 3.14*26

25. The Apple displays the output from a PRINT statement at three predetermined positions across the display. A comma in a PRINT statement causes the next item to appear at the next available standard print positions. This is similar to having preset tabs on a typewriter. Look at the example below and fill in the blanks.

You type: PRINT 1,2,3
It types: 1   2   3
          ↑
    Position 1   Position ____   Position ____

— — — — — — — —

2; 3

26. What happens if there are more than three items in a PRINT statement and the items are separated by commas? Look at the direct statement below and also at how the computer displayed it.

```
You type:   ? 1,2,3,4,5,6,7,8,9,10,11,12
It types:   1              2              3
            4              5              6
            7              8              9
            10             11             12
```

Describe the output displayed by the direct statement. _____

_____

The computer printed the 12 numbers on 4 lines, with 3 numbers on each line.

27. Following the rules for items or expressions separated by commas, show what the computer will print in response to the following PRINT statement.

```
You type:   ? 1,2,3,4,5,6,7,8
It types:
```

_____

```
            1              2              3
            4              5              6
            7              8
```

28. Instead of commas, we can also use *semicolons* as separators in a PRINT statement. Watch what happens.

```
You type:   ]? 1;2;3;4;5
It types:   12345

You type:   ]? 1; 2; 3; 4; 5; 6; 7
It types:   1234567
```

Semicolon spacing *catenates* numbers. That is, it directs the computer to print numbers *close together*, in a linked series. *Comma* spacing causes numbers to be printed in *predetermined print positions*. So, to print results close together, use

_____.

_____

semicolons

29. The usual display for the Apple has 40 columns, or *character positions*, across the line. If you wanted to, you could type X's across the screen and count them. Other terminals, such as printers, may have from 32 to 132 character positions across a line, with 80 being the popular number. On our Apple video display, the character positions are numbered from 1 to 40, starting at the left margin. Complete the diagram by filling in the blanks.

Read the numbers up and down, like this: $\begin{array}{c}1\\4\end{array}$ = 14.

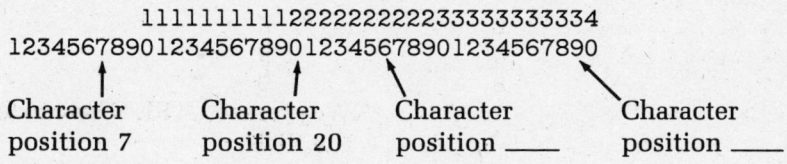

26; 39

30. The three *standard print positions*, used in comma spacing, begin at character positions 1, 17, and 33. We've marked print position 1; you mark print positions 2 and 3 on the diagram below.

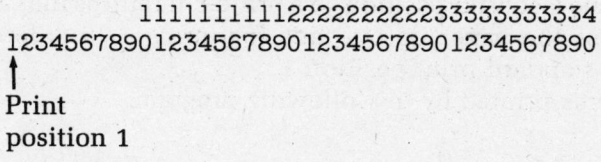

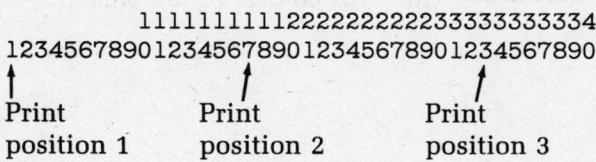

31. Now watch what happens when we put a comma at the *end* of a PRINT statement.

```
10 LET N=1
20 PRINT N,————————— Comma
30 LET N=N+1
40 GOTO 20
```

```
]RUN
1            2            3
4            5            6
7            8            9
10           11           We pressed CTRL/C here to terminate
                          the RUN.

BREAK IN 20
```

Remember what the comma does. It tells the computer to move to the next standard print position. So, after printing number 1, the computer moves to print position 2; after printing 2, the computer moves to standard print position 3. As you have seen, after displaying something at standard print position 3, the computer "wraps around" to the next line and starts again at the first print position. After using the last print position on a printer, it returns the carriage to the left margin, spaces the paper up one line (performs a "line feed"), and continues printing at standard print position 1.

Show the first 8 items printed by the following program.

```
10 LET N=1
20 PRINT N,
30 LET N=N+2 ←———————— Note this change in line 30.
40 GOTO 20

RUN
```

— — — — — —

```
]RUN
1            3            5
7            9            11
13           15
```

32. A print zone is the character positions from the beginning of print position 1 (character position 1) up to character position 16; the second print zone starts at print position 2 at character position 17, and includes up to 32; then print zone 3 starts and continues to the right margin. Mark print zones 1, 2, and 3 with brackets.

```
         1111111111222222222233333333334
1234567890123456789012345678901234567890
```

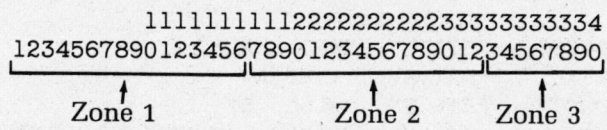

33. Unfortunately, life is not quite so simple. Consider the display caused by the following long PRINT statement.

You type:
? 1,12,123,1234,12345,123456,1234567,12345678,123456789,1234567890

It types:
```
1                  12                 123
1234               12345              123456
1234567            12345678
123456789          1.23456789E+09
```
←— In the third display line, this print zone was skipped.

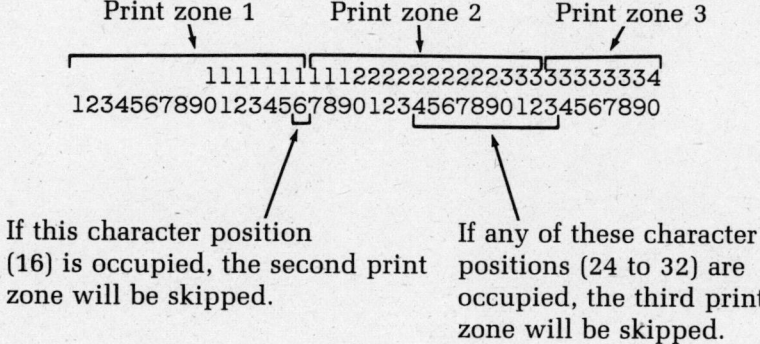

If this character position (16) is occupied, the second print zone will be skipped.

If any of these character positions (24 to 32) are occupied, the third print zone will be skipped.

This is important information to have when using commas in PRINT statements. For example, the headings for a three-column chart to be displayed across the screen will only work if:

1. The first heading, and any information displayed under it, occupy 15 characters or less (positions 1 to 15 only)
2. The second heading, and any information displayed it, occupy 7 characters or less (positions 17 to 23 only); and
3. The third heading, and any information displayed under it, occupy 8 characters or less (positions 33–40). If positions past 40 are needed, the first print zone on the next line down will be used.

Which of the following PRINT statements will provide the headings for a three-column table on the display screen?

(a) 130 PRINT "PRODUCT", "RETAIL", "WHOLESALE"
(b) 130 PRINT "RAINFALL", "DAY.AV.", "MO.AV."
(c) 130 PRINT "PRODUCT", "RET. $", "WLSL. $"
(d) 130 PRINT "RAINFALL", "DAILY AVERAGE", "MONTHLY AVERAGE"

(b), (c)

34. Now, what do you suppose happens if we put a semicolon at the end of a PRINT statement? As always with computers, if we don't know, we EXPERIMENT. Let's try it.

```
10 LET N=1
20 PRINT N;
30 LET N=N+1
40 GOTO 20
RUN
123456789           We pressed CTRL/C again to stop the RUN.

BREAK IN 20
```

READ AND DATA WORK TOGETHER   163

Remember, with semicolon spacing, the computer prints positive numbers one immediately after the other. When it gets to the end of a line, it wraps around to start at the beginning of the next line down on the display. On a printer, when it gets to the end of a line, it returns the carriage, indexes up one line (still another way of saying it does a "line feed"), and keeps chunking away. Show what happens if we RUN the following program.

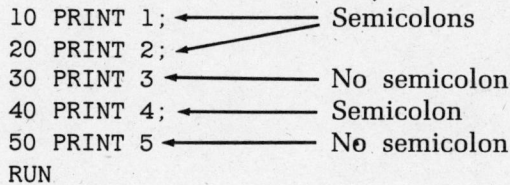

```
10 PRINT 1;            Semicolons
20 PRINT 2;
30 PRINT 3             No semicolon
40 PRINT 4;            Semicolon
50 PRINT 5             No semicolon
RUN
```

```
123      Printed by lines 10, 20, 30
 45      Courtesy of lines 40 and 50
```

Since there was no semicolon at the end of the statement PRINT 3 (line 30) to hold the display on the same line, the computer went on to the next line, as it normally does at the end of a PRINT statement that has no comma or semicolon at the end.

35. Write a program using *two* PRINT statements, to compute and print the values of 2*2, 3*3, 4*4, 5*5, and 6*6. When you RUN your program, the results should be printed as follows.

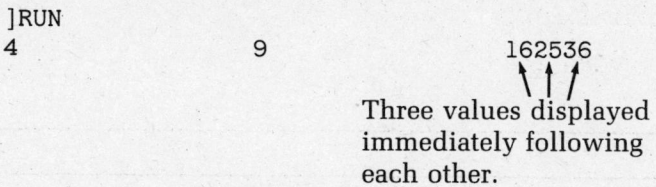

```
]RUN
4            9            162536
```
                                  ↖↑↗
                          Three values displayed
                          immediately following
                          each other.

Method 1:

```
10 PRINT 2*2, 3*3, 4*4;
20 PRINT 5*5; 6*6
```

Method 2:

```
10 PRINT 2*2, 3*3,
20 PRINT 4*4; 5*5; 6*6
```

Method 3:

```
10 PRINT 2*2,
20 PRINT 3*3, 4*4; 5*5; 6*6
```

You might have thought of still more ways to do it!

36. Now let's look at a way to put a space between a series of numbers displayed with semicolon spacing, to separate things a bit. We use a blank space enclosed by quotation marks. Note that this is *not* a null string, because it does contain one character: a space.

```
10 LET N = 1
20 PRINT N;" ";
30 LET N = N + 1
40 GOTO 20
```

Examine line 20, then show a RUN for the first 27 numbers produced and displayed by this program before CTRL/C is used to stop the RUN.

RUN

```
]RUN
1 2 3 4 5 6 7 8 9 10 11 12 13 14 15 16 1
7 18 19 20 21 22 23 24 25 26 27
```

CTRL/C used here

37. We have spent some time with comma spacing and semicolon spacing with numbers. Next, let's try *strings*.

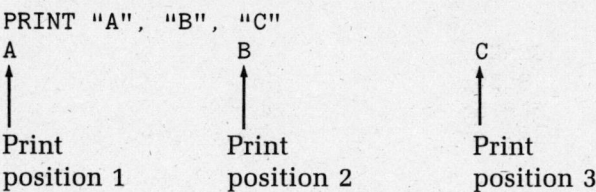

Your turn. Complete the output for this direct statement the way the computer would do it.

```
PRINT "A", "B", "C", "D", "E", "F", "G", "H"
A              B              C
_____
_____
```

- - - - - - - - - - -

```
A              B              C
D              E              F
G              H
```

With strings, as with numbers, the comma causes the computer to move to the next standard print position.

38. Comma spacing is useful for printing *headings*. For example, here is a rewrite of our inches-to-centimeters program in frame 6.

```
10 REM **INCHES VERSUS CENTIMETERS TABLE
20 PRINT "INCHES", "CENTIMETERS"
30 READ I
40 PRINT I, 2.54*I
50 GOTO 30
90 DATA 1, 8, 12

]RUN
INCHES              CENTIMETERS
1                   2.54
8                   20.32
12                  30.48

?OUT OF DATA ERROR IN 30
```

Note the use of comma spacing in lines 20 and 40. The numeric values printed by line 40 line up nicely under the headings printed by line 20.

Your turn. Rewrite the ounces-to-grams program (frame 7), so that a RUN looks like the following one.

```
]RUN
OUNCES          GRAMS
1               28.35
13              368.55
16              453.6

?OUT OF DATA ERROR IN 30
```

```
10 REM **OUNCES TO GRAMS TABLE
20 PRINT "OUNCES", "GRAMS"
30 READ Z
40 PRINT Z,28.35*Z
50 GOTO 30
90 DATA 1, 13, 16
```

39. Now, let's look at semicolon spacing with strings.

```
PRINT "A"; "B"; "C"; "D"; "E"
ABCDE  ←——————— Look ma! No spaces.
```

Semicolon spacing causes the computer to catenate strings, that is, to print them one after the other with no spaces.

Show what happens when the computer executes the following PRINT statement.

```
PRINT "THIS"; "IS"; "COMPUTER"; "PROGRAMMING?"
```

```
THISISCOMPUTERPROGRAMMING?
```

40. The output in frame 39 was rather crowded and hard to read. If you want spaces between strings, you must put them where you want them. For example:

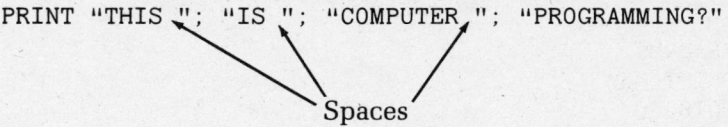

Show what the computer will print this time.

_____

— — — — — — — — — —

      THIS IS COMPUTER PROGRAMMING?

41. Let's try a program that uses strings stored by string variables to print information.

```
10 LET A$="COMPUTERS "
20 LET B$="ARE"
30 LET C$=" INTERESTING."
40 PRINT A$;B$;C$
50 PRINT A$,B$,C$
```

Note the spaces inside the quotation marks in lines 10 and 30.

Show what the computer will print when the program is RUN.

    RUN

_____

_____

_____

— — — — — — — — — —

```
]RUN
COMPUTERS ARE INTERESTING.
COMPUTERS      ARE           INTERES
TING.
```

42. You may have guessed by now that a READ statement may also be used to assign strings to string variables. Show how you think the RUN for the following program to print the names of computer club members will look.

```
10 READ M$
20 PRINT M$
30 GOTO 10
40 DATA JERRY,PAUL,MARY,DANNY
50 DATA MIMI,KARL,BOBBY,WHO?
```

```
]RUN
JERRY
PAUL
MARY
DANNY
MIMI
KARL
BOBBY
WHO?

?OUT OF DATA ERROR IN 10
```

43. We have made a special point of explaining how strings and values are printed when semicolons and colons are used to separate items in PRINT statements. Now we would like to emphasize how strings assigned to string variables from DATA statements must be handled in order to leave the desired spacing between printed strings.

```
10 READ L$,M$,N$
20 PRINT L$;M$;N$
30 DATA     COMPUTERS,    ARE,     INTERESTING.
RUN
COMPUTERSAREINTERESTING.
```

Notice that even though we left leading spaces around the string items in the DATA statement, the computer ignored those spaces when it assigned the string characters to the string variables. We replaced line 30 with the following line and ran the program again.

```
30 DATA COMPUTERS," ARE ", INTERESTING

RUN
COMPUTERS ARE INTERESTING
```

Based upon your examinations of the two DATA statements and RUNs, explain how you can include leading and/or trailing spaces in strings assigned to variables from DATA statements. _____

_____

_____

_ _ _ _ _ _ _ _ _ _

Enclose strings in quotation marks, and include leading or trailing spaces, in order to assign strings to string variables that will include leading or trailing spaces.

Note: Applesoft BASIC will include *trailing* spaces in a DATA string. For example, line 30 could also be written as follows.

```
30 DATA COMPUTERS ,ARE ,INTERESTING
                 ↑    ↑
              trailing spaces

10 READ L$,M$,N$
20 PRINT L$;M$;N$
30 DATA COMPUTERS ,ARE ,INTERESTING

]RUN
COMPUTERS ARE INTERESTING
```

However, to include *leading* spaces, you must enclose the string in quotation marks.

44. And now, it's your turn again to write a program. You have probably used dice before, either in "board" games or other games. We want you to apply your accumulated knowledge of BASIC to write a program that simulates (imitates) the roll of a die. (A "die" is one of a pair of "dice.") Below is a RUN of our program. Examine it and use it as a guide to writing a program that will produce a RUN similar to this one. Use standard print positions. Take your time, and try your solution on a computer before looking at ours, if possible.

Hint: Use ON . . . GOTO to branch to six different PRINT statements.

```
]RUN

HOW MANY ROLLS? 7

ONE             FOUR            FIVE
FOUR            FOUR            ONE
TWO

HOW MANY ROLLS? 2

FIVE            FOUR

HOW MANY ROLLS?        And so on.
```

```
100 REM **DIE ROLLER
110 PRINT : INPUT "HOW MANY ROLLS? "; R
120 K=1 : PRINT
200 REM **'ROLL THE DIE' R TIMES
210 S=INT(6*RND(1))+1
220 ON S GOTO 230, 240, 250, 260, 270, 280
230 PRINT "ONE",   : GOTO 290
240 PRINT "TWO",   : GOTO 290
250 PRINT "THREE" ,  : GOTO 290
260 PRINT "FOUR",  : GOTO 290
270 PRINT "FIVE",  : GOTO 290
280 PRINT "SIX",
290 IF K<R THEN LET K=K+1 : GOTO 210
300 PRINT : GOTO 110
```

Self-Test

Try this Self-Test, so you can evaluate how much you have learned so far.

1. Pretend that you are the computer and complete each RUN.

    (a) 10 READ A
         20 PRINT A
         30 DATA 27
         RUN

    (b) 10 READ A
         20 READ B
         30 PRINT A−B
         40 DATA 27, 15
         RUN

    (c) 10 READ A,B
         20 PRINT A−B
         30 DATA 27, 15
         RUN

    (d) 10 READ A,B
         20 PRINT A−B
         30 DATA 27
         40 DATA 15
         RUN

2. Show the RUNs for the following programs.

    (a) 10 READ X
         20 PRINT X, ←——— Comma at end of PRINT statement
         30 GOTO 10
         40 DATA 3,7,0,−2,5,−1,7,8,0,−3
         RUN

(b) 10 READ X
    20 PRINT X; ←——— Semicolon at end of PRINT statement
    30 GOTO 10
    40 DATA 3,7,0,-2,5,-1,7,8,0,-3
    RUN

3. Complete each RUN as if you were the computer.

   (a) 10 READ X
       20 IF X >= 0 THEN PRINT "X ="; X, ←——— Comma
       30 GOTO 10
       40 DATA 3,7,0,-2,5,-1,7,8,0,-3
       RUN

   (b) 10 READ X
       20 IF X >= 0 THEN PRINT "X ="; X; ←——— Semicolon
       30 GOTO 10
       40 DATA 3,7,0,-2,5,-1,7,8,0,-3
       RUN

   (c) 10 READ X
       20 IF X >= 0 THEN PRINT "X = ";X;" "; ←——— Space in quotes
       30 GOTO 10   and semicolon
       40 DATA 3,7,0,-2,5,-1,7,8,0,-3
       RUN

4. Show the results if we RUN the following short program. Watch out! We are using comma spacing and the 40-character video display lines with the standard Applesoft print positions.

```
420 PRINT "ANSWER","NO. OF","% OF"
430 PRINT "(YES OR NO)","ANSWERS","TOTAL"
RUN
```

5. Modify the questionnaire analysis program beginning in frame 18 so that the results are printed as follows.

```
]RUN

ANSWER            NO.OF            % OF
(YES OR NO)       ANSWERS          TOTAL

YES:              23               46
NO:               27               54
TOTAL:            50               100
```

Hint: Rewrite lines 120, 420, and 430. Add a blank PRINT statement at 435 to separate the heading from the rest of the table. We added lines 440, 450, and 460. The required information is printed under the three headings in the standard print positions.

6. Write a program, using READ and DATA statements, to compute the distance traveled in one turn of the rear wheel for bicycles with various wheel diameters. Use the following DATA statement with the line number of your choice.

   DATA 16,20,24,26,27 ←——————— Wheel diameters

   The following is a RUN of our program.

   ```
   RUN

   WHEEL DIAMETER: 16
   DISTANCE IN ONE TURN: 50.24

   WHEEL DIAMETER: 20
   DISTANCE IN ONE TURN: 62.8

   WHEEL DIAMETER: 24
   DISTANCE IN ONE TURN: 75.36

   WHEEL DIAMETER: 26
   DISTANCE IN ONE TURN: 81.64

   WHEEL DIAMETER: 27
   DISTANCE IN ONE TURN: 84.78

   ?OUT OF DATA ERROR IN 10
   ```

   Remember, distance in one turn is circumference of the wheel. C = 3 where D = diameter of the wheel.

7. Write a program to simulate coin flipping. The program should direct the computer to do the following steps. Type H for HEADS and T for TAILS *across* the page as shown in the RUN below. Also ask *how many* flips the user wants and do exactly that many, then stop. In other words, count the flips, and, when the count has reached the number requested, stop. Here are two RUNs of our program.

RUN

HOW MANY FLIPS? 20

Note the spaces between flips

H H H H T T T H T H H T T H T T T T H T

RUN

HOW MANY FLIPS? 100

H H H H T T H T T T H H H T H T T H T T
T H T H H T T T H T H H T T H H H T H H
H T H H H H H T T T T H T H T H H T T
T T H H H T H T T H T T H H T H H H H
H T H H T T H H H T H H H T H H T H

The first RUN of our program on our computer produced 9 heads (H) and 11 tails (T). The second RUN produced 57 heads (H) and 43 tails (T). Your computer may give quite different results.

8. Why not let the computer count the number of heads and the number of tails? Modify your program for question 7 so that the computer counts the number of heads and tails. Use the variable H to keep track of the number of heads and the variable T to keep track of the number of tails. Two RUNs of the modified program are shown below.

```
RUN

HOW MANY FLIPS? 20

T H H T T H H H T H H H T H H T T T H T

11 HEADS AND 9 TAILS

RUN

HOW MANY FLIPS? 100

H T H H H T T T H T T H T T T H H H H T
T H H H H T H T T T T T T T T H T T H T
H H H T T H T T T T T T H T H H H H H H
H T T H T T T H H H H T T H T H T H T H
T T T T T T T H T T H T H H H T T T H H

43 HEADS AND 57 TAILS
```

9. Write a program to *count* the numbers in all the DATA statements in a program. Do *not* count the *flag!* For example, if the following DATA statements are in the program, the computer should dutifully tell us that there are 25 numbers.

   ```
   150 DATA 2,3,5,7,11,13,17,19,23,29,31,37,41
   160 DATA 43,47,53,59,61,67,71,73,79,83,89,97,1E38
                                                  ↑
                                              The flag
   ```

   Our program RUNs like this.

   ```
   RUN
   THERE ARE 25 ITEMS IN THE DATA STATEMENTS.
   ```

10. Now write a program that will print a pattern of asterisks according to a plan entered as DATA statement values. This might be a way of laying a pattern of floor tiles, or loom weaving patterns, or just "computer art." Use a flag to avoid an out-of-data error message. Following are our DATA statement values and the pattern produced by our program. Our program prints five different lines of asterisks and spaces.

3,4,4,5,1,5,1,5,1,5,2,2,2,5,1,5,1,5,1,5,4,4,3 ←—DATA values

RUN

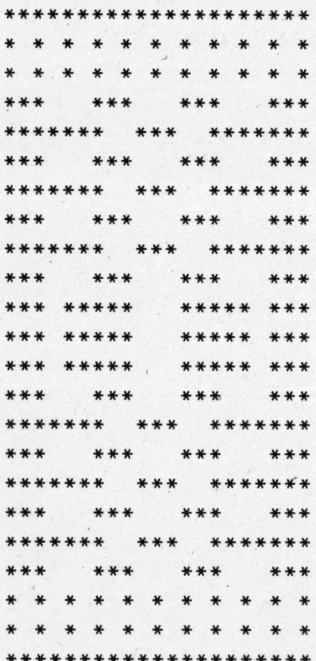

Hint: The pattern consists of five different types of lines. The first and last lines are "type 3" lines. The first and last numbers in the DATA statement are 3. Got the idea?

Answers to Self-Test

The frame numbers in parentheses refer to the frames in the chapter where the topic is discussed. You may wish to refer to these for quick review.

1. (a) RUN
     27
   (b) RUN
     12
   (c) RUN
     12
   (d) RUN
     12

   (frames 1–6)

2. (a)]RUN
     3   7   0
     -2   5   -1
     7   8   0
     -3
     ?OUT OF DATA ERROR IN 10

   (b)]RUN
     370-25-1780-3
     ?OUT OF DATA ERROR IN 10

   (frames 1–10, 33, 34)

3. (a)]RUN
     X =3   X =7   X =0
     X =5   X =7   X =8
     X =0
     ?OUT OF DATA ERROR IN 10

   (b)]RUN
     X =3X =7X =0X =5X =7X =8X =0
     ?OUT OF DATA ERROR IN 10

   (c)]RUN
     X = 3 X = 7 X = 0 X = 5 X = 7 X = 8 X = 0
     ?OUT OF DATA ERROR IN 10

   (frames 11, 33–36)

4.]RUN

   ANSWER   NO.OF   % OF
   (YES OR NO)   ANSWER   TOTAL

   (frames 33, 38)

5.
```
100 REM ***QUESTIONNAIRE ANALYSIS PROGRAM
110 REM ***INITIALIZE: SET COUNTING VARIABLES TO ZERO
120 Y = 0:N = 0:T = 0
200 REM ***READ AND COUNT VOTES
210 READ A: IF A = -1 THEN 410
220 IF A = 1 THEN LET Y = Y + 1 : GOTO 210
230 IF A = 2 THEN LET N = N + 1 : GOTO 210
400 REM ***PRINT THE RESULTS
410 PRINT
420 PRINT "ANSWER","NO.OF","% OF"
430 PRINT "(YES OR NO)","ANSWERS","TOTAL"
435 PRINT
440 PRINT "YES:",Y,(Y / (Y + N))* 100
450 PRINT "NO:",N,(N / (Y + N)) * 100
460 PRINT "TOTAL:",N + Y, (N + Y) / (N + Y) * 100
900 REM ***DATA * 1=YES, 2=NO, -1=END OF DATA
910 DATA 1,2,2,2,1,2,1,2,1,2
920 DATA 2,1,1,1,2,1,2,2,2,1
930 DATA 2,2,2,1,2,1,2,2,1,2
940 DATA 1,1,1,1,2,1,2,2,1,1
950 DATA 2,2,2,2,1,1,1,2,1,2,-1
```

(frames 35-40)

6.
```
100 REM **DISTANCE IN ONE TURN OF A WHEEL
110 READ D
120 PRINT
130 PRINT "WHEEL DIAMETER: ";D
140 PRINT "DISTANCE IN ONE TURN: ";3.14*D
150 GOTO 110
160 DATA 16,20,24,26,27
```

(frames 11, 38)

7.
```
100 REM **COIN FLIPPER
110 PRINT : INPUT "HOW MANY FLIPS? ";N
120 IF N<1 THEN END
130 REM **FLIP COIN N TIMES
140 K=0 : PRINT
150 C=INT(2*RND(1))
160 IF C=0 THEN PRINT "T ";
170 IF C=1 THEN PRINT "H ";
180 K=K+1
190 IF K<N THEN 150
```

There is more than one way to write this program. In ours, we use the variable K to count the number of times the coin has been flipped. In line 140, we set K to zero. Then, each time through the loop, we increase K by 1 (line 180) and compare K with N (line 190). If K is still less than N, we increase K by 1 and go around again. If N is less than 1, no flips are done-this is checked by line 120. Your program may be entirely different. If it works, you have solved the problem!

(frames 18–20, 44)

8. We modified our program of question 7. The complete program is shown below. The variable T is used to count the number of tails and the variable H to count the number of heads. Look for T and H in lines 140, 160, 170, and 210.

```
100 REM **COIN FLIPPER
110 PRINT : INPUT "HOW MANY FLIPS? ";N
120 IF N<1 THEN END
130 REM **FLIP COIN N TIMES
140 K=0 : T=0 : H=0 : PRINT
150 C=INT(2*RND(1))
160 IF C=0 THEN PRINT "T "; : T=T+1
170 IF C=1 THEN PRINT "H "; : H=H+1
180 K=K+1
190 IF K<N THEN 150
200 PRINT : PRINT
210 PRINT H;" HEADS AND ";T;" TAILS"
```

(frames 33, 38, 43, 44)

9.
```
100 REM **COUNT ITEMS IN DATA STATEMENTS, EXCEPT FLAG
110 K=0
120 READ N
130 IF N<>1E38 THEN LET K=K+1 : GOTO 120
140 IF N=1E38 THEN PRINT "THERE ARE ";K;
    " ITEMS IN THE DATA STATEMENTS."
150 DATA 2,3,5,7,11,13,17,19,23,29,31,37,41
160 DATA 43,47,53,59,61,67,71,73,79,83,89,97,1E38
```

Do you recognize the numbers in the DATA statements? They are all the prime numbers (those numbers with themselves and 1 as their only factors) less than 100. (frames 10, 11, 18–20)

10.
```
100 REM **PATTERN PRINTING PROGRAM
110 READ X : IF X=-1 THEN END
120 ON X GOTO 210,220,230,240,250
200 REM **PATTERN LINES
210 PRINT "*******   ***   *******" : GOTO 110
220 PRINT "***  *****   *****  ***" : GOTO 110
230 PRINT "***********************" : GOTO 110
240 PRINT "* * * * * * * * * * *" : GOTO 110
250 PRINT "***   ***   ***   ***" : GOTO 110
300 REM **DATA TO MAKE A RUG DESIGN
310 DATA 3,4,4,5,1,5,1,5,1,5,2,2,2,5,1,5,1,5,1,5,4,4,3,-1
RUN
```

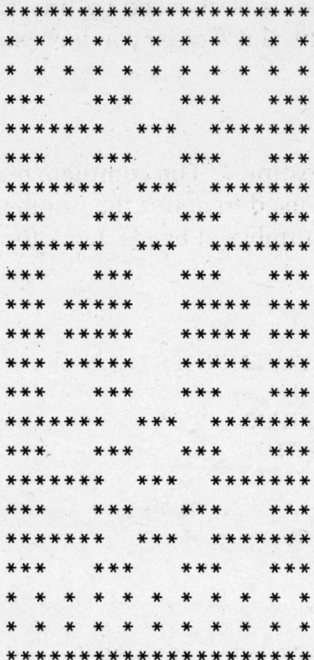

Here is another way to do it.

```
10 REM **PATTERN PRINTING PROGRAM
20 READ X
30 IF X=-1 THEN END
40 IF X=1 THEN 100
50 IF X=2 THEN 120
60 IF X=3 THEN 140
70 IF X=4 THEN 160
80 IF X=5 THEN 180
90 GOTO 20
100 PRINT "******* *** ******* "
110 GOTO 20
120 PRINT "*** *****   ***** *** "
130 GOTO 20
140 PRINT "******************** "
150 GOTO 20
160 PRINT "* * * * * * * * * * "
170 GOTO 20
180 PRINT "***    ***    ***    *** "
190 GOTO 20
900 DATA 3,4,4,5,1,5,1,5,1,5,2,2
910 DATA 2,5,1,5,1,5,1,5,4,4,3,-1
```

(frames 18, 19, 38, 42, 44)

CHAPTER SIX

FOR-NEXT Loops

In this chapter we introduce another important computer programming concept: the FOR-NEXT loop. The IF-THEN statement and the FOR-NEXT loop greatly extend the usefulness of the computer as a tool. Close attention to the explanation and problems in this chapter will help you understand the functions of these statements in BASIC and will open a new dimension in your computer programming capability. When you complete this chapter you will be able to:

- Use the FOR and NEXT statements
- Use the STEP clause in FOR statements

1. The following Loop Demonstration Program is a counting program that prints the value for F as we increase F from 1 through 8. Line 10 merely initializes F at 1. To initialize, remember, means to assign the first value to a variable. Line 20 prints the current value for F. Line 30 increases F by 1 each time through the program.

Line 40 is an IF statement that tests the value of F. As long as F is less than or equal to 6, line 40 sends the computer back to line 20 to print the value of F. Once F exceeds 6, the program will stop since there are no more statements in the program.

```
5 REM***LOOP DEMONSTRATION
10 LET F=1
20 PRINT "F = " ; F
30 LET F=F+1
40 IF F <= 6 THEN 20

RUN
F = 1
F = 2
F = 3
F = 4
F = 5
F = 6
```

Just for practice, rewrite the program using multiple statements in one line. But think carefully: Can you do the *entire* program in just one line?

```
10 LET F=1
20 PRINT "F = " ; F : LET F=F+1 : IF F <= 6 THEN 20
RUN
F = 1
F = 2
F = 3
F = 4
F = 5
F = 6
```

This means go back and start executing line 20 again (only if the comparison is true, of course). Notice that line 10 would also fit on this line, but the value for F would get "initialized" back to 1 every time the statement was executed. So we could *not* put the entire program in just one line.

2. The space-saving, time-saving FOR-NEXT loop accomplishes a given number of *iterations* or repetitions more easily. Look at the FOR-NEXT loop below. Instead of IF-THEN, this time we use the FOR and NEXT statements to tell the computer how many times to go through the loop.

```
 5 REM **FOR-NEXT LOOP DEMONSTRATION
10 FOR F=1 TO 6
20 PRINT "F = "; F
30 NEXT F
RUN
F = 1
F = 2
F = 3
F = 4
F = 5
F = 6
```

In every FOR-NEXT loop, the FOR statement is the beginning point of the loop and the NEXT statement is always the last statement in the loop. The statement or statements between FOR and NEXT are executed, in order, over and over again, with the FOR statement indicating to the computer how many times the loop is to be executed.

(a) You can see from the RUN of the FOR-NEXT loop that each time through the loop the value of F is automatically increased by _____.

(b) How many times did the computer go through the loop? _____

(c) Why did the computer stop after going through the loop the above number of times? _____

(d) What other statement must you have? _____

(a) 1
(b) 6
(c) because the FOR statement told it to go from 1 to 6
(d) a NEXT statement

3. As you can see in the program below, the computer will continue with the rest of the program when it has completed the loop as specified by the FOR statement.

```
 5 REM***ANOTHER FOR-NEXT LOOP
10 FOR D=5 TO 10              Note that the loop doesn't have to start
20 PRINT "D = "; D            with 1.
30 NEXT D
40 PRINT
50 PRINT "AHA! OUT OF THE LOOP BECAUSE"
60 PRINT "D = "; D; " WHICH EXCEEDS 10."

RUN
D = 5
D = 6
D = 7
D = 8
D = 9
D = 10

AHA! OUT OF THE LOOP BECAUSE
D = 11 WHICH EXCEEDS 10.
```

In the program, the FOR-NEXT loop occupies which lines?_____

lines 10, 20, and 30

4. How does the FOR-NEXT loop work? Follow the arrows.

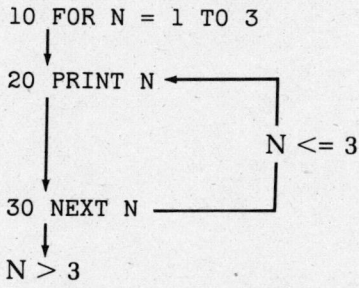

In line 10, N is set equal to 1.

In line 30, N is increased by one, and the computer compares the increased value of N to the upper limit for N indicated in the FOR statement.

Let's look at the FOR statement.

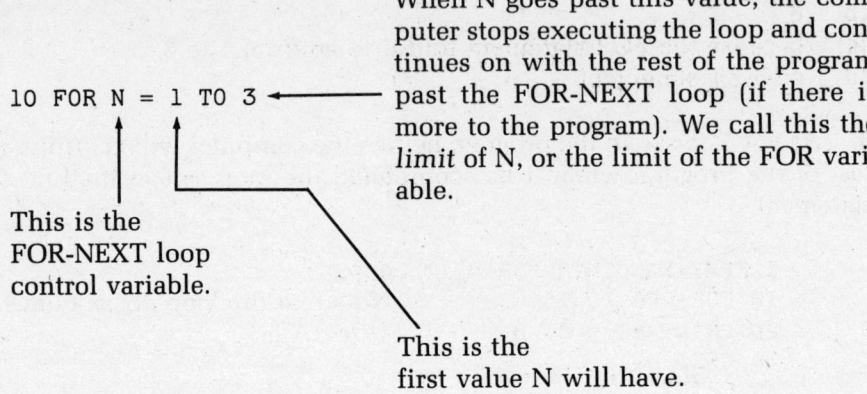

Here is a RUN of the program above.

```
10 FOR N=1 TO 3
20 PRINT N
30 NEXT N
RUN
1
2
3
```

Each time the computer comes to a NEXT N statement, it increases the value of N by one, and checks the new value against the limit for N. In this case, the limit is 3, because the FOR statement reads: FOR N = 1 TO 3. When the value of N is greater than 3, the computer continues on to the next statement after the NEXT statement, if there is one. If not, the computer has finished executing the program and stops. Got that? Let's see.

Statement 10 means that for the first time through the loop, N = 1. The second time through, N = N + 1 = 1 + 1 = 2. The third time through,

N = _____ = _____ = _____.

__ __ __ __ __ __ __ __ __

N = N + 1 = 2 + 1 = 3

5. Write a program with three statements that will print the word LOOP six times. Use a FOR-NEXT loop, and use C as the FOR-NEXT loop control variable. Show what your program will print when it is RUN.

_____

_____

_____

RUN

_____

_____

_____

_____

_____

_____

_ _ _ _ _ _ _ _ _

```
10 FOR C = 1 TO 6
20 PRINT "LOOP"
30 NEXT C
RUN
LOOP
LOOP
LOOP
LOOP
LOOP
LOOP
```

6. FOR-NEXT statements can be used in a multiple-statement line. Here is a FOR-NEXT program, all on one line. Follow the arrows.

```
10 FOR N = 1 TO 5 : PRINT N;" ";: NEXT N : PRINT "N NOW EQUALS " ; N
```

RUN

1 2 3 4 5 N NOW EQUALS 6

When the computer had finished the FOR-NEXT loop and had made its exit from the loop, what was the value for N? _____

―――――――――

6

Notice that the value for N after loop exit is one more than the upper limit for N as given in the FOR statement. That is how the computer recognized that it had performed the proper number of loops and was ready to go on to the next statement in the program beyond the FOR-NEXT loop.

7. You can use FOR-NEXT in DIRECT mode, too. Remember in direct mode you can enter a one-line statement without a line number, and the computer executes the statement as soon as you press RETURN. Let's say you enter the following multiple-statement line.

```
PRINT "TESTING"; : FOR X = 1 TO 4 : PRINT X; : NEXT X
```

What would your computer print when you pressed RETURN?_____

―――――――――

```
TESTING1234
```

8. Finish writing this program so that the computer will produce the RUN shown. Use a FOR-NEXT loop with Y as the control variable.

```
10 PRINT "THIS YEAR CATHY IS 10 YEARS OLD"
20_____
30_____
40_____

RUN
THIS YEAR CATHY IS 10 YEARS OLD
AND THE NEXT YEAR SHE WILL BE 11
AND THE NEXT YEAR SHE WILL BE 12
AND THE NEXT YEAR SHE WILL BE 13
AND THE NEXT YEAR SHE WILL BE 14
```

―――――――――

```
20 FOR Y = 11 TO 14
30 PRINT "AND THE NEXT YEAR SHE WILL BE " ; Y
40 NEXT Y
```

9. Another thing to notice about FOR-NEXT loops is that variables may be used instead of numbers, providing, of course, that the variables have been assigned values earlier in the program. In the example below, values are assigned by LET statements. Values could also have been assigned by INPUT or READ statements.

```
10 A=3 : B=8
20 FOR C=A TO B
30 PRINT C; " ";       ← Semicolon keeps printout on one line.
40 NEXT C
RUN
3  4  5  6  7  8
```

Rewrite the FOR statement (line 20), substituting numerical values for variables A and B. Use the values that were assigned by the program above.

   20_____

- - - - - - - - - - -

```
20 FOR C = 3 TO 8
```

10. Play computer and show the RUN for this FOR-NEXT demonstration program.

```
10 X=0 : Y=4
20 FOR Z=X TO Y
40 PRINT Z; " ";
50 NEXT Z
RUN
```
   _____

- - - - - - - - - - -

```
RUN
0  1  2  3  4
```

11. Now you write a program where variables are used to set the initial and upper limits of the FOR-NEXT loop control variable. Have your program READ the values to be used for the initial and upper limits from a DATA statement.

(Problem continued on the next page.)

Use Z for the control variable, and use X and Y for the variables that set the initial and upper limits. Select your DATA statement values so that your program will produce the following RUN.

```
RUN
100  101  102  103  104  105
```

```
10 READ X
20 READ Y
30 FOR Z=X TO Y
40 PRINT Z; " ";
50 NEXT Z
60 DATA 100,105
```

Statements 10 and 20 could be combined in one statement: 10 READ X, Y.

12. In this next program, an INPUT value (line 40) is used to establish the upper limit of the FOR statement (line 100), which tells the computer how many times to repeat "X = ? " When the program is RUN, the PRINT statements in lines 10–80 tell the user how to use the program.

```
5 REM **FRIENDLY MEAN FROM INPUT VALUES
10 PRINT "FOR MY NEXT ENCORE I WILL COMPUTE"
20 PRINT "THE MEAN (AVERAGE) OF A LIST OF NUMBERS."
30 PRINT
40 INPUT "HOW MANY NUMBERS IN THE LIST? " ; N
50 PRINT
60 PRINT "EACH TIME I TYPE 'X =?' YOU TYPE IN"
70 PRINT "ONE NUMBER AND THEN PRESS THE RETURN KEY."
80 PRINT
90 T=0
100 FOR K=1 TO N
110 INPUT "X =? "; X
120 T=T+X
130 NEXT K
140 M=T/N
150 PRINT
160 PRINT "TOTAL = " ; T
170 PRINT "MEAN = " ; M
```

(a) In the program above, the FOR-NEXT loop occupies lines _____

(b) What is the FOR-NEXT loop control variable? _____
(c) The upper limit for the control variable is determined by the value assigned to which other variable? _____

— — — — — — — — — —

(a) 100, 110, 120, 130
(b) K
(c) N

13. In the program of frame 12, which line in the FOR-NEXT loop will keep a running tally of the values entered for line 110? _____

— — — — — — — —

    120 T = T + X

14. This is a RUN of the program in frame 12.

```
RUN
FOR MY NEXT ENCORE, I WILL COMPUTE
THE MEAN (AVERAGE) OF A LIST OF NUMBERS.

HOW MANY NUMBERS IN THE LIST? 5

EACH TIME I TYPE 'X =?' YOU TYPE IN
ONE NUMBER AND THEN PRESS THE RETURN KEY.

X =? 16  ⎤
X =? 46  |
X =? 38  ⎬ ←———— Values entered by user.
X =? 112 |
X =? 23  ⎦

TOTAL = 235
MEAN  = 47
```

Show the numerical values in the FOR statement for the above RUN.

    100 FOR K = _____ TO _____

— — — — — — — — — —

    1 TO 5 (The value entered for INPUT N was 5.)

15. Here is the beginning of another RUN of the same program.

```
RUN
FOR MY NEXT ENCORE, I WILL COMPUTE
THE MEAN (AVERAGE) OF A LIST OF NUMBERS.

HOW MANY NUMBERS IN THE LIST? 4
```
←—Value entered by user.

How many times will "X=?" be printed?____How many times will the statements between the FOR-NEXT statements be executed?____

———————————

4; 4

Just to prove it to you, this is the rest of the same RUN.

```
EACH TIME I TYPE 'X =?' YOU TYPE IN
ONE NUMBER AND THEN PRESS THE RETURN KEY.

X =? 2
X =? 4
X =? 6
X =? 8

TOTAL = 20
MEAN = 5
```

16. Do you remember this program from frame 39 in Chapter 3?

```
100 REM **CHANGE OF ADDRESS PROGRAM
110 PRINT
120 PRINT "DEAR FRIENDS, MY NEW ADDRESS IS:"
130 PRINT
140 PRINT "IRENE BROWNSTONE"
150 PRINT "605 PARK AVENUE"
160 PRINT "NEW YORK, NY 10016"
170 PRINT
180 GOTO 110
```

Show how you would modify this program to use a FOR-NEXT loop that will ask the user how many messages to print, and then print just that many address change messages. Insert, replace, or delete lines as needed. A RUN should look like this.

```
RUN
HOW MANY TIMES? 2

DEAR FRIENDS, MY NEW ADDRESS IS:

IRENE BROWNSTONE
605 PARK AVENUE
NEW YORK, NY 10016

DEAR FRIENDS, MY NEW ADDRESS IS:

IRENE BROWNSTONE
605 PARK AVENUE
NEW YORK, NY 10016
```

- - - - - - - - - -

```
105 INPUT "HOW MANY TIMES? " ; T
115 FOR X=1 TO T
180 NEXT X
```

Line numbers need not be the same as those we used. However, the INPUT statement *must* be inserted between lines 100 and 110, and the FOR statement *must* appear between lines 110 and 120. Also, you might have used another letter for the FOR-NEXT loop control variable where we used X, or for the INPUT variable T.

17. Complete the following program to compute the product (P) of N numbers. Think carefully about the effect of your statements when the program is RUN. (A *product* is the result of multiplication.)

```
5 REM **PRODUCT CALCULATED FROM A LIST OF NUMBERS
10 PRINT "YOU WANT STILL ANOTHER ENCORE? I'M FLATTERED!"
20 PRINT "I'LL COMPUTE THE PRODUCT OF A LIST OF NUMBERS."
30 PRINT
40 INPUT "HOW MANY NUMBERS IN THE LIST? " ; N
50 PRINT
60 PRINT "EACH TIME I TYPE 'X =? ' YOU TYPE IN"
70 PRINT "ONE NUMBER AND THEN PRESS THE RETURN KEY."
80 PRINT


100_____

110_____
120 INPUT "X =? " ; X
130 P=P*X


140_____
150 PRINT : PRINT "PRODUCT = " ; P

RUN
YOU WANT STILL ANOTHER ENCORE? I'M FLATTERED!
I'LL COMPUTE THE PRODUCT OF A LIST OF NUMBERS.

HOW MANY NUMBERS IN THE LIST? 5

EACH TIME I TYPE 'X =?' YOU TYPE IN
ONE NUMBER AND THEN PRESS THE RETURN KEY.

X =? 7
X =? 12
X =? 4
X =? 3
X =? 19

PRODUCT = 19152
```

— — — — — — — — —

```
100 LET P=1
110 FOR K=1 TO N
140 NEXT K
```

Consider what would happen if P = 0 the first time through the loop: in line 140, P*X would be zero for the first time through the loop *and* every time after that. No matter what value X had, zero times X would always be zero!

18. Any BASIC expression may be used to set both the initial and the maximum value of a FOR-NEXT loop control variable. The computer evaluates these expressions (that is, does the arithmetic) *before* the loop is executed the first time and does *not* recompute these values each time through the loop.

Look at the FOR statement in this next program, and then decide whether the computer executed the loop the proper number of times.

```
10 Q=4
20 FOR P=Q TO 2*Q-1
30 PRINT P; " ";
40 NEXT P

RUN
 4  5  6  7  ←───────── The computer was right!
```

In the following program, fill in the blanks in line 20 with expressions using the variable Q, so that when the program is RUN, it will produce the printout shown below.

```
10 Q=4

20 FOR P=_____TO_____
30 PRINT P; " ";
40 NEXT P

RUN
 2  3  4  5  6  7  8  9  10  11  12
```

— — — — — — — — — —

       20 FOR P=Q/2 TO Q*3   or   20 FOR P=Q-2 TO Q+8

Note: If your answer is different and you think it is correct, try it on a computer and see if you get the same RUN that we did.

19. In the FOR-NEXT loops you have seen so far, the FOR-NEXT loop control variable takes the first value given in the FOR statement and keeps that value until the computer comes to the NEXT statement. Then the FOR variable increases its value by one each time through the loop until it reaches the maximum value allowed by the FOR statement.

               FOR X = 5 TO 10
                    ↗   ↖
First value of X   Maximum value for X

X = 5, then 6, then 7, then 8, then 9, and then 10

However, you can write a FOR statement that causes the value of the FOR-NEXT loop control variable to increase by multiples of other than one, or by fractional increments. You can also have the value of the FOR-NEXT variable *decrease* each time through the loop.

```
10 FOR X=1 TO 10 STEP 2
```

Tells the computer to increase the value of X by 2 every time through the FOR-NEXT loop, until X is greater than 10.

```
10 FOR Y=3 TO 6 STEP 1.5
```

Tells the computer to increase the value of Y by 1.5 every time through the FOR-NEXT loop, until Y is greater than 6.

```
10 FOR Z=10 TO 5 STEP -1
```

Note that Z will start at Z = 10 and go to Z = 5

Tells the computer to decrease the value of Z by 1 each time through the FOR-NEXT loop, until Z is less than 5.

Some demonstration programs will show the effects of STEP in action.

```
10 FOR B=1 TO 10 STEP 2
20 PRINT B; " " ;
30 NEXT B
40 PRINT
50 PRINT
60 PRINT "LOOP TERMINATES BECAUSE"
70 PRINT "B = "; B; ", WHICH IS GREATER THAN 10."

RUN
1  3  5  7  9

LOOP TERMINATES BECAUSE
B = 11, WHICH IS GREATER THAN 10.
```

The PRINT statement in line 40 "bumps" the computer off the line where it is held by the semicolon at the end of line 20. The PRINT statement in line 50 causes the space before line 60 is printed.

Note that the loop starts with the first value in the FOR statement (1) and increases by increments of 2, until the value of B = 11 which exceeds the maximum value allowed (10). At that point, the computer terminates the loop and continues running the rest of the program.

Play computer again, and fill in the RUN for this program.

```
10 D=3 : FOR F=D TO 4*D STEP D : PRINT F; " "; :NEXT F
RUN
```

----

3 6 9 12

20. In this example, the STEP in the FOR statement is followed by a negative number. STEP may be used to decrease the value of the FOR variable in any size step, going from a large value to a smaller one.

```
10 FOR J=100 TO 10 STEP -10
20 PRINT J; " ";
30 PRINT J
RUN
100  90  80  70  60  50  40  30  20  10
```

Now you write one where the FOR-NEXT loop control variable E decreases in steps of 3 from 27 to 18. Show the program and the RUN.

```
10 FOR E =27 TO 18 STEP -3
20 PRINT E; " ";
30 NEXT E

RUN
27  24  21  18
```

or

```
10 FOR E = 27 TO 18 STEP -3 : PRINT E; " "; : NEXT E
RUN
27  24  21  18
```

21. As we mentioned, the steps in a FOR-NEXT loop can be fractional values, as in the following example.

```
10 FOR X = 5 TO 7.5 STEP .25
20 PRINT X; " ";
30 NEXT X
RUN
5  5.25  5.5  5.75  6  6.25  6.5  6.75  7  7.25  7.5
```

Show the RUN for this program if we changed line 10 to the following.

```
10 FOR X = 5 TO 7.5 STEP .5
RUN
```

— — — — — — — —

```
RUN
5  5.5  6  6.5  7  7.5
```

22. Here's another useful trick. You don't *have* to use the control variable name in the NEXT statement. If no variable is used, the computer assumes you are referring to the most recent FOR statement. For example:

```
10 INPUT "HOW MANY TIMES? "; T
20 FOR K=1 TO T : PRINT "*"; : NEXT
```
           The computer assumes NEXT K

Write a program using a FOR-NEXT loop and all the space-saving, time-saving tricks introduced thus far in this book to print 20 random whole numbers between 1 and 50.

— — — — — — — —

```
10 FOR X=1 TO 20 : PRINT INT(50*RND(1))+1; : NEXT
```

23. The FOR-NEXT loop is useful for such things as repeated calculations, counting or keeping tallies, and dealing with cyclical or recurring events.
 One such recurring event is the monthly compounding of interest on a savings account or other financial investment.
 In the program on the following page, monthly interest (I) is calculated in line 170 by multiplying the initial amount of money (P for Principal) by the Rate of interest (R).
 The rate of interest is converted to a decimal fraction: R = 5% = 5/100 = .05

Since 5 percent is the yearly rate of interest, only 1/12 the calculated amount of interest is added to the principal each month.

```
1 REM USES PRESS 'RETURN' TO CONTINUE TECHNIQUE
100 REM ***MONTHLY INTEREST COMPOUNDING
110 INPUT "PRINCIPAL TO START? $";P
120 INPUT "YEARLY INTEREST RATE (IN %) ";R
130 INPUT "HOW MANY MONTHS? ";M
140 PRINT
150 FOR K = 1 TO M
160 LET I = (P * (R / 100)) / 12
170 PRINT "MONTH: ";K: PRINT "PRINCIPAL: ";P
180 PRINT "INTEREST: ";I
190 PRINT "PRINCIPAL + INTEREST: ";P + I: LET P = P + I
200 INPUT "";R$: PRINT : NEXT K

]RUN
PRINCIPAL TO START? $1000
YEARLY INTEREST RATE (IN %) 14
HOW MANY MONTHS? 10

MONTH: 1
PRINCIPAL: 1000
INTEREST: 11.6666667
PRINCIPAL + INTEREST: 1011.66667

MONTH: 2
PRINCIPAL: 1011.66667
INTEREST: 11.8027778
PRINCIPAL + INTEREST: 1023.46944

MONTH: 3
PRINCIPAL: 1023.46944
INTEREST: 11.9404769
PRINCIPAL + INTEREST: 1035.40992

MONTH: 4
PRINCIPAL: 1035.40992
INTEREST: 12.0797824
PRINCIPAL + INTEREST: 1047.4897
```

(The RUN continues to month 10.)

(a) Which lines are included in the FOR-NEXT loop?_____
(b) Which variable keeps track of and is used to print the number corresponding to the month for each line in the table?_____
(c) Which line keeps a running tally of principal plus interest?_____

(a) 150, 160, 170, 180, 190, 200
(b) the FOR variable K
(c) 190

Note: If you want to brush up on your business math, a useful book would be Locke, *Business Mathematics: A Self-Teaching Guide*, John Wiley & Sons, New York, 1972.

24. Can you have a FOR-NEXT *inside* another FOR-NEXT loop? Absolutely. It is called *nested* FOR-NEXT loops and is perfectly "legal" provided you follow the rule illustrated below.

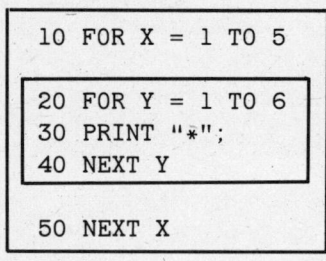

This *inside* loop must be completely *inside* the other or outside loop. Otherwise you'll get an error message.

```
RUN
*******************************
```

Count the stars. How many are there? Do you see any relationship between the number of stars printed and the numbers 5 and 6 which appear in the two FOR statements?

A loop within a loop is called a _____ FOR-NEXT loop. The inside loop must be_____the outside loop.

———————————

nested; inside

25. Here are two programs using nested FOR-NEXT loops.

```
5 REM **PROGRAM A          5 REM**PROGRAM B
10 FOR N=5 TO 9            10 FOR N=5 TO 9
20 FOR L=1 TO 3            20 FOR L=1 TO 3
30 PRINT "NESTED"          30 PRINT "NESTED"
40 NEXT L                  40 NEXT N
50 PRINT "       LOOP"     50 PRINT "       LOOP"
60 NEST N                  60 NEXT L
```

Which program (A or B) has correctly nested FOR-NEXT loops?_____

———————————

program A

26. Program A in frame 25 produces a repeated pattern of printout. Look at the program closely and then show what the computer will print when the program is RUN.

```
RUN
NESTED
NESTED
NESTED
     LOOP
NESTED
NESTED
NESTED
     LOOP
NESTED
NESTED
NESTED
     LOOP
NESTED
NESTED
NESTED
     LOOP
NESTED
NESTED
NESTED
     LOOP
```

27. Another time-saving, space-saving trick available to you is the ability to use two NEXT statements at once. In a program where nested FOR-NEXT loops end in successive statements, we would replace two NEXT statements with just one, as below.

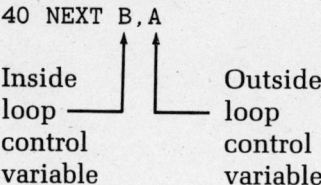

```
40 NEXT B,A
```

Inside loop control variable — Outside loop control variable

Following is a program with nested loops that will print the multiplication table from 0 × 0 to 9 × 9.

```
10 FOR X=0 TO 9
20 FOR Y=0 TO 9
30 PRINT X; "X"; Y "="; X*Y,
40 NEXT Y
50 NEXT X
]RUN
```

0×0=0	0×1=0	0×2=0
0×3=0	0×4=0	0×5=0
0×6=0	0×7=0	0×8=0
0×9=0	1×0=0	1×1=1
1×2=2	1×3=3	1×4=4
1×5=5	1×6=6	1×7=7
1×8=8	1×9=9	2×0=0
2×1=2	2×2=4	2×3=6
2×4=8	2×5=10	2×6=12
2×7=14	2×8=16	2×9=18
3×0=0	3×1=3	3×2=6
3×3=9	3×4=12	3×5=15
3×6=18	3×7=21	3×8=24
3×9=27	4×0=0	4×1=4
4×2=8	4×3=12	4×4=16
4×5=20	4×6=24	4×7=28
4×8=32	4×9=36	5×0=0
5×1=5	5×2=10	5×3=15
5×4=20	5×5=25	5×6=30
5×7=35	5×8=40	5×9=45
6×0=0	6×1=6	6×2=12
6×3=18	6×4=24	6×5=30
6×6=36	6×7=42	6×8=48
6×9=54	7×0=0	7×1=7
7×2=14	7×3=21	7×4=28
7×5=35	7×6=42	7×7=49
7×8=56	7×9=63	8×0=0
8×1=8	8×2=16	8×3=24
8×4=32	8×5=40	8×6=48
8×7=56	8×8=64	8×9=72
9×0=0	9×1=9	9×2=18
9×3=27	9×4=36	9×5=45
9×6=54	9×7=63	9×8=72
9×9=81		

Write a *single* NEXT statement that will be correct for this program. _____

— — — — — — — — —

```
40 NEXT Y,X
```

28. Do your kids, friends, or family hound you for arithmetic problems? Ours sure do. The following is a little program to generate multiplication problem *worksheets*. Fill in the blanks.

```
10 REM **PERSONALIZED MULTIPLICATION WORKSHEET
20 INPUT "WHAT IS YOUR NAME? "; A$
30 INPUT "HOW MANY PROBLEMS? "; T
40 INPUT "HOW MANY DIGITS IN EACH NUMBER(1,2 OR 3)? "; D
50 PRINT : PRINT "MULTIPLICATION WORKSHEET FOR "; A$

60 FOR P=_____
70 FOR M=1 TO 2
80 PRINT INT (10^D*RND(1))

90_____
100 PRINT "-------" : PRINT : PRINT : PRINT

110_____
```

```
RUN
WHAT IS YOUR NAME? BETTE
HOW MANY PROBLEMS? 3
HOW MANY DIGITS IN EACH NUMBER(1,2 OR 3)? 3


MULTIPLICATION WORKSHEET FOR BETTE
 278
 496
-------


 750
 378
------


 734
 128
-------
```
_ _ _ _ _ _ _ _ _ _

60 FOR P = 1 TO T
90 NEXT (You might also have said NEXT M.)
110 NEXT P (You must have the P; otherwise, the computer assumes the most recent FOR and that was FOR M.)

29. Look again at the program in frame 28.
(a) Which lines contain the FOR-NEXT statements to limit the number of problems?_____
(b) What does line 100 do?_____

— — — — — — — — — —

(a) Lines 60 and 110 contain the FOR and NEXT statements. All the statements between are inside the loop with the control variable P.
(b) Line 100 prints a line below which you place your answer and prints spaces (or does three line feeds) between problems.

30. Sometimes our line 80 from the program in frame 28 produces random numbers with only 2 digits when we asked for 3, or only 1 digit when we asked for 2, as in this RUN.

```
RUN
WHAT IS YOUR NAME? MIKE
HOW MANY PROBLEMS? 2
HOW MANY DIGITS IN EACH NUMBER(1,2 OR 3)? 2

MULTIPLICATION WORKSHEET FOR MIKE
  4
 89
-------


  1
  5
-------
```

We want you to fix our program so that won't happen, using an IF-THEN statement to check the number generated by line 80. If the number does not have the proper number of digits, direct the computer to generate another number. Notice the 10∧D in line 80. If D = 1, then 10∧1 = 10. If D = 2, then 10∧2 = 100. If D = 3, then 10∧3 = 1000. This way of using the INPUT value of D will be useful in writing the IF-THEN statement. Remember, if D = 2, we don't want 9 or less to be printed, and if D = 3, we don't want 99 or less to be used in a problem. Write your changes below.

— — — — — — — — — —

Our changes: 80 N=INT(10∧D*RND(1)) : IF N<10∧(D−1) THEN 80
             90 PRINT N : NEXT M

Now a RUN always has the correct number of digits in the problem. If your answer doesn't look like ours but you think it is right, try it on a computer! You'll be seeing and using a lot more FOR-NEXT loops as you continue on in this book.

```
RUN
WHAT IS YOUR NAME? KATHY
HOW MANY PROBLEMS? 4
HOW MANY DIGITS IN EACH NUMBER(1,2 OR 3)? 2

MULTIPLICATION WORKSHEET FOR KATHY
 42
 10
 -------


 28
 14
 -------


 51
 76
 -------


 67
 21
 -------
```

Self-Test

Now that you have completed Chapter 6, you have acquired enough understanding of computer programming to be able to learn a lot more by experimenting at a computer terminal. As you look at our demonstration programs, you may see some possibilities that we do not specifically deal with. Build on your knowledge by trying out your own ideas.

But right now, find out if you really know how to use FOR-NEXT loops by doing the following programs.

1. Show what will be printed if we RUN the following program.

```
10 S=0
20 FOR K=1 TO 4
30 S=S+K
40 NEXT K
50 PRINT S
RUN
```

2. Show what will be printed if we RUN the following program.

   ```
   10 P=1 : FOR K=1 TO 4 : P=P*K : NEXT K : PRINT P
   RUN
   ```

3. Examine this program. Which of the three RUNs was produced by the program?____

   ```
   10 N=1
   20 FOR K=1 TO N
   30 PRINT "*";
   40 NEXT K
   50 PRINT
   60 N=N+1
   70 IF N>10 THEN END
   80 GOTO 20
   ```

   ```
        RUN 1              RUN 2              RUN 3
          *               ********              *
         ***              ********              **
        *****             ********              ***
       *******            ********              ****
      *********           ********              *****
     ***********          ********              ******
    *************         ********              *******
   ***************        ********              ********
                                                *********
                                                **********
   ```

4. Write a program to print a table of N, N^2, and N^3. Use INPUT statements to indicate what list of numbers you wish included in the table. A RUN should look like this.

    ```
    ]RUN
    FIRST NUMBER?40
    LAST NUMBER?45

    N                N-SQR'D           N-CUBED
    40               1600              64000
    41               1681              68921
    42               1764              74088
    43               1849              79507
    44               1936              85184
    45               2025              91125
    ```

   (*Hint*: the slight error in the calculation of squares and cubes using exponentiation can be controlled by using INT in an intelligent way.)

5. Show what will be printed if we RUN the following program.

    ```
    10 S=0
    20 FOR K=1 TO 7 STEP 2
    30 S=S+K
    40 NEXT K
    50 PRINT S
    RUN
    ```

6. Complete the following program to print a table projecting growth rate of a population at specified intervals over a given time period (years). The formula for population growth is:

$$Q = P(1 + R/100)^N$$

where N is the number of years.

```
100 REM **REQUEST DATA AND PRINT HEADING
110 INPUT "INITIAL POPULATION? "; P
120 INPUT "GROWTH RATE? "; R
130 INPUT "INITIAL VALUE OF N? "; A
140 INPUT "FINAL VALUE OF N? "; B
150 INPUT "STEP SIZE? ": H
160 PRINT : PRINT " N", "POPULATION" : PRINT
200 REM **COMPUTE AND PRINT TABLE

210_____

220_____

230_____

240_____

RUN
INITIAL POPULATION? 230
GROWTH RATE? 1
INITIAL VALUE OF N? 0
FINAL VALUE OF N? 100
STEP SIZE? 25

 N          POPULATION
 0          230
 25         294.959
 50         378.263
 75         485.095
 100        622.1

RUN
```

(The RUN is shown on the next page.)

```
          INITIAL POPULATION? 205      For the United States, 1970 (in mil-
                                       lions of people)
          GROWTH RATE? 1
          INITIAL VALUE OF N? 0
          FINAL VALUE OF N? 100
          STEP SIZE? 10

          N           POPULATION       Results are expressed in millions.
          0           205
          10          226.447
          20          250.139
          30          276.309
          40          305.217
          50          337.149
          60          372.422
          70          411.386
          80          454.426
          90          501.968
          100         554.485
```

7. Write a program to compute and print the sum of whole numbers from 1 to N where the value of N is supplied in response to an INPUT statement. A RUN might look like the following one.

```
RUN
GIVE ME A WHOLE NUMBER (N) AND I WILL COMPUTE
AND PRINT THE SUM OF THE WHOLE NUMBERS FROM 1 TO N.

WHAT IS N? 3
THE SUM IS 6          Because 1 + 2 + 3 = 6

WHAT IS N? 5
THE SUM IS 15         Because 1 + 2 + 3 + 4 + 5 = 15

WHAT IS N?

BREAK IN 30
```

8. Look back at the simple number guessing game in Chapter 1, frame 5. Use a FOR-NEXT loop to modify the program so that the user has only eight chances to guess the number. If he fails in eight guesses, print an appropriate message before starting over again.

Answers to Self-Test

The frame numbers in parentheses refer to the frames in the chapter where the topic is discussed. You may wish to refer back to these for a quick review.

1. RUN
   10

   The answer is the *sum* of the values of K defined by the FOR statement (K = 1, 2, 3, and 4). (frames 1–7)

2. RUN
   24

   The answer is the *product* of the values of K defined by the FOR statement (K = 1, 2, 3, and 4). (frames 1–6, 13)

3. RUN 3. The FOR-NEXT loop (lines 20, 30, 40) causes the computer to print a *row* of N stars. The loop is done for N = 1, 2, 3, . . ., 10. (frames 1–6, 20)

4. ```
   10 INPUT "FIRST NUMBER? ";A
   20 INPUT "LAST NUMBER? ";B
   30 PRINT
   40 PRINT "N", "N-SQR'D", "N-CUBED"
   50 FOR N = A TO B
   60 PRINT N, INT (N ^ 2), INT (N ^ 3)
   70 NEXT N
   ```

   (frames 9, 23)

5. RUN
   16

   Similar to question 1, but this time the values of K defined by the FOR statement are K = 1, 3, 5, and 7. (frame 19)
   ```

6. ```
200 REM **COMPUTE AND PRINT TABLE
210 FOR N=A TO B STEP H
220 LET Q=P*(1+R/100)^N
230 PRINT N,Q
240 NEXT N
```

(frames 19, 23)

7. ```
10 PRINT "GIVE ME A WHOLE NUMBER (N) AND I WILL COMPUTE"
20 PRINT "AND PRINT THE SUM OF THE WHOLE NUMBERS FROM 1 TO N."
30 PRINT
40 PRINT "WHAT IS N? ";
50 INPUT N
55 LET S=0
60 FOR W=1 TO N
70 LET S=S+W
80 NEXT W
90 PRINT "THE SUM IS ";S
100 GOTO 30
```

(frame 23)

8. ```
100 REM **THIS IS A SIMPLE COMPUTER GAME
110 LET X=INT (100*RND(1))+1
120 PRINT
130 PRINT"I'M THINKING OF A NUMBER FROM 1 TO 100."
140 PRINT"GUESS MY NUMBER!!!"
150 FOR A=1 TO 8 : INPUT"YOUR GUESS? ";G
160 IF G<X THEN PRINT"TRY A BIGGER NUMBER" : GO TO 190
170 IF G>X THEN PRINT"TRY A SMALLER NUMBER": GO TO 190
180 IF G=X THEN PRINT"THAT'S IT!!! YOU GUESSED MY NUMBER." :
          GO TO 110
190 NEXT A : PRINT"TOO MANY GUESSES. THE NUMBER WAS ";X :
             GO TO 110
```

(frames 2, 4)
```

CHAPTER SEVEN

Low-Resolution Graphics

In this chapter you will be introduced to the low-resolution graphics instructions for the Apple and to the system of coordinates used to instruct the computer as to where on the screen to display the graphics.

When you complete this chapter you will be able to use the following instructions:

    GR
    TEXT
    HOME
    PLOT
    HLIN
    VLIN

You will also learn:

- How to cause and control delays in the length of time a display remains on the screen, using FOR-NEXT
- How to create images that appear to blink or move around the screen
- How to create block letters and numbers in graphics mode
- How to use variables to change the placement of an image on the screen
- How to use FOR-NEXT loops to automate the creation and control of images

1. Up to now you have been writing and using programs in TEXT mode. Another mode available for control by Applesoft BASIC is called low-resolution graphic mode. "Low-resolution" means that you get a limited degree of detail in your images.

The two-letter instruction GR (for GRaphic) tells the computer to change from TEXT mode to GRaphic mode. The instruction TEXT does the opposite: it tells the computer to leave GRaphic mode and return to TEXT mode.

In text mode, the screen displays 24 lines (or rows) of alphanumeric characters (letters, numbers, symbols, and/or spaces) in 40 columns (or character positions) across the screen. In GRaphic mode, the display also has 40 columns across the screen where a dot can be displayed. This dot is actually a small square or block, the size of the top half of the famous flashing cursor. The top 20 rows or lines of the alphanumeric TEXT mode display are converted into 40 rows in GRaphic mode. (The bottom four text lines are discussed shortly.) Therefore, the smallest point or block you can control in low-resolution graphics is half the size of an alphanumeric character.

(a) What is the Applesoft BASIC instruction that activates the low-resolution graphic mode? _____

(b) How many rows are displayed in text mode?_____
In graphic mode?_____

(c) How many columns are used in graphic mode? ____

__ __ __ __ __ __ __

(a) GR
(b) Text: 24; rows or lines; GRaphic: 40 rows
(c) 40 columns

2. In GR mode, the 40 columns across the screen are numbered from 0 to 39, starting at the left edge of the display. The 40 rows are also numbered from 0 to 39, with the top row being row 0 (zero) and the bottom row 39. You can think of this as a system similar to rectangular Cartesian coordinates, often used in graphs, or as a numbered grid, like this one.

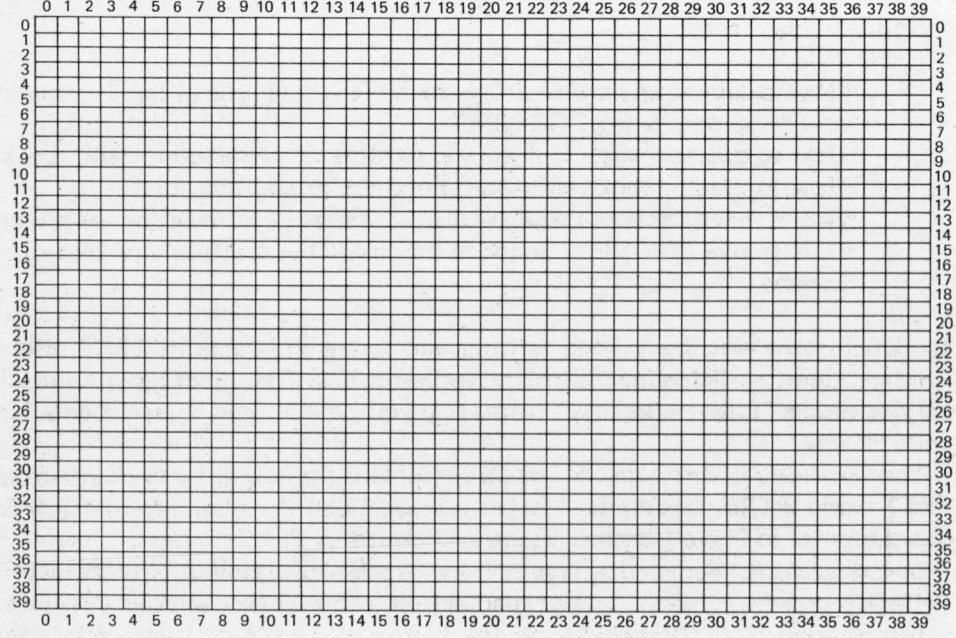

Using this number system, you can specify to the computer exactly where on this grid to "turn on" a particular colored block (and also turn off a block). It is important that you become familiar with this number system, as it is used extensively in GR mode instructions. In fact, using the numbered grid as an aid, you can "draw" complicated figures and identify the coordinates on the grid for use in program statements that reproduce that figure on the display.

The coordinates for the little block at the upper left corner of the 40-by-40 grid is column 0 (zero), row 0 (zero). The block at the bottom left corner is at column 0, row 39. Referring to the grid, you fill in the blanks that follow. The block at the upper right corner is at column ____, row ____; the block at the lower right corner is at column ____, row ____.

— — — — — — — —

column 39; row 0
column 39; row 39

3. To determine the color to be displayed in a particular block on the grid, the BASIC instruction COLOR= is used. Low-resolution graphic mode allows you to choose from 16 colors, numbered from 0 (zero) to 15, as shown in the chart. The program statement

    20 COLOR= 2

tells the computer to use dark blue as the color for all blocks in the grid "turned on" by the program statements that follow. This COLOR= instruction stays in effect until another COLOR= statement changes the color to be displayed.

Apple Low-Resolution GRaphic Mode Color Codes

- 0 = black (also called video black—absence of any color on the screen)
- 1 = magenta (a purplish red, as close to red as you can obtain in GR mode)
- 2 = dark blue
- 3 = purple (a light purple or lavender)
- 4 = dark green
- 5 = grey
- 6 = medium blue
- 7 = light blue
- 8 = brown
- 9 = orange
- 10 = grey
- 11 = pink
- 12 = green
- 13 = yellow
- 14 = agua (blue-green)
- 15 = white

Note: These are the colors displayed by a color TV or color video monitor when the tint and color balance are properly adjusted on a well-functioning set.

Referring to the chart, write the color selected by the following BASIC statements.

(a) 20 COLOR= 9 _____
(b) 20 COLOR= 12 _____
(c) 20 COLOR= 15 _____
(d) 20 COLOR= 1 _____
(e) 20 COLOR= 0 _____

(a) orange
(b) green
(c) white
(d) magenta (red)
(e) black (video black)

4. If the computer is in TEXT mode, then when the computer executes the statement

```
10 GR
```

the screen is cleared and all blocks in the grid are displayed in video black, and COLOR is automatically set to zero (black), until a COLOR= statement in the program is executed to change the color setting.

With this background, we are now ready to create low-resolution color graphics programs. The first instruction we will use to actually "turn on" colored blocks on the display is PLOT. Because it turns on a block of color specified by the position where a numbered column and a numbered row cross, PLOT acts like plotting a point on a graph. The format of the PLOT statement is as follows:

PLOT grid column number, grid row number

For example,

```
30 PLOT 10,15
```

tells the computer to "turn on" a block a light at the place on the grid where column 10 is crossed by row 15. Find this place on the grid in frame 2. Now enter and RUN this program.

```
10 GR
20 COLOR= 12
30 PLOT 10,15
RUN
```

(a) What color is the dot or block displayed by this program? _____

(b) Where on the graphics display grid does this block appear? _____

— — — — — — — — —

(a) green
(b) column 10, row 15

5. When the program in the previous frame is executed, the screen goes blank (actually "black"), and a green dot appears in the upper left quarter of the display screen. The Applesoft "prompt" bracket] and the flashing cursor appear at the left toward the bottom of the screen. In this low-resolution graphics mode, there is a text window at the bottom of the screen. As we mentioned earlier, the top 20 (out of 24) display lines in TEXT mode are converted into the 40 numbered rows on the graphics grid. The bottom 4 lines of the 24-line text display remain in TEXT mode. Type LIST (and hit RETURN), and the last two lines of your three-statement program will be displayed in the text window. (Do it!) Line 10 was also displayed, but was *scrolled* (pushed up) out of the text window. To see individual statement lines from the program, type LIST followed by the line number.

Error messages as well as strings from PRINT or INPUT statements in the program can also appear in the text window.

Now modify the program by replacing line 20 with this statement:

```
20 COLOR= 1
```

and LIST the program again. You should see your new line 20 in the program listing in the text window. Notice that you can enter, change, or delete a program without leaving GRaphic mode.

Now RUN the modified program.

(a) What color is the block plotted and displayed by the program? _____

(b) Where on the screen is the block displayed? _____

(c) What must you type to see program line 10 in the text window? _____

— — — — — — — — —

(a) magenta (red)
(b) same as before, where row 15 intersects column 10
(c) LIST 10

6. To change from GRaphic mode back to TEXT mode, type the word TEXT and hit RETURN. You should see a screen of @ signs, with the cursor remaining in its text window position. You can clear the screen of unwanted clutter in TEXT mode by typing the word HOME. The display is cleared, and the cursor positioned at the top left of the otherwise blank screen.

Now type the instructions that follow. Note that they are separated by colons.

You type: TEXT:HOME:LIST

Describe the display now. _____

_____

— — — — — — — — —

The program is LISTed at the top of an otherwise blank display.

Note: You will find this sequence of instructions handy when creating, correcting, or modifying graphics programs, since you usually cannot see an entire program in the four-line text window in GR mode.

7. To develop your ability to use the grid coordinates (column and row numbers) for creating graphic instruction statements, fill in the blanks in the following chart.

A block located at:	Has grid coordinates at:	
	Column	Row
(a) Lower right corner	_____ ,	_____
(b) Upper left corner	_____ ,	_____
(c) Upper right corner	_____ ,	_____
(d) Lower left corner	_____ ,	_____
(e) Approx. center of grid	_____ ,	_____

— — — — — — — — —

(a)   39, 39
(b)   0, 0
(c)   39, 0
(d)   0, 39
(e)   19, 19 (or 20, 20)

8. Now write one program to place a dot at each corner of the screen, and one in the middle, each a different color.

- - - - - - - - - -

```
1 REM ** DOTS IN CORNER
10 GR
20 COLOR= 1
30 PLOT 0,0
40 COLOR= 3
50 PLOT 0,39
60 COLOR= 5
70 PLOT 39,0
80 COLOR= 7
90 PLOT 39,39
100 COLOR= 9
110 PLOT 19,19
```

9. The column and row numbers specified in a PLOT statement can be variables or calculated expressions. But notice that no value less than zero (no negative numbers) or values greater than 39 can be used. Examine this program.

```
10 GR
20 COLOR= 15
30 LET C=5
40 LET R=8
50 PLOT C,R
60 PLOT C,R - C
70 PLOT C * 8,R * 5
```

Where will the block be displayed for (a), (b), and (c):

(a) Line 50? _____

(b) Line 60? _____

(c) Line 70? _____

(d) What color are the blocks displayed by this program? _____

(a) column 5, row 8
(b) column 5, row 3
(c) none plotted; illegal quantity error because C * 8 = 40
(d) white

10. The program below uses a PLOT statement inside a FOR-NEXT loop. The FOR control variable X is used to determine the column number for each block.

```
10 GR
20 COLOR= 2
30 FOR X = 0 TO 39
40 PLOT X,10
50 NEXT X
```

Describe the display produced by this program. _____

----

a horizontal blue line across row 10

11. Below is a modification for the previous program, where the FOR-NEXT loop control variable is used to automate the display of a number of blocks, but using only one PLOT statement. Replace line 40 with this new line 40:

```
40 PLOT X,X
```

Describe the display now produced by the program. _____

----

a diagonal line of blue blocks from the upper left corner to the bottom right corner of the graphic display area

12. A single strategically placed PLOT statement in a program can fill the entire display with color. This is accomplished with nested FOR-NEXT loops, with one variable used to set the column number, the other to set the row number. Borrowing a term from painters, this is often referred to as a "wash." Try this program.

```
10 GR
20 COLOR= 13
30 FOR X = 0 to 39
40 FOR Y = 0 to 39
50 PLOT X,Y
60 NEXT Y,X
RUN
```

Describe the display produced by this program. _____
_____

— — — — — — — — —

The graphic display area is "washed" or filled with yellow.

13. Now add the statements below to the previous program to make a dark green box appear in the display. This box will be composed of four blocks.

```
70 COLOR= 4
80 PLOT 18,19
90 PLOT 19,19
100 PLOT 18,20
110 PLOT 19,20
RUN
```

In what general section of the display will the green box appear? _____

— — — — — — — — —

near the center

Remember: To see a complete listing of the program, type

TEXT:HOME:LIST.

14. To make a particular image disappear from the display, without disturbing the remainder of the screen, simply replot the same blocks that make up the image, using the background color for replotting. Complete this addition to the previous program to make the green box "disappear."

```
120 COLOR= 13
130 _____
140 _____
150 _____
160 _____
```

— — — — — — — — —

```
130 PLOT 18,19
140 PLOT 19,19
150 PLOT 18,20
160 PLOT 19,20
```

15. Now add one statement to the end of the previous program to make the green box blink on and off in a yellow background. (We suggest you SAVE this program after testing it.)

    170 _____

— — — — — — — — —

    170 GOTO 70

Note: Since this is a continuous GOTO loop, use CTRL/C to stop a RUN.

16. The following program places a purple dot in the middle of the screen.

    10 GR
    20 COLOR= 3
    30 PLOT 19,19

Provide the statements needed to make this dot disappear.

— — — — — — — — —

    40 COLOR= 0
    50 PLOT 19,19

17. The amount of time that anything appears on the display can be controlled by the use of the time delay technique shown next. This technique merely instructs the computer to count to itself before continuing with the rest of the program. The "counting" is done with a program loop. What statements are usually used to automatically start and stop the repeated execution of a section

    of a program? _____

— — — — — — — — —

FOR and NEXT

18. Examine this multiple-statement line:

    150 FOR D = 1 TO 100: NEXT D

The computer must go through the loop 100 times before continuing to the next line-numbered statement, thus creating a delay in the execution of the rest of the program.
    What part of the statement can be changed to create longer or shorter delays?

_____

_____

the (starting and upper) limits you give in the FOR statement

19. Using the delay technique just discussed, write a program to cause a white dot to blink on and off at position 19,19.

```
10 GR
20 COLOR= 15
30 PLOT 19,19
40 FOR D = 1 TO 100: NEXT D
50 COLOR= 0
60 PLOT 19,19
70 FOR D = 1 TO 100: NEXT D
80 GOTO 20
```

20. Referring to your program solution for the previous frame, which of the following statements would cause the slowest blinking, (a) or (b)?

(a) FOR D = 1 TO 50: NEXT D
(b) FOR D = 50 TO 150: NEXT D

(b)

21. Return now to the program you constructed that causes a green square to flash in a yellow background. (LOAD it if you SAVEd it.) You can slow the blinking of the green square by writing two delay statements, inserted between the proper existing lines in the program (see frames 12, 13, and 14). Between which lines should the delay statements be inserted? _____

between lines 110 and 120, and between lines 160 and 170 (Do a test RUN.)

22. Now we want you to write a program that causes a colored block to appear to run around the inside edge of the graphics display area, like the lights on a theater marquee. Inside FOR-NEXT loops, a block should be plotted, then turned off, for each grid position along the top of the screen, from left to right. Then the block should "run" down the right side, then from the lower right corner across the bottom to the lower left corner, then up the left side. From there, repeat forever (or until CTRL/C is used). *Hint:* Our solution, without using multiple statements per line, has 26 statements. We also use STEP −1 in two FOR-NEXT loops.

```
10 GR
20 FOR D = 0 TO 39
30 COLOR= 13
40 PLOT D,0
50 COLOR= 0
60 PLOT D,0
70 NEXT D
90 FOR D = 1 TO 38
100 COLOR= 13
110 PLOT 39,D
120 COLOR= 0
130 PLOT 39,D
140 NEXT D
150 FOR D = 39 TO 0 STEP -1
160 COLOR= 13
170 PLOT D,39
180 COLOR= 0
190 PLOT D,39
200 NEXT D
210 FOR D = 38 TO 1 STEP -1
220 COLOR= 13
230 PLOT 0,D
240 COLOR= 0
250 PLOT 0,D
260 NEXT D
270 GOTO 20
```

Note: Lines 90 and 210 start or end at positions 1 and 38 to avoid "double blinks" at the corner positions.

23. Examine this program.

```
10 GR
20 COLOR= 11
30 FOR X = 0 TO 39: PLOT 19,X: NEXT
40 COLOR= 12
50 FOR Y = 0 TO 39: PLOT Y,19: NEXT
```

Describe what it will display. _____

_____

a pink vertical line crossed by a green horizontal line

24. Here are two more graphics instructions to make your graphics programming life easier: HLIN and VLIN. Both operate in a manner similar to PLOT. HLIN "draws" horizontal lines. The H in HLIN stands for horizontal, the LIN stands for line. VLIN draws (wouldn't you know it) vertical lines. Both HLIN and VLIN use the same numbered grid of column and row coordinates as PLOT to specify where the lines will appear on the display, as well as where the end points of the lines will be, to determine line length.

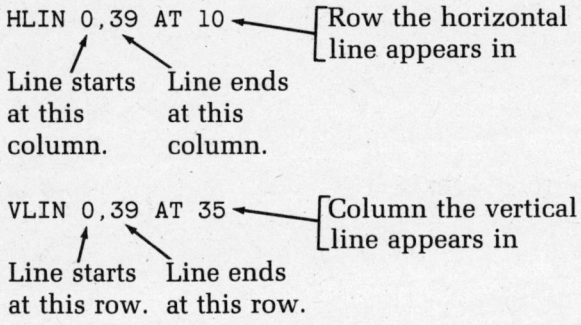

In GR mode, the statement

    40 HLIN 10,30 AT 19

draws a horizontal line which starts in column 10 and ends in column 30, going across row 19 (the middle of the screen). Similarly, the statement

    50 VLIN 5,39 AT 19

draws a vertical line from row 5 (near, but not at, the top of the screen) to the bottom of the graphic display area, the line being located in column 19.

For your first practice in applying the grid coordinates to HLIN and VLIN, do the following:

(a) Write a statement to draw a line at the top of the graphics display area from the left side to the middle. _____

(b) Write a statement to draw a line along the entire right side of the graphic display area. _____

— — — — — — —

(a)   HLIN 0,19 AT 0
(b)   VLIN 0,39 AT 39

25. Earlier you used a program to cover the screen with a yellow wash (background color), using PLOT inside nested FOR-NEXT loops. Write a similar, but simpler, program to cover the screen in aqua, using HLIN.

```
10 GR
20 COLOR= 14
30 FOR R = 0 TO 39
40 HLIN 0,39 AT R
50 NEXT
```

Note: Lines 30, 40, and 50 could appear as one multiple statement line. This results in slightly faster execution of the program.

26. As with PLOT, the grid coordinate numbers for HLIN and VLIN can be variables or expressions to calculate. Remember, values less than 0 or greater than 39 in HLIN and VLIN statements will result in errors; so be especially cautious with calculated values. Consider the line produced by this example program.

```
10 C = 10
20 R = 39
30 GR
40 COLOR= 9
50 HLIN C,39 - C AT R
```

(a) How many "grid blocks" long will this line be? _____

(b) Where will it be located on the screen? _____

(c) What color will it be? _____

(a) 20
(b) the middle of the bottom edge of the graphic display area
(c) orange

27. Another example program:

```
10 GR
20 COLOR= 5
30 FOR C = 0 TO 19
40 HLIN 19,39 - C AT 39 - C
50 HLIN C,19 AT 39 - C
60 NEXT C
```

Exercise your brain cells by predicting the shape of this display before you RUN the program. Examine lines 40 and 50, and see what the coordinates would be for C = 0, C = 1, C = 2, to get the idea. Using the grid may help you to "play computer" and visualize the display produced by the program. _____

_____

a pyramid, with the base at the bottom of the display area and the top near the center

28. Write another program routine, or section, to be added to the above program. This time use VLIN to make a sideways pyramid with the "base" along the left edge of the graphic display area.

```
70 COLOR= 2
80 _____
90 _____
100 _____
110 _____
```

_____

```
70 COLOR= 2
80 FOR R = 0 TO 19
90 VLIN 19,39 - R AT R
100 VLIN R,19 AT R
110 NEXT R
```

29. Let's complete the picture with pyramids from the top down to the center, and from the right edge out to the center.

```
120 COLOR= 3
130 _____
140 _____
150 _____
160 _____
170 COLOR= 4
180 _____
190 _____
200 _____
210 _____
```

```
120 COLOR= 3
130 FOR C = 0 TO 19
140 HLIN C,19 AT C
150 HLIN 19,39-C AT 19
160 NEXT C
170 COLOR= 4
180 FOR R = 0 TO 19
190 VLIN 19,R AT 39 - R
200 VLIN 39 - R, 19 AT 39 - R
210 NEXT R
```

30. Now let's add a fancy feature to this program. Instead of specifying the color for each pyramid, have the computer choose a color at random (from the 16 available) for each section or routine in this program. Write the instruction to produce a random integer from 0 to 15 for each of the following statement lines.

```
 20 COLOR= _____
 70 COLOR= _____
120 COLOR= _____
170 COLOR= _____
```

```
 20 COLOR= INT(16 * RND(1))
 70 COLOR= INT(16 * RND(1))
120 COLOR= INT(16 * RND(1))
170 COLOR= INT(16 * RND(1))
```

230 BASIC FOR THE APPLE II

31. One final touch to this work of art will cause the pyramids to continually change colors, chosen at random. Write the required loop statement for the end of the program. Then add your latest statement and the random COLOR statements to the program and RUN it.

220 _____

— — — — — — — —

220 GOTO 20

Note: Name this program ODE TO THE MAYA and SAVE it.

32. Where would the COLOR statements have to be moved to have the color of each "row of blocks" in each pyramid chosen at random?_____

_____

— — — — — — —

between lines 30 and 40; 80 and 90; 130 and 140; and between 180 and 190 (Note: Change the line number reference of the GOTO statement if you remove line 20. Try out the program.)

33. Now let us consider a different sort of graphic programming problem. Instead of interesting patterns, we want to create letters or numbers. The same techniques also apply to creating other representational images, such as a house, car, or other such figures.

Alphanumeric characters, such as those appearing in PRINT statement strings, cannot be made to appear in the graphic display area, only in the text window. So to display the word YES in the graphic area, the letters must be constructed with HLIN, VLIN, and PLOT. Look at the diagram.

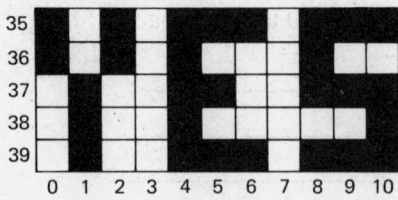

What section of the display area is represented by this partial grid?_____

_____

— — — — — — —

lower left corner of the graphic display area

34. Let's start with the "Y" in YES. Our block letter Y is composed of three vertical lines. Here is the program segment to produce this block Y.

```
10 GR
20 COLOR= 11
30 VLIN 35,36 AT 0
40 VLIN 35,36 AT 2
50 VLIN 37,39 AT 1
```

Now you write two more program segments or routines so that the completed program will produce the word YES in block letters, all of the same color.

```
60 _____
70 _____
80 _____
90 _____

100 _____
110 _____
120 _____
130 _____
140 _____
```
- - - - - - - - - - - -

```
60  VLIN 35,39 AT 4
70  HLIN 4,6 AT 35
80  HLIN 4,5 AT 37 (or 80 PLOT 5, 37)
90  HLIN 4,6 AT 39

100 VLIN 35,37 AT 8
110 VLIN 37,39 AT 10
120 HLIN 8,10 AT 35
130 HLIN 8,10 AT 37
140 HLIN 8,10 AT 39
```

35. Now use the diagram below to help you write a program, using HLIN, VLIN, and/or PLOT, to display the word NO in block letters at the upper right corner of the graphic display area. Use the diagram as a guide.

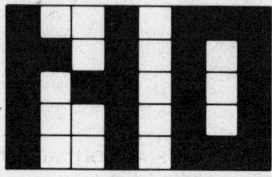

First, number the columns and rows for the upper right-hand corner of the display on the grid.

———————————

At the top, from left to right, number from 32 to 39. From the top down on the right side, number from 0 (zero) to 4.

36. Using the partial grid in the previous frame, write a continuation of the YES program to place NO in magenta at the upper right corner of the graphic display area.

```
150 _____
160 _____
170 _____
180 _____
190 _____
200 _____
210 _____
220 _____
230 _____
```

———————————

```
150 COLOR= 1
160 VLIN 0,4 AT 32
170 VLIN 0,4 AT 35
180 HLIN 32,33 AT 1
190 HLIN 34,35 AT 2
200 HLIN 37,39 AT 0
210 HLIN 37,39 AT 4
220 VLIN 0,4 AT 37
230 VLIN 0,4 AT 39
```

37. Below is a modification of the NO section of the previous program. A variable has been added to each grid position specified to create parts of the "N" and the "O." To shift the entire word along the rows, a negative value for variable X is needed (see line 530). To shift the entire word to a lower position on the display, choose a positive value for the other INPUT variable Y. Remember, the strings from PRINT and INPUT statements appear in the text window. The program is numbered from line 500 so that it can be used with the previous program or by itself.

```
500 REM ** ROUTINE TO CHANGE THE POSITION OF 'NO'
510 GR
520 COLOR= 1
530 INPUT "NO. OF UNITS TO THE LEFT? ";X: LET X = -X
540 INPUT "NO. OF UNITS DOWN? ";Y
550 VLIN 0 + Y,4 + Y AT 32 + X
560 VLIN  + Y,4 + Y AT 35 + X
570 HLIN 32 + X,33 + X AT 1 + Y
580 HLIN 34 + X,35 + X AT 2 + Y
590 HLIN 37 + X,39 + X AT 0 + Y
600 HLIN 37 + X,39 + X AT 4 + Y
610 VLIN 0 + Y,4 + Y AT 37 + X
620 VLIN 0 + Y,4 + Y AT 39 + X
630 GOTO 530
```

(a) What value must be assigned to X and Y for the word NO to appear in the upper left corner? _____

(b) Upper right corner? _____

(c) Lower left corner? _____

(d) Lower right corner? _____

(e) In the approximate center? _____

(f) So that the upper left corner block in the letter O is located at grid position (column) 28, (row) 8? _____

(g) What is the maximum values that can be assigned to INPUT variables X and Y? _____

(h) In line 530, why is the value of X changed to –X? _____

(a) X = 32 (number of units to the left), Y = 0 (number of units down)
(b) X = 0, Y = 0
(c) X = 32, Y = 34
(d) X = 0, Y = 34
(e) X = 15, Y = 17 (approximately—your answer could be slightly different)
(f) X = 11, Y = 8
(g) maximum X = 32, maximum Y = 34
(h) Because of the position of No in the upper left corner. (*Logic:* While rows start numbering from the top down, columns are numbered from the left edge to the right. Therefore, counting each column position to move NO to the left is like subtracting 1 from the original column position of NO.)

The Self-Test that follows provides several interesting projects to demonstrate and consolidate your skills in "lo-res" (low-resolution) graphics programming on the Apple.

The use of high-resolution graphics on the Apple computer requires more knowledge of the inner workings and memory structure of the Apple than is appropriate or feasible to include in this beginner's text in BASIC programming fundamentals. If using graphics is of particular interest to you, then you may have the motivation and patience to acquire the necessary knowledge and programming techniques for this somewhat detailed (and possibly tedious) pursuit. Commercially available Apple "hi-res" graphic programming software and special hardware such as graphic tablets allow you to take real advantage of the Apple's hi-res graphic capabilities. Consult the Apple reference materials, check through the computer magazines and journals, and inquire at book stores and computer retailers for materials specifically on Apple lo-res and hi-res graphics.

Self-Test

The following programming projects can be done a variety of ways. Your solution is correct if it "works." We urge you to try out and correct your solutions before looking at our way of doing it.

1. Write a program to place a large red (magenta) cross in the middle of a dark blue background. The vertical part of the cross should go from the top of the display area to the bottom and be 11 columns wide. Select the width of the horizontal part of the cross to appear approximately equal to the vertical dimension, and make it 7 rows wide.

2. Write a program to draw the American flag. Each stripe should be three rows wide. The blue field should extend from the left edge of the display area to column 20. We use two sets of nested FOR-NEXT loops to place the white "stars" (actually one white block for each star) in the blue field, because the first, third, fifth, and seventh rows have nine stars each, while the second, fourth, and sixth rows have only eight stars.

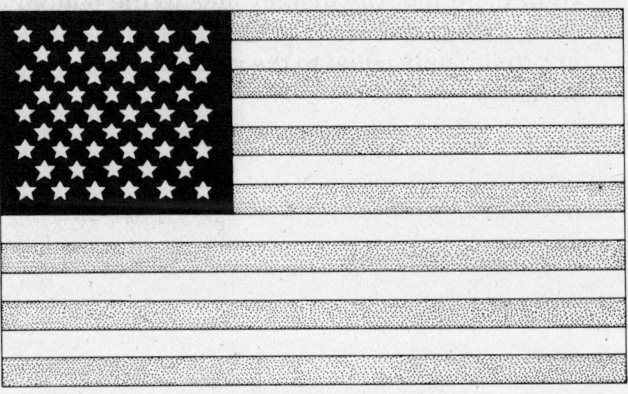

3. Write one program with three sections. We suggest you test out the first section before adding the second, etc.

   (a) Create the number 0 (zero) in "block number" style. The zero should be three blocks wide and five blocks tall. The lower left corner of the zero should be at column 6 in row 0 (zero).
   (b) Create the number 100 in block numbers. The "1" should be 1 column wide and 5 rows tall. The zeros should be the same size as in (a). The number should be located in the upper left corner of the display area.
   (c) Have the computer draw a vertical line from row 32 to the top of the display in column 10. Have the computer also draw a horizontal line from column 10 to the right edge in row 32.

   Use line numbers for this program starting at 700, so that you can use it with programs in later chapters. Don't forget to SAVE it if you have a disk drive or cassette.

Answers to Self-Test

1.
```
 1   REM ***RED CROSS ON BLUE
10   GR
20   COLOR= 2
30   FOR X = 0 TO 39
40   HLIN 0,39 AT X
50   NEXT X
60   COLOR= 2
70   FOR X = 14 TO 24
80   HLIN 7,31 AT X
90   NEXT X
100  FOR X = 16 TO 22
110  VLIN 0,39 AT X
120  NEXT X
```

2. 1   REM ***U.S. FLAG
    10 GR
    20 FOR R = 0 TO 38
    30 COLOR= 1
    40 HLIN 0,39 AT R
    50 NEXT R
    60 FOR W = 3TO 38 STEP 6
    70 COLOR= 15
    80 FOR X = 0 TO 2
    90 HLIN 0,39 AT W + X
    100 NEXT X,W
    110 FOR B = 0 TO 20
    120 COLOR= 2
    130 HLIN 0,19 AT B
    140 NEXT B
    150 FOR S = 1 TO 18 STEP 3
    160 FOR ST = 1 TO 18 STEP 4
    180 COLOR= 15
    190 PLOT S,ST
    200 NEXT ST,S
    210 FOR S = 2 TO 15 STEP 3
    220 FOR ST = 3 TO 15 STEP 4
    230 PLOT S,ST
    240 NEXT ST,S

3. 1   REM ***GRAPH 0 TO 100
    710 GR
    720 COLOR= 9
    730 HLIN 6,8 AT 39
    740 HLIN 6,8 AT 34
    750 VLIN 34,39 AT 6
    760 VLIN 34,39 AT 8
    770 VLIN 0,5 AT 0
    780 HLIN 2,4 AT 0
    790 HLIN 2,4 AT 5
    800 VLIN 0,5 AT 2
    810 VLIN 0,5 AT 4
    820 HLIN 6,8 AT 0
    830 HLIN 6,8 AT 5
    840 VLIN 0,5 AT 6
    850 VLIN 0,5 AT 8
    860 VLIN 0,32 AT 10
    870 HLIN 10,39 AT 32

CHAPTER EIGHT
String Variables and String Functions

In Chapter 3, we showed you a few ways to use alphanumeric string variables. We also used string variables in the chapters that followed as we introduced new programming concepts. In this chapter we will review what you already know about string variables and introduce you to some new goodies as well. Generally you will find that there is as wide a range of manipulation for string variables as for a numeric variable.

When you have completed this chapter you will be able to use the RESTORE statement with READ and DATA statements. You will also be able to use the following string functions with the string variables you will learn about in this chapter.

    VAL
    STR$
    CHR$
    ASC
    MID$
    LEFT$
    RIGHT$
    LEN

1. So far, our use of alphanumeric (mixed alphabetic and numeric) phrases has mostly been limited to the use of strings in PRINT statements such as the following.

    `10 PRINT "THIS IS A STRING"`

Now let's explore another feature of BASIC, the string variable.

    `10 LET T$="STRING FOR THE STRING VARIABLE T$"`
           ↑
    This is a string variable.

You identify a string variable by using any legal variable name followed by a dollar sign ($). String variables permit you to manipulate alphanumeric data with greater ease. String variable instructions include LET, PRINT, INPUT, READ, DATA, and IF-THEN, plus special string functions.

A string variable may be assigned a string with zero (a null string) to 255 characters. How many characters are in the string assigned to the string variable T$ on the previous page? _____ (Did you count blank spaces?)

— — — — — — — —

33 characters

2. As you know, you can assign values to a string variable using an INPUT statement that asks for one or more string variables to be entered by the user.

```
10 INPUT "WHAT IS YOUR NAME? "; N$
10 INPUT "YOUR NAME AND SUN SIGN? " ; N$, S$
10 INPUT "YOUR NAME, CITY, AND STATE YOU LIVE IN? " ; N$,C$,S$
```

You may also assign numeric and string variables in the same INPUT statement as shown here.

```
10 INPUT "WHAT IS YOUR NAME AND AGE? " ; N$,A
```

If, however, you want to INPUT a string variable with an imbedded comma (a comma included as part of the string) or if you want leading or trailing space(s) in the string, you must enter the string variable enclosed in quotes.

Show how you would respond to this computer prompt.

ENTER YOUR NAME, LAST NAME FIRST? _____

— — — — — — — —

"ARMITIGE, PAUL" (your name inside quotes)

3. Write a program to enter and print an auto license plate that has a three-letter alphabetic string and a three-digit number (such as SAM 123). Enter the letters as a string variable and the number as a numeric variable.

— — — — — — — —

```
10 INPUT A$,B
20 PRINT A$;B

]RUN
?SAM,123
SAM123

]RUN
?SAM,-123
SAM-123
```

If you enter a negative number (which you normally wouldn't for this problem), it will look like this.

4. You can also enter string variables by using READ and DATA statements.

```
1 REMARK **STRING READ/DATA COURSE LIST
10 PRINT "COURSE","HOURS","GRADE"
20 READ A$,B,C$
30 PRINT A$,B,C$
40 GOTO 20
50 DATA ENGLISH 1A,3,B,SOC 130,3,A
60 DATA BUS ADM 1A,4,B,STAT 10,3,C
70 DATA HUMANITIES,3,A,HISTORY 17A,3,B
80 DATA CALCULUS 3A,4,C

]RUN
COURSE                  HOURS           GRADE
ENGLISH 1A              3               B
SOC 130                 3               A
BUS ADM 1A              4               B
STAT 10                 3               C
HUMANITIES              3               A
HISTORY 17A             3               B
CALCULUS 3A             4               C

?OUT OF DATA ERROR IN 20
```

Look at the output produced by line 30 in the program above. What is the function of the comma in a string variable PRINT statement? _____

_____

— — — — — — — — — —

The comma causes the output to be displayed in up to three columns across the line, just as with numeric variables. But remember, if character position 16 is used, the second print zone (starting at 17) is skipped, and if character positions 24 to 32 are used, the third print zone (starting at 33) is skipped.

5. The string LET assigns a particular string to a string variable. Note that you must enclose the string in quotes as in these two examples.

```
20 LET A$=" GOOD EXAMPLE"
30 LET B$=" THIS IS A "

20 LET A$="YES"
30 LET B$="NO"
40 LET C$=A$   ←————————   C$ now contains "YES".
```

Write a string LET statement that assigns the book name BASIC FOR THE APPLE II to the variable S$.

```
10 LET S$="BASIC FOR THE APPLE II"
```

6. Now write a program similar to the one in frame 4. Instead of courses and grades, the data should be books contained in your home library. Your DATA should include author, title, and number of pages. Your RUN should look like this (with your books, of course).

```
]RUN
TITLE                AUTHOR          PAGES
INSTANT BASIC        BROWN           196
HOME COMPUTERS       DIDDAY          279
APPLE DATA FILE      FINKEL          300
INTRO TO MICROS      OSBORNE         384
COMPUTER LIB         NELSON          186
101 BASIC GAMES      AHL             180
APPLE BASIC          BROWN           334
```

```
10 REM ***STRING/DATA HOME LIBRARY LIST
15 PRINT "TITLE","AUTHOR","PAGES"
20 READ A$,T$,P: IF A$ = "END" THEN STOP
30 PRINT T$,A$,P: GOTO 20
40 REM AUTHOR, TITLE,PAGES
50 DATA BROWN, INSTANT BASIC, 196
60 DATA DIDDAY, HOME COMPUTERS, 279
70 DATA FINKEL, APPLE DATA FILE, 300
80 DATA OSBORNE, INTRO TO MICROS, 384
90 DATA NELSON, COMPUTER LIB, 186
100 DATA AHL, 101 BASIC GAMES, 180
110 DATA BROWN, APPLE BASIC, 334
120 DATA END, END,1
```

7. Modify the program you just wrote for frame 6 so that it will only print those books with fewer than 200 pages. Our RUN looked like this.

```
]RUN
TITLE                   AUTHOR          PAGES
INSTANT BASIC           BROWN           196
COMPUTER LIB            NELSON          186
101 BASIC GAMES         AHL             180

25 _____
```

———————————

25 IF P >= 200 THEN 20

8. The string IF-THEN allows you to compare the contents of two string variables.

```
15 LET B$ = "NO"
20 INPUT "DO YOU WANT INSTRUCTIONS? YES OR NO" ; A$
30 IF A$ = B$ THEN 140
40 PRINT "THIS SIMULATION PERMITS YOU TO REGULATE . . ."
```

Let's say that someone typed YES for the INPUT question during a RUN. Line 30 compares the contents of the string variable A$ (YES) to the contents of string variable B$ (NO). If you responded YES to the INPUT statement, A$ and B$ are not equal (they do not have the same contents). The computer will execute the next statement, line 40, which in this case will print the instructions. If you respond NO to line 20 above, the program would branch to line 140 and continue execution there.

The comparison in line 30 is between _____.

———————————

the contents of two string variables, A$ and B$

9. You can compare the contents of a string variable to a string enclosed in quotes.

```
10 INPUT "DO YOU WANT INSTRUCTIONS? YES OR NO" ; A$
20 IF A$="NO" THEN 140
30 PRINT "THIS SIMULATION PERMITS YOU TO REGULATE . . ."
```

The comparison in line 20 above is between a _____ and a _____.

———————————

string assigned to a string variable (the contents of a string variable) and a string enclosed in quotes

10. You *cannot* compare a numeric variable to a string variable.

```
110 IF A$ = B THEN 140
```
← This is not permitted.

But you *can* change a string variable into its numeric equivalent using the VAL($) function. In the above example, if A$ contained a number (entered as a string variable), you could compare it with numeric variable B by changing line 110 to read as follows.

```
110 IF VAL(A$) = B THEN 140
```

Look at this demonstration program.

```
10 LET S$="3.14159"
20 PRINT S$
30 LET S=VAL(S$)
40 PRINT S

]RUN
3.14159
3.14159
```

Here is another demonstration program. Which is the correct RUN for the program?

```
10 LET A$="32" : LET B$="1.115" : LET C$="-10"
20 PRINT A$ : PRINT VAL(A$)
30 PRINT B$ : PRINT VAL(B$)
40 PRINT C$ : PRINT VAL(C$)
```

RUN	RUN	RUN
32	32	32
32	32	32
1.115	1.115	1.115
1.115	1.115	1.115
−10	−10	−10
−10	−10	−10

- - - - - - - - -

The first RUN (on the Left) is correct.

11. Using the STR$ function, you can convert a numeric variable to a string or place a numeric variable into a string variable.

```
10 PRINT STR$(X)
```
← Will print the string equivalent of the numeric content of variable X

```
20 LET A$ = STR$(X)
```
← Will place into string variable A$ the numeric content of variable X

STRING VARIABLES AND STRING FUNCTIONS   **245**

Which is the correct RUN for this demonstration program?

```
10 V = 112 : PRINT V : PRINT STR$(V)
```

RUN	RUN	RUN	RUN
112	112	112	112
112	112	112	112

— — — — — — — — —

The first RUN (on the left) is the correct one.

12.   In a string IF-THEN, the comparison is made one character at a time. For example, if a space is introduced in the wrong place, it may cause a comparison other than what you expect.

```
10 INPUT A$
20 IF A$ = "MCGEE" THEN 140
```

If the user enters MC GEE in response to the computer's INPUT prompt message during the RUN, the comparison will not be equal. Why will this comparison not be equal? _____

_____

— — — — — — — — —

The space between C and G is a character which is not present in "MCGEE."

13.   You can compare strings using the same symbols you used earlier: <>, <, >, <=, >=, and =. It's a little tricky so you should use caution with these comparisons. The comparison is still made one character at a time from left to right. The *first* difference found determines the relationship. The relationship is based on position in the alphabet; C is "less than" S; T is "greater than" M.

```
10 LET A$ = "SMITH"
20 LET B$ = "SMYTH"
30 IF A$ < B$ THEN 100
```

In line 30 above, will the program branch to line 100 or continue to the next statement in sequence? _____

— — — — — — —

It will jump to line 100. The first difference is the third character, and since I is "less than" Y, the IF-THEN condition is TRUE.

14. Here is another example.

```
120 LET D$ = "COMPUTE"
130 LET E$ = "COMPUTER"
140 IF D$ < E$ THEN 180
150 PRINT D$
    .
    .
    .
180 PRINT E$
```

Which statement will be executed after the comparison in line 140? _____

— — — — — — —

Line 180. D$ is "less than" E$. It is smaller in size, therefore "less than" E$.

15. Change line 140 in frame 14 to read as follows.

```
140 IF D$ = E$ THEN 180
```

Now which statement will be executed after the comparison of line 140?

_____

— — — — — — —

Line 150. D$ is not equal to E$.

16. In frame 14 change line 140 to read as follows.

```
140 IF E$ > D$ THEN 180
```

Which statement will be executed after the comparison? _____

— — — — — — —

Line 180. E$ is "greater than" D$.

17. To expand your understanding of string comparisons, we would like to introduce you to the ASCII (pronounced ASKEE) code. Who's ASCII, you ask? ASCII stands for the American Standard Code for Information Interchange. For each character you type on the keyboard, an ASCII code number for that character is sent to the computer. The computer sends back an ASCII code number for each character that appears on your printer or screen. That's the "information interchange" referred to by ASCII.

The version of BASIC we are using allows us to enter ASCII code numbers instead of keyboard characters with the use of the CHR$ function and allows us to convert a character into its ASCII code number using the ASC function.

- CHR$(X)   The ASCII number to be converted is placed in X before you use this function. Or you can place the number directly into the parentheses instead of X, as in CHR$(65).
- ASC(X$)   The string character to be converted to ASCII code is placed in X$ before execution.

For example, the uppercase letters we use in BASIC correspond to ASCII code numbers 65 to 90 inclusive: A = 65, B = 66, C = 67, ..., X = 88, Y = 89, Z = 90. A complete table of Apple ASCII code numbers and the characters they represent can be found in the Appendix, page 399.

The following program prints a quotation from John Wayne that is found in the DATA statement in ASCII code numbers.

```
10 READ X : IF X = -1 THEN END
20 PRINT CHR$(X) ; : GOTO 10
30 DATA 89,85,80,-1

RUN
YUP
```

Referring to that table of ASCII code numbers, tell what the following program will print when RUN.

```
10 READ A : IF A = -1 THEN END
20 PRINT CHR$(A) ; : GOTO 10
30 DATA 72,65,80,80,89,32,67,79,77,80,85,84,73,78,71,-1
```

```
RUN
HAPPY COMPUTING
```

18. Using the ASC function you can find out the ASCII code number for a string character. Here's a demonstration.

```
10 LET X$ = "A" : LET Y$ = "B" : LET Z$ = "C"
20 PRINT "A = " ; ASC(X$), "B = "; ASC(Y$), "C = "; ASC(Z$)

RUN
A = 65     B = 66     C = 67
```

Write a program using the ASC function to provide you with the ASCII code for the following characters, so that the RUN looks like this.

```
RUN
CHARACTER   ASCII CODE

  $           36
  =           61
  ?           63
```

Here are two possible solutions.

```
10 A$ = "$" : B$ = "=" : C$ = "?"
20 PRINT "CHARACTER", "ASCII CODE" : PRINT
30 PRINT A$, ASC(A$)
40 PRINT B$, ASC(B$)
50 PRINT C$, ASC(C$)

10 PRINT "CHARACTER", "ASCII CODE" : PRINT
20 PRINT "$", ASC("$")
30 PRINT "=", ASC("=")
40 PRINT "?", ASC("?")
```

19. Now let's return to string comparisons using the IF-THEN statement. Strings are compared using a character by character process and the computer uses ASCII code numbers to do the comparing. For example, in frame 12, we saw this program segment.

```
10 INPUT A$
20 IF A$ = "MCGEE" THEN 140
```

When the program is RUN and the user enters MC GEE, the computer compares ASCII code numbers as follows.

"MCGEE"	A$ (user-entered)
M = 77	M = 77
C = 67	C = 67
G = 71	space = 32
E = 69	G = 71
E = 69	E = 69
	E = 69

The computer finds the two strings equal for the first two characters, but the third character comparison is unequal (71 vs. 32).

Show how the computer, using ASCII codes, will compare the strings in the following segment.

```
10 INPUT "DO YOU WANT INSTRUCTIONS? YES OR NO:" ; A$
20 IF A$ = "NO" THEN 140

RUN
DO YOU WANT INSTRUCTIONS? YES OR NO:YES
```

A$ "NO"
_____
_____
_____
_____

Is the comparison true or false? _____

— — — — — — — — — —

A$	"NO"
Y = 89	N = 78
E = 69	O = 79
S = 83	

The comparison is false.

20. Before you proceed, we need to introduce the RESTORE statement and its use in connection with READ and DATA statements. A READ statement causes the next item(s) of data to be read from the DATA statements. You may find that you want the program to read through the data from the beginning again. To do so, use a RESTORE statement, which causes the next DATA item to be READ to be the first piece of data in the *first* DATA statement. See line 15 below.

Now that you have seen how to use string variable comparisons, you can understand this simple information retrieval program that permits retrieving information from DATA statements.

The program in frame 4 prints courses, hours, and grades. The program below permits the operator to enter the course: the computer will then print the course, hour, and grade.

```
1 REM    ***STRING COURSE INFO RETRIEVAL
10 INPUT "ENTER COURSE NAME:" ; D$
15 RESTORE
20 READ A$, B, C$ : IF A$=D$ THEN 40
30 GOTO 20
40 PRINT A$, B, C$ : PRINT : GOTO 10
50 DATA ENGLISH 1A,3,B, SOC 130,3,A
60 DATA BUS ADM 1A,4,B, STAT 10,3,C
70 DATA HUMANITIES,3,A, HISTORY 17A,3,B
80 DATA CALCULUS 3A,4,C

]RUN
ENTER COURSE NAME:HUMANITIES
HUMANITIES      3               A

ENTER COURSE NAME:STAT 10
STAT 10         3               C

ENTER COURSE NAME:ECON 1A

?OUT OF DATA ERROR IN 20
```
⟵ Whoops, no such course. The computer read through all the data and found no such course; therefore, it printed this error message.

Let's look at another RUN of the program.

```
]RUN
ENTER COURSE NAME:SOC130

?OUT OF DATA ERROR IN 20
```

Why did we get an error message this time? _____

The course name is stored in line 50 as SOC 130, but the user typed SOC130 without a space between SOC and 130.

21. Refer back to the program in frame 20.
(a) What is the purpose of this part of line 20?

    ...IF A$ = D$ THEN 40

(b) Under what conditions will line 30 (30 GOTO 20) be executed?

(a) to test whether or not the course read from the DATA statement is the course requested in the INPUT statement
(b) when the course READ is not the course requested in the INPUT statement

22. Modify the program in frame 20 so it will print the message NO SUCH COURSE instead of the data error message, indicating that the course entered by the user does not exist in the computer's information system. You might try putting a flag at the end of the regular data.

    25 _____
    90 _____

Add these statements (or ones similar to them).

```
25 IF A$ = "END" THEN PRINT "NO SUCH COURSE" : GOTO 10
90 DATA END,0,END
```

Remember, the end-of-data signal must contain a string, followed by a numeric value, followed by a string, because the READ statement calls for three variables at once.

23. It's your turn. Write a program that contains the names and phone numbers of your friends and business associates that you would like to "retrieve" using your computer. When you type in a name, the computer should respond with the correct phone number, as shown below, or with the message NAME NOT IN FILE, instead of an error message.

```
NAME? ADAM OZ

ADAM OZ          415-555-2222

NAME? JUDY WIL

JUDY WIL         112-555-0075

NAME? JERRY
NAME NOT IN FILE

NAME?
```

```
1 REM **STRING TELEPHONE RETRIEVAL SYSTEM
10 INPUT "NAME? " ; N$
20 RESTORE
30 READ D$,T$ : IF N$ = D$ THEN PRINT : PRINT D$,T$ : PRINT : GOTO 10
35 IF D$ = "END" THEN PRINT "NAME NOT IN FILE" : GOTO 10
40 GOTO 30
50 DATA TONY BOD, 415-555-8117
60 DATA MARY JAY, 213-555-0144
70 DATA MARY MMM, 213-555-1212
80 DATA JUDY WIL, 112-555-0075
90 DATA ADAM OZ, 415-555-2222
100 DATA BOBBY ALL, 312-555-1667
110 DATA END, END
```

24. Next, we will show you some new functions that allow you to manipulate and examine parts of strings, called *substrings*. The rules for these functions get a little complicated, so we suggest that you do all the exercises in this section but don't worry about memorizing the rules. Once you have a good general idea about how they work, you can always look back to this section to recall the exact rules.

The MID$ function will cause the computer to produce part of a string beginning with a specified character. Thus, MID$(A$,N) will give you that part of the string A$ beginning with character number N and continuing to the end of the string. For example, if A$ is HELLO, then H is character 1, E is character 2, and so on. If N is 4, then the statement PRINT MID$(A$,N) tells the computer to print the substring starting with character 4 and continuing to the end of the string. In this case the computer will print LO.

Here is a demonstration program. Remember, a space is counted as one character.

```
10 LET A$ = "MY HUMAN UNDERSTANDS ME"
20 PRINT MID$(A$,10)

RUN
UNDERSTANDS ME
```

Replace line 20 with PRINT MID$(A$,15). What will be printed when the new line 20 is RUN? _____

— — — — — — — — — —

```
STANDS ME
```

25. Now let's look at some more examples of the MID$ function. To isolate one character, you need to use two values in the MID$ function. The first numeric value in the parentheses tells the computer where to start the substring, just as before. The second numeric value tells the computer how *many* characters beyond the starting point to include in the substring. Thus, to isolate and print just one character in a substring, the second numeric value in the parentheses would be one (1). Here's a sample progam and RUN.

```
10 LET A$ = "MY HUMAN UNDERSTANDS ME"
20 PRINT MID$(A$,4,1)

RUN
H
```

In the example below, we print a substring that starts at character 1 and continues through character 8 (inclusive).

```
10 LET A$ = "MY HUMAN UNDERSTANDS ME"
20 PRINT MID$(A$,1,8)
RUN
MY HUMAN
```

Suppose we change line 20 above to read 20 PRINT MID$(A$,4,8). What will be printed when the new line 20 is executed? _____

— — — — — — — — —

    HUMAN

26. What will be printed by the following program?

```
20 LET A$ = "GAMES COMPUTERS PLAY"
30 PRINT MID$(A$,7,9), MID$(A$,17), MID$(A$,1,5)
RUN
```

_____

— — — — — — — — —

```
RUN
COMPUTERS      PLAY       GAMES
```

Notice that the second MID$ function in the program, MID$(A$,17), does not specify how many characters to print; therefore, it will automatically print to the end of the string A$.

27. Here are parts of a program to PRINT the string variable A$ backward, one character at a time. Fill in the blanks and show the RUN.

```
10 LET A$ = "ABCDEFGHIJKLMNOPQRSTUVWXYZ"
20 FOR X = _____ TO _____ STEP −1
30 PRINT MID$(A$, _____, _____);
40 _____
RUN
```

_____

— — — — — — — — —

```
20 FOR X = 26 TO 1 STEP −1
30 PRINT MID$(A$,X,1);
40 NEXT X
RUN
ZYXWVUTSRQPONMLKJIHGFEDCBA
```

STRING VARIABLES AND STRING FUNCTIONS

28. Let's go all the way back to frame 5 of Chapter 1 and change our number-guessing game to a *letter*-guessing game. Here's the old program. All its logic should still apply.

```
100 REM **THIS IS A SIMPLE COMPUTER GAME
110 LET X = INT(100*RND(1))+1
120 PRINT
130 PRINT "I'M THINKING OF A NUMBER FROM 1 TO 100."
140 PRINT "GUESS MY NUMBER!!!"
150 PRINT : INPUT "YOUR GUESS? " ; G
160 IF G<X THEN PRINT "TRY A BIGGER NUMBER" : GOTO 150
170 IF G>X THEN PRINT "TRY A SMALLER NUMBER" : GOTO 150
180 IF G=X THEN PRINT "THAT'S IT!!! YOU GUESSED MY NUMBER." : GOTO 110
```

We should first add line 105, a LET statement with all the letters of the alphabet assigned to one string variable, A$.

105 _____

——————————

```
105 LET A$ = "ABCDEFGHIJKLMNOPQRSTUVWXYZ"
```

29. Now change line 110 to randomly select a number between 1 and 26.

110 _____

——————————

```
110 LET X = INT(26*RND(1))+1
```

30. Let's place our selected choice into X$.

115 LET X$ = _____

——————————

```
115 LET X$ = MID$(A$,X,1)
```

31. You complete lines 140 and 150.

```
130 PRINT "I'M THINKING OF A LETTER FROM A TO Z"
```
140 _____
150 _____

——————————

```
140 PRINT "GUESS MY LETTER!!!"
150 PRINT : INPUT "YOUR GUESS? " ; G$
```

32. Change lines 160, 170, and 180 as necessary. RUN your new game.

    160 _____

    170 _____

    180 _____

— — — — — — — — — —

Here's the entire LIST and, following it, a RUN.

```
100 REM ARK***THIS IS A SIMPLE COMPUTER GAME
105 LET A$ = "ABCDEFGHIJKLMNOPQRSTUVWXYZ"
110 LET X = INT(26*RND(1))+1
115 LET X$ = MID$(A$,X,1)
120 PRINT
130 PRINT "I'M THINKING OF A LETTER FROM A TO Z"
140 PRINT "GUESS MY LETTER!!!"
150 PRINT : INPUT"YOUR GUESS? "; G$
160 IF G$<X$ THEN PRINT "TRY A BIGGER LETTER." : GOTO 150
170 IF G$>X$ THEN PRINT "TRY A SMALLER LETTER." : GOTO 150
180 IF G$=X$ THEN PRINT "THAT'S IT!!! YOU GUESSED MY LETTER." : GOTO 110

RUN
I'M THINKING OF A LETTER FROM A TO Z
GUESS MY LETTER!!!

YOUR GUESS? L
TRY A SMALLER LETTER.

YOUR GUESS? G
TRY A BIGGER LETTER.

YOUR GUESS? H
TRY A BIGGER LETTER.

YOUR GUESS? K
TRY A SMALLER LETTER.

YOUR GUESS? I
TRY A BIGGER LETTER.

YOUR GUESS? J
THAT'S IT!!! YOU GUESSED MY LETTER.
```

33. You can manipulate the left and right portion of a string using the LEFT$ and RIGHT$ functions. It's really not all that complicated. Complete the RUN below.

```
10 LET A$ = "ABCDEFGHIJKLMNOPQRSTUVWXYZ"
20 PRINT LEFT$(A$,5)  ←——— Print the leftmost five characters of A$.
30 PRINT RIGHT$(A$,5) ←——— Print the rightmost five characters of A$.
RUN

ABCDE
```

_____

VWXYZ (In practice we have found many more uses for MID$ than for LEFT$ and RIGHT$.)

34. Using the data from the program in frame 23, write a program that will print a list of phone numbers of people whose first name begins with the letter M.

```
RUN
MARY JAY        213-555-0144
MARY MMM        213-555-1212

?OUT OF DATA ERROR IN 30
```

```
1 REM **STRING TELEPHONE DIRECTORY
20 RESTORE
30 READ D$,T$ : IF LEFT$(D$,1) = "M" THEN PRINT D$,T$ : GOTO 30
40 GOTO 30
50 DATA TONY BOD,415-555-8117
60 DATA MARY JAY,213-555-0144
70 DATA MARY MMM,213-555-1212
80 DATA JUDY WIL,112-555-0075
90 DATA ADAM OZ,415-555-2222
100 DATA BOBBY ALL,312-555-1667
110 DATA END,999
```

35. Modify your program in frame 34 so that the computer will print telephone numbers and names located in area code 415 (you are going there for a visit and want to call old friends).

```
RUN
415-555-8117   TONY BOD
415-555-2222   ADAM OZ

?OUT OF DATA ERROR IN 30
```

```
1 REM **STRING TELEPHONE DIRECTORY
20 RESTORE
30 READ D$,T$ : IF LEFT$(T$,3) <> "415" THEN 30
40 PRINT T$,D$ : GOTO 30
50 DATA TONY BOD,415-555-8117
60 DATA MARY JAY,213-555-0144
70 DATA MARY MMM,213-555-1212
80 DATA JUDY WIL,112-555-0075
90 DATA ADAM OZ,415-555-2222
100 DATA BOBBY ALL,312-555-1667
110 DATA END,999
```

36. Sometimes we need to know the length of the contents of a string variable (how many characters). And, of course, BASIC has a special function, LEN, to help you find the answer. LEN(A$) will tell you the number of characters, including blanks, in the string A$. Here is an example.

```
10 LET A = LEN(A$)
20 PRINT LEN(C$)
30 IF LEN (A$)<>LEN(B$) . . .
```

Predict the number which the computer will count for each of the following program segments.

(a) `10 PRINT LEN("HELLO DOLLY")`_____
(b) `10 LET A$ = "HOW LONG AM I?"`

   `20 PRINT LEN(A$)`_____

— — — — — — — — — —

(a) 11
(b) 14

37. You can use the MID$ and LEN functions in combination to search for a short string (a substring) of one or more characters in a longer string. For example, if we wanted to find the word UNDER in the sentence MY COMPUTER UNDERSTANDS ME, we could use a program like this:

```
10 A$ = "MY COMPUTER UNDERSTANDS ME"
20 FOR K = 1 TO LEN(A$) +4   ←——— Use value 4 for complete
                                   string record.
30 IF MID$(A$,K,5) = "UNDER" THEN 50
40 NEXT K
50 PRINT "I FOUND THE WORD "; MID$(A$,K,5)
RUN
I FOUND THE WORD UNDER
```

Here is a second version of the same program, with the substring UNDER assigned to B$, and more uses for LEN.

```
10 A$ = "MY COMPUTER UNDERSTANDS ME": B$ = "UNDER"
20 FOR K = 1 TO LEN(A$) — LEN(B$) + 1
30 IF MID$(A$,K,LEN(B$)) = B$ THEN 50
40 NEXT K
50 PRINT "I FOUND THE WORD "; MID$(A$,K,LEN(B$))
RUN
I FOUND THE WORD UNDER
```

(a) In line 20, what is the value of LEN(A$) − LEN(B$) + 1? _____

(b) Rewrite the MID$ function in line 30, giving the numeric values in parentheses for the first trip through the FOR-NEXT loop.

    MID$(A$, ____ , ____)

- - - - - - - - - -

(a) 26 − 5 + 1 = 22
(b) MID$(A$,1,5)

38. You can use this technique to check answers entered to questions, "edit" responses to INPUT statements, and a host of other things. Here is a school quiz program for you to complete. The program asks a question, requests a student's response, then checks the answer and makes an appropriate remark. Fill in the missing parts.

```
10 REM *** U.S. HISTORY TEST
20 INPUT "WHO WAS THE FIRST PRESIDENT OF THE U.S.A.?"; A$
30 FOR X = 1 TO _____
40 IF _____ = "WASHINGTON" THEN PRINT "CORRECT": END
50 NEXT X
60 PRINT "SORRY, THAT IS NOT CORRECT"
```

- - - - - - - - - -

    30 FOR X = 1 TO LEN(A$) − 9
    40 IF MID$(A$,X,10) = "WASHINGTON" THEN PRINT "CORRECT": END

39. How will this program respond to the student answer WASHINGTON IRVING? _____

- - - - - - - - - -

    CORRECT

40. The LEN function can be used to "edit" data entered by users that might have to be a certain size, and no bigger because of forms you use or because of the size of your computer memory. Examine the example below and answer the questions which follow.

```
10 INPUT "ENTER YOUR NAME: "; N$
20 IF LEN(N$)>20 THEN PRINT "LIMIT YOUR NAME TO 20 CHARACTERS
   PLEASE" : GOTO 10
30 INPUT "ENTER YOUR ADDRESS: " ; A$
40 IF LEN(A$)>15 THEN PRINT "PLEASE ABBREVIATE YOUR ADDRESS" :
   GOTO 30
```

How many characters are allowed for name? ____ For address? ____

— — — — — — — — — —

20; 15

Self-Test

Try this Self-Test, so you can evaluate how much you have learned so far.

1. Write a program to permit INPUT of a five-letter word and then print the word backward.

2. Write a program to read a series of four-letter words from DATA statements and print only those words that begin with the letter A.

3. Modify the program in question 2 to print only words that begin with A and end with S.

   20 _____

   25 _____

4. Some years ago, the auto industry was hard-pressed to come up with names for new cars. They used a computer to generate a series of five-letter words. Write a program to generate 100 five-letter words with randomly selected consonants in the first and third and fifth places and randomly selected vowels in the second and fourth places.

5. You have the following DATA statements containing names in last-name-first order. Write a program to print these names first-name-first without the comma.

   ```
   9000 DATA "BUTLER, LINDA", "OLIVER, RACHELLE"
   9010 DATA "DANIELS, JAMES", "JOHNSON, DIANE"
   9020 DATA "CASH, BETTY", END
   ```

Answers to Self-Test

The frame numbers in parentheses refer to the frames in the chapter where the topic is discussed. You may wish to refer back to these for quick review.

1.  ```
    10 REM ** STRING SELF-TEST 8-1
    20 INPUT A$
    30 FOR X = 5 TO 1 STEP -1 : PRINT MID$(A$,X,1); : NEXT X
    40 PRINT : GOTO 20
    ```

    (frames 25–27)

2.  ```
    10 REM ** STRING SELF-TEST 8-2
    20 READ A$ : IF LEFT$(A$,1) <> "A" THEN 20
    30 PRINT A$ : GOTO 20
    40 DATA ANTS,GNATS,LOVE,BALD,APES
    50 DATA BAKE,MIKE,KARL,BARD,ALAS
    ```

    (frame 33)

3.  ```
    20 READ A$ : IF RIGHT$(A$,1) <> "S" THEN 20
    25 IF LEFT$(A$,1) <> "A" THEN 20
    ```

    (frame 33)

4.  ```
    1 REM ** STRING SELF-TEST 8-4
    10 LET A$ = "AEIOU"
    20 LET B$ = "BCDFGHJKLMNPQRSTVWXYZ"
    25 FOR X = 1 TO 100
    30 FOR Z = 1 TO 2
    40 LET B = INT(21*RND(1))+1
    50 PRINT MID$(B$,B,1);
    60 LET A = INT(5*RND(1))+1
    70 PRINT MID$(A$,A,1);
    75 NEXT Z
    80 LET B = INT(21*RND(1))+1
    90 PRINT MID$(B$,B,1),
    95 NEXT X
    ```

    (frames 25, 33)

5.  ```
    1 REM ** STRING SELF-TEST 8-5
    20 READ N$ : IF N$ = "END" THEN END
    30 FOR X = 1 TO 20 : IF MID$(N$,X,1) = "," THEN 40
    35 NEXT X : GOTO 20
    40 PRINT MID$(N$,X+1),LEFT$(N$,X-1)
    50 GOTO 20
    9000 DATA "BUTLER,LINDA","OLIVER, RACHELLE"
    9010 DATA "DANIELS, JAMES","JOHNSON, DIANE"
    9020 DATA "CASH, BETTY",END

    RUN
    LINDA      BUTLER
    RACHELLE   OLIVER
    JAMES      DANIELS
    DIANE      JOHNSON
    BETTY      CASH
    ```

    (frames 25, 33)
    ```

CHAPTER NINE

Subscripted Variables

In Chapters 9 and 10 we will present another useful tool, the *subscripted variable*. First we will discuss BASIC variables with a *single* subscript.

You will learn, for example, how to count votes from a survey and how to accumulate or count dollars and assign them to different groupings. And you will get lots more practice using FOR-NEXT loops and making more attractive printed reports.

The only completely new BASIC statement is the DIMension statement, but many new programming ideas are introduced in this chapter. Read the chapter slowly and carefully. Experiment on your computer, if you have one—you will find that these new techniques give you much more range and flexibility. When you complete this chapter, you will be able to:

- Recognize and use subscripted variables with a single (one) subscript
- Assign values to subscripted variables
- Use subscripted variables with variables for subscripts
- Use one-dimensional arrays to store the values of subscripted variables
- Use the DIM statement to tell the computer the maximum size of the array(s) used by a program.

1. The concept we discuss here will require your close attention. Take it slowly, and read carefully as we enter the mysterious realm of *subscripted variables*.

Until now, we have used only *simple* BASIC variables. A simple variable consists of a letter (any letter A to Z) or a letter *followed* by a single digit (any digit 0 to 9). For example, the following are simple variables.

    P   R   K   P1   P2

Now we want to introduce a new type of variable, called a subscripted variable.

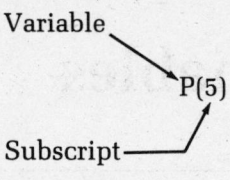

Say it: "P sub 5"

A subscripted variable consists of a letter (any letter A to Z) followed by a subscript enclosed in *parentheses*. P(3) is a subscripted variable; P3 is *not* a subscripted variable.

Which of the following are subscripted variables?

    X(1)   X   X1   C(23)   D

X(1), C(23)

Note: X, X1, and X(1) are three distinct variables. All three can appear in the same program. They may confuse *you*, but the computer will recognize them as three different variables, referring to three different memory storage locations.

2. A *subscripted* variable (like the simple variables we have been using) names a memory location inside the computer. You can think of it as a box, a place to store a number.

P(0)
P(1)
P(2)
P(3)
P(4)
P(5)
P(6)
P(7)
P(8)

A set of subscripted variables is also called an *array*. This set of subscripted variables is a *one-way dimensional array*, also known as a vector. In Chapter 10, we will discuss two-dimensional arrays.

Pretend you are the computer, and LET P(2) = 36. In other words, use your pencil or pen and write the number in the box labeled P(2) in the drawing. Then LET P(3) = 12. (Do it.) Now LET P(7) + P(2) + P(3). Check yourself by looking at our answer following the dashed line.

P(0)	
P(1)	
P(2)	36
P(3)	12
P(4)	
P(5)	
P(6)	
P(7)	48
P(8)	

3. Subscripted variables can have variables for subscripts. The subscripted variable Y(J) has the variable J for a subscript.

If J = 1, then Y(J) is Y(1)
If J = 2, then Y(J) is Y(2)
If J = 7, then Y(J) is Y(7)

Let us assume that the values in the following boxes have been assigned to the corresponding variables. Note that both simple and subscripted variables are shown here.

Y(1)	4	Z(1)	4.7	A	1		
Y(2)	−3	Z(2)	9.2	B	2		
Y(3)	5	X(1)	2	C	3		
Y(4)	6	X(2)	3	D	4		

Write the value of each variable below.

Y(1) = ___   A = ___   Y(A) = ___
Y(2) = ___   B = ___   Y(B) = ___
Y(C) = ___   X(A) = ___   X(B) = ___
Z(A) = ___   Z(B) = ___   Y(D) = ___

```
_ _ _ _ _ _ _ _
 4      1      4
-3      2     -3
 5      2      3
 4.7    9.2    6
```

4. So far we have only used single variables as subscripts. However, the subscript can be more complex. Below are two examples, still using the variables and values in the boxes in frames 3.

$$Y(A + 1) = Y(1 + 1) = Y(2) = -3$$

$$Y(2*B) = Y(2*2) = Y(4) = 6$$

Notice that the expressions inside the subscript parentheses are computed using the same rules for BASIC arithmetic as an expression in a PRINT statement, or inside a function parentheses.

Now you complete some examples as we did above, showing both the value calculated for the subscript and the value assigned to the subscripted variable with that subscript. (Refer to the boxes in frame 3, p. 267.)

$Y(A + 2) = $ _____

$Y(2*A - 1) = $ _____

$Y(A + B) = $ _____

$Y(B*C - D) = $ _____

$Y(A + 3) = $ _____

$Y(D - 3) = $ _____

$Y(D - C + A) = $ _____

$Y((C + D) - (A + B)) = $ _____

$Y(A + 2) = Y(1 + 2) = Y(3) = 5$
$Y(2*A - 1) = Y(2*1-1) = Y(2 - 1) = Y(1) = 4$
$Y(A + B) = Y(1 + 2) = Y(3) = 5$
$Y(B*C - D) = Y(2*3 - 4) = Y(6 - 4) = Y(2) = -3$
$Y(A + 3) = Y(1 + 3) = Y(4) = 6$
$Y(D - 3) = Y(4 - 3) = Y(1) = 4$
$Y(D - C + A) = Y(4 - 3 + 1) = Y(1 + 1) = Y(2) = -3$
$Y((C + D) - (A + B)) = Y((3 + 4) - (1 + 2)) = Y(7 - 3) = Y(4) = 6$

5. So how can subscripted variables contribute to the ease and versatility of programming in BASIC? One common use of subscripted variables is to store a list of numbers entered via INPUT or READ statements. This can be done with a FOR-NEXT loop. The *control variable* can also be used as the *variable for the subscript* in a subscripted variable, causing the subscript to *increase by one* each time through the loop. To illustrate, again we will turn to the World's Most Expensive Adding Machine.

```
100 REM **WORLD'S MOST EXPENSIVE ADDING MACHINE (AGAIN)
110 PRINT
120 INPUT "HOW MANY NUMBERS? " ; N
130 PRINT
140 FOR K=1 TO N
150 INPUT "X =? " ; X(K)     ←— N Numbers are entered by the user and
160 NEXT K                        stored in X(1) through X(N).
170 T=0                      ←— First T is set to zero. Then the numbers
180 FOR K=1 TO N                  in X(1) through X(N) are added to T.
190 LET T=T+X(K)
200 NEXT K
210 PRINT "THE TOTAL IS " ; T

RUN

HOW MANY NUMBERS? 5

X =? 37
X =? 23
X =? 46
X =? 78
X =? 59
THE TOTAL IS 243
```

For the RUN shown, N is 5. Therefore, 5 numbers will be entered by the operator and stored in X(1) through _____.

X(5)

6. Suppose the computer is running the program in frame 5. It has just completed the FOR-NEXT loop in lines 140 to 160. The numbers entered by the user are now stored as follows.

N	5
X(1)	37
X(2)	23
X(3)	46
X(4)	78
X(5)	59

The computer is ready to proceed with line 170. This statement initializes the variable T, that is, gives T its first value. Show the value of T after line 170 has been executed.

T	

T	0

7. Next, the computer will execute the FOR-NEXT loop in lines 180 to 200. How many times will the FOR-NEXT loop be executed? _____

----

5 times, because line 180 says FOR K = 1 TO N and N is equal to 5.

8. The FOR-NEXT loop in lines 180 to 200 will be done 5 times, first for K = 1, then for K = 2, K = 3, K = 4, and finally for K = 5. Let's look at line 190, where K is used as a subscript.

```
190 LET T = T + X(K)
```

This statement tells the computer to add the value of X(K) to the *old* value of T and then assign the result as the *new* value of T.

What is the value of T after line 190 has been executed for K = 1?____ For K = 2?____ For K = 3?____ For K = 4?____ For K = 5?____

37; 60; 106; 184; 243

9. The program in frame 5 is shown the "long way" to aid your understanding of subscripted variables. Let's rewrite that program together to take advantage of BASIC's super ability to crunch a program down to size. Lines 100–130 reduce to the following.

```
100 REM***WORLD'S MOST EXPENSIVE ADDING MACHINE (AGAIN)
110 PRINT : INPUT "HOW MANY NUMBERS? " ; N : PRINT
```

Lines 140–160 reduce to a single line.

```
120 FOR K=1 TO N : INPUT "X =? "; X(K) : NEXT K
```

Lines 170–210? Your turn.

130 _____

140 _____

— — — — — — — — —

```
130 LET T=0 : FOR K=1 TO N : LET T=T+X(K) : NEXT K
140 PRINT "TOTAL IS ": T
```

10. Since the use of the word LET is optional in a LET statement (also called an assignment statement), line 130 could be shortened even further. Show how it would look.

130 _____

— — — — — — — — —

```
130 T=0 : FOR K=1 TO N : T=T+X(K) : NEXT K
```

We could also leave off the K in NEXT K to save additional time and computer memory space.

11. Let's use the World's Most Expensive Adding Machine to compute the sum of whole numbers 1 through 12.

```
RUN

HOW MANY NUMBERS? 12

X =? 1
X =? 2
X =? 3
X =? 4
X =? 5
X =? 6
X =? 7
X =? 8
X =? 9
X =? 10
X =? 11

?BAD SUBSCRIPT ERROR IN 120
```

This time we got an error message telling us that we had a bad subscript. What was the largest subscript for X(K) that the computer would accept *before* it gave us an error message? _____

— — — — — — — — — —

10

12. The computer does *not* permit a subscript to be *greater than 10*, unless we specify otherwise.

If subscripts greater than 10 are to be used, special instructions must be included in the program to reserve space for a larger array of subscripted variables. We must tell the computer the *largest* subscript it is to permit in a subscripted variable by using a DIM statement. ("DIM" is the abbreviation for "dimensions" of an array of subscripted variables.)

```
              105 DIM X(100)
```

Variable for which space is being reserved ↗   ↖ Maximum subscript to be permitted

The above DIM statement specifies a subscripted variable which can have a maximum subscript of _____.

— — — — — — — — — —

100

13. Suppose we wanted to specify that the maximum subscript is 50. Write the DIM statement.

      105_____

— — — — — — — — —

      105 DIM X(50)

14. We will add the DIM statement from frame 12 to the program from frame 9. Below is a LIST and RUN using the 12 numbers that gave us trouble before.

```
100 REM **WORLD'S MOST EXPENSIVE ADDING MACHINE (AGAIN)
105 DIM X(100)
110 PRINT : INPUT "HOW MANY NUMBERS? "; N : PRINT
120 FOR K=1 TO N : INPUT "X =? "; X(K) : NEXT K
130 T=0 : FOR K=1 TO N : LET T=T+X(K) : NEXT K
140 PRINT "THE TOTAL IS "; T

RUN

HOW MANY NUMBERS? 12

X =? 1
X =? 2
X =? 3
X =? 4
X =? 5
X =? 6
X =? 7
X =? 8
X =? 9
X =? 10
X =? 11
X =? 12
THE TOTAL IS 78
```

Now the program can be used to compute the sum of *at most* how many numbers?_____

— — — — — — — — —

100. If 100 numbers are entered, they will be stored in X(1) through X(100), the limit specified by the DIM statement in line 105. We can, of course, also use the program to compute the sum of fewer than 100 numbers.

15. A DIM statement may have its dimensions assigned by a variable. Look at the examples below.

    DIM X(N)   DIM A$(B)   DIM D(Y+2)

This is called dynamic dimensioning, because it is done during the execution of the program. But there is a catch. An array can be dimensioned *only once* during the RUN of a program, and the computer will give you an error message and stop executing the program if it comes to a DIM statement for the same array a second time and tries to redimension the array during the same RUN. Therefore, never place a DIM statement inside a program loop.

Look at the program segment below and the beginning of the RUN.

    100 INPUT "HOW MANY NUMBERS? "; N
    110 DIM X(N) : FOR K=1 TO N : LET X(K)=0 : NEXT K
    RUN
    HOW MANY NUMBERS? 8

What will be the dimensioned size of the array during this RUN of the program? _____

— — — — — — — — —

8 (the value assigned to N by the INPUT statement)

16. Look at the first FOR-NEXT loop (line 120) in the program in frame 14. The first value assigned to K is 1, so the first subscripted variable X(K) is X(1). Since the array *could* start with X(0), an array dimensioned as DIM X(100) can actually hold how many values? _____

Show how we could modify the FOR statement so that we could take advantage of every element (subscripted variable value) in the array for storing values, provided that N = 100. _____

— — — — — — — — —

    101
    FOR K = 0 TO N

17. Instead of using an INPUT statement to get values for X(1), X(2), and so on, we can use READ and DATA statements. We'll put the value of N and the values of X(1) through X(N) in a DATA statement, as follows.

    DATA 5, 37, 23, 46, 78, 59
         ╱   ╲ ↑   ↑   ↑   ╱
    Value of N   Values of X(1) through X(5)

The following is the program. Note that line 210 is *outside* any program loop, so this statement only reads one value (the first one) from the DATA statements. However, the subscripted variable for the X array is *inside* a FOR-NEXT loop, so an entire series of values are assigned to the subscripted values.

```
100 REM **WORLD'S MOST EXPENSIVE ADDING MACHINE (AGAIN)
110 DIM X(100)
200 REM **READ N AND X(1) THROUGH X(N)
210 READ N
220 FOR J=1 TO N
230 READ X(J)
240 NEXT J
300 REM **PRINT VALUES OF N AND X(1) THROUGH X(N)
310 PRINT "N =? " ; N
320 PRINT "X(1) THROUGH X(" ; N; ") ARE:"
330 FOR K=1 TO N
340 PRINT X(K);
350 NEXT K
360 PRINT
400 REM **COMPUTE TOTAL OF X(1) TO X(N)
410 T=0
420 FOR L=1 TO N
430 T=T+X(L)
440 NEXT L
500 REM **PRINT TOTAL AND GO BACK FOR NEW DATA
510 PRINT "THE TOTAL IS " ; T
520 PRINT
530 GOTO 210
900 REM **HERE ARE TWO SETS OF DATA
910 DATA 5, 37, 23, 46, 78, 59
920 DATA 12, 1, 2, 3, 4, 5, 6, 7, 8, 9, 10, 11, 12
```

In the first FOR-NEXT loop (lines 220–240), we used J as the subscript. This choice was entirely arbitrary. What subscript did we use in lines 330 to 350? _____ In lines 420 to 440? _____

- - - - - - - - - -

K; L

18. The following questions refer back to the program in frame 17.
(a) For the second set of data, which statement assigns the first item in the DATA statement to a variable?_____
(b) Which statement assigns the rest of the data to a subscripted variable? _____

(c) Which statement prints values stored in an array instead of from the DATA statement?_____
(d) Which statement tallies or adds up all the values stored in the array? _____

(a) 210 READ N
(b) 230 READ X(J)
(c) 340 PRINT X(K);
(d) 430 T=T+X(L)

19. If we had wanted to, could we have used J as the subscript in all three places? _____

Yes. These are three separate and distinct FOR-NEXT loops. We could have used *any* variable as the subscript except N or T.

20. Suppose we RUN the program in frame 17. Show what the RUN will look like. (*Hint:* Check all the PRINT statements.)

```
]RUN
N = 5
X(1) THROUGH X(5) ARE:
37 23 46 78 59
THE TOTAL IS 243

N = 12
X(1) THROUGH X(12) ARE:
1 2 3 4 5 6 7 8 9 10 11 12
THE TOTAL IS 78

?OUT OF DATA ERROR IN 210
```

21. So that you can better understand and use subscripted variables in your programming, here's a little more practice at doing what a computer does when dealing with subscripted variables.

For this segment of a computer program, fill in the following boxes, showing the values of D(G) at the affected locations after this FOR-NEXT loop has been run.

```
10 FOR G=1 TO 3
20 D(G)=2*G-1
30 NEXT G
```

D(1) [ ]   D(2) [ ]   D(3) [ ]

D(1)	1	For G = 1, $2*G - 1 = 2*1 - 1 = 2 - 1 = 1$
D(2)	3	For G = 2, $2*G - 1 = 2*2 - 1 = 4 - 1 = 3$
D(3)	5	For G = 3, $2*G - 1 = 2*3 - 1 = 6 - 1 = 5$

22. For the following FOR-NEXT loop, fill in the boxes showing the values in R(1) through R(4) after the loop has been carried out.

```
10 FOR R=1 TO 4
20 R(R)=R^2
30 NEXT R
```

R(1) [ ]   R(2) [ ]   R(3) [ ]   R(4) [ ]

R(1)	1	For R = 1, $R\wedge 2 = 1\wedge 2 = 1$
R(2)	4	For R = 2, $R\wedge 2 = 2\wedge 2 = 4$
R(3)	9	For R = 3, $R\wedge 2 = 3\wedge 2 = 9$
R(4)	16	For R = 4, $R\wedge 2 = 4\wedge 2 = 16$

23. Let's do one more of these. Show what values will be in the boxes after this FOR-NEXT loop has been executed.

```
10 FOR N=1 TO 6
20 P(N)=2^N
30 NEXT N
```

P(1) [ ]   P(2) [ ]   P(3) [ ]

P(4) [ ]   P(5) [ ]   P(6) [ ]

P(1) [2]   P(2) [4]   P(3) [8]

P(4) [16]   P(5) [32]   P(6) [64]

24. Next, assume that numbers are stored in C(1) through C(5), as follows:

C(1) | 18 | C(2) | 34 | C(3) | 12 |
C(4) | 20 | C(5) | 17 |

What will be printed if the following FOR-NEXT loop is carried out?

```
45 FOR A=1 TO 5
53 PRINT C(A) ; " ";
67 NEXT A

RUN
```

```
RUN
18  34  12  20  17
```

25. Suppose numbers are stored in C(1) through C(5) as shown in frame 24. What will be printed if the following FOR-NEXT loop is carried out?

```
45 FOR A=5 TO 1 STEP -1
53 PRINT C(A);" ";
67 NEXT A

RUN
```

```
RUN
17  20  12  34  18
```

The values are printed in reverse order. If you missed this, review Chapter 6, frames 19 and 20.

26. Assume that an election is approaching and you have conducted a poll among your friends, using the following questionnaire.

> Who will you vote for in the coming election? Circle the number to the left of your choice.
> 1. Sam Smoothe
> 2. Gabby Gruff

Let's write a program to count the votes each candidate received in the poll. You have 35 responses to your questonnaire, each response being either a 1 or a 2. First, record the votes in a DATA statement.

```
910 DATA 1,1,2,2,2,1,1,2,2,2,1,1,1,2,1,2,1,1
920 DATA 2,2,1,1,1,2,1,2,2,2,1,1,2,1,1,2,1,-1
                                            ↑
                                End-of-data flag (not a vote)
```

How many votes did Sam Smoothe receive?_____

——————————

19

27. In frame 26, how many votes did Gabby Gruff receive?_____(Do your answers total 35?)

——————————

16

28. To answer those last two questions, you probably counted the 1s in the DATA statements to find out how many votes Sam Smoothe received. Then you counted the 2s to find out how many votes Gabby Gruff received.

Your computer can count votes by using subscripted variables to keep a running total of the 1s and 2s read from the DATA statements. When it comes to the end-of-data flag (−1) it stops counting and prints the results. Following is a program to count the votes.

```
100 REM **VOTE COUNTING PROGRAM
110 REM **INITIALIZE
120 DIM C(2) : C(1)=0 : C(2)=0
200 REM **READ AND COUNT VOTES
210 READ V
220 IF V=-1 THEN 310
230 C(V)=C(V) + 1
240 GOTO 210
300 REM **PRINT RESULTS
310 PRINT "SAM SMOOTHE: "; C(1)
320 PRINT "GABBY GRUFF: "; C(2)
910 DATA 1,1,2,2,2,1,1,2,2,2,1,1,1,2,1,2,1,1
920 DATA 2,2,1,1,1,2,1,2,2,2,1,1,2,1,1,2,1,-1

RUN
SAM SMOOTHE: 19
GABBY GRUFF: 16
```

280 BASIC FOR THE APPLE II

Is the DIM statement really necessary? Why or why not?_____

_____

― ― ― ― ― ― ― ― ― ―

No, since only C(1) and C(2) are involved, no subscript exceeds 10. However, some people feel it is good practice *always* to use a DIM statement.

29. After the computer executes line 120, what are the values of C(1) and C(2)?

C(1) ☐

C(2) ☐

― ― ― ― ― ― ― ― ― ―

Both have a value of 0. These are the initial values prior to counting votes. We call the process *initializing*, as shown in the REMark statement in line 110.

30. The entire line 120 is unnecessary for this particular program. It is good programming practice to include it anyway and a good habit for you to practice. Although our BASIC sets variables to zero if no other assignment is made, you should get in the habit of including the initializing process so the next user of your program, on whatever computer, will be able to "see" the procedure from your program. When your programs get so long that they start exceeding the computer's memory capacity, delete the initializing process (and REMarks) to save memory space.

To save memory space, which statements could be delete from the program and still have it RUN as shown in frame 28?_____

― ― ― ― ― ― ― ― ― ―

100, 110, 120, 200, and 300

31. Look again at the crucial vote-counting statement from frame 28.

```
230 LET C(V) = C(V)+1
```

It is the subscripted variable equivalent of a similar statement which has been used in earlier programs to keep count.

```
LET N = N+1
```

Note how the variable *subscript* of C is used to determine whether either the value of C(1) is increased by 1, or the value of C(2) is increased by 1. Since V can have only two values, either 1 or 2, line 230 is actually a double-purpose line. Depending on the value of V, line 230 is actually equivalent to

```
LET C(1) = C(1)+1     or     LET C(2) = C(2)+1
```

SUBSCRIPTED VARIABLES **281**

When the preceding program is RUN, what values will the computer have stored for C(1) and C(2) after the *first* vote has been read and processed? (That is, lines 210 through 230 have been done for the first vote in the first DATA statement.)

C(1) [   ]   C(2) [   ]

What values will be stored for C(1) and C(2) after the *second* vote has been read and processed?

C(1) [   ]   C(2) [   ]

What values will be stored in C(1) and C(2) after the third vote has been read and processed?

C(1) [   ]   C(2) [   ]

— — — — — — — — — —

C(1) [1]   C(2) [0]

C(1) [2]   C(2) [0]

C(1) [2]   C(2) [1]

32. In the program we have been discussing (frame 28), line 220 checks for the end-of-data flag with the following statement.

    IF V = −1 THEN 310

If we switch lines 220 and 230, this section of the program would look like this:

```
210 READ V
220 LET C(V)=C(V)+1
230 IF V=-1 THEN 310
240 GOTO 210
```

(a) What would be the last value assigned to V from the DATA statement? _____

(b) If the computer used this value for V in line 220, what would the subscripted variable look like? _____

(c) Since negative subscripts are not allowed, what error message would our computer print? _____

(a) −1
(b) C(−1)
(c) ?BAD SUBSCRIPT ERROR IN 220   Moral: Beware of *where* you place the test for the end-of-data flag. The best place is usually right after the READ or INPUT statement where the flag might appear.

33. Suppose the following poll is conducted.

> Which candidate will you vote for in the coming election? Circle the number to the left of your choice.
>   1. Sam Smoothe
>   2. Gabby Gruff
>   3. No opinion

The results of this poll are shown below.

       2,2,2,1,2,1,1,2,1,1,3,2,1,3,2,1
       1,3,1,3,2,2,1,1,3,2,1,3,1,1,2,1,2,1,1,

Modify the vote-counting program from frame 28 to process this data. You will have to add a line to set C(3) to zero and a PRINT statement to print the NO OPINION total. You will also have to change the DATA statements for the new data, as well as the DIM statement. Here is how it should RUN.

```
RUN
SAM SMOOTHE: 17
GABBY GRUFF: 12
NO OPINION: 6
```

Write your program below.

Here are the modifications.

```
120 DIM C(3) : C(1)=0 : C(2)=0 : C(3)=0
330 PRINT "NO OPINION: " ; C(3)
910 DATA 2,2,2,1,2,1,1,2,1,1,3,2,1,3,2,1
920 DATA 1,3,1,3,2,2,1,1,3,2,1,3,1,1,2,1,2,1,1,-1
```

Did you remember the flag?

The complete program now looks like this.

```
100 REM **VOTE COUNTING PROGRAM
110 REM **INITIALIZE
120 DIM C(3) : C(1)=0 : C(2)=0 : C(3)=0
200 REM **READ AND COUNT VOTES
210 READ V
220 IF V=-1 THEN 310
230 C(V)=C(V)+1
240 GOTO 210
300 REM **PRINT RESULTS
310 PRINT "SAM SMOOTHE: "; C(1)
320 PRINT "GABBY GRUFF: "; C(2)
330 PRINT "NO OPINION: "; C(3)
910 DATA 2,2,2,1,2,1,1,2,1,1,3,2,1,3,2,1
920 DATA 1,3,1,3,2,2,1,1,3,2,1,3,1,1,2,1,2,1,1,-1
```

34. Suppose we have a questionnaire with 4 possible answers, or 5 or 6. Instead of writing a separate program for each, let's write one program to count votes for a quetionnaire with N possible answers. The value of N will appear in a DATA statement prior to the actual answers, or votes. For example, the data for the questionnaire in frame 26 would look like this.

```
900 REM **THE DATA
901 REM **FIRST DATA STATEMENT TELLS NUMBER OF POSSIBLE ANSWERS
910 DATA 2
919 REM **THE VOTES AND THE FLAG (-1)
920 DATA 1,1,2,2,2,1,1,2,2,2,1,1,1,2,1,2,1,1
930 DATA 2,2,1,1,1,2,1,2,2,2,1,1,2,1,1,2,1,-1
```

Line 910 is the value of N. In this case, N is 2 and possible votes are 1 or 2. How would the data for the questionnaire in frame 33 be placed in DATA statements?

```
900 REM **THE DATA
901 REM **FIRST DATA STATEMENT TELLS NUMBER OF POSSIBLE ANSWERS
910 DATA_____
919 REM **THE VOTES AND THE FLAG (-1)
920_____
930_____
```

```
910 DATA 3
920 DATA 2,2,2,1,2,1,1,2,1,1,3,2,1,3,2,1
930 DATA 1,3,1,3,2,2,1,1,3,2,1,3,1,1,2,1,2,1,1,-1
```

This time N = 3 (line 910), and possible votes are 1, 2, or 3.

35. Your turn. Write a program to read and count votes for a questionnaire with N different possible answers (votes), where N is less than or equal to 20. You will have to do the following things.

(1) DIMension for the *maximum* subscript for C. Remember, we said N is less than or equal to 20.
(2) Read the value of N.
(3) Set C(1) through C(N) to zero. (Use a FOR-NEXT loop.)
(4) Read and count votes until a flag is read.
(5) Print the results, as shown in the sample runs below.

```
Example: N = 2              Example: N = 5

RUN                         RUN
ANSWER #1:19                ANSWER #1:12
ANSWER #2:16                ANSWER #2:7
                            ANSWER #3:9
                            ANSWER #4:9
                            ANSWER #5:10
```

Here's a good opportunity to practice writing multiple statements per line. Our sample runs above were produced using these two sets of data.

```
900 REM **THE DATA
901 REM **FIRST DATA STATEMENT TELLS NUMBER OF POSSIBLE ANSWERS
910 DATA 2
919 REM **THE VOTES AND THE FLAG (-1)
920 DATA 1,1,2,2,2,1,1,2,2,2,1,1,1,2,1,2,1,1
930 DATA 2,2,1,1,1,2,1,2,2,2,1,1,2,1,1,2,1,-1

900 REM **THE DATA
901 REM **FIRST DATA STATEMENT TELLS NUMBER OF POSSIBLE ANSWERS
910 DATA 5
919 REM **THE VOTES AND THE FLAG (-1)
920 DATA 4,3,4,2,4,1,1,5,5,3,5,4,5,1,3,2,5,5,4,4,5,1,2,3
930 DATA 3,3,5,2,2,3,1,5,4,1,1,1,2,3,1,4,1,5,1,2,3,4,1,-1
```

Write your program below. (You need not show the DATA statements.)

```
100 REM **VOTE COUNTING PROGRAM
110 REM **INITIALIZE
120 DIM C(20) : READ N : FOR K=1 TO N : C(K)=0 : NEXT K
200 REM **READ AND COUNT VOTES
210 READ V : IF V <> -1 THEN LET C(V)=C(V)+1 : GOTO 210
300 REM **PRINT RESULTS
310 FOR K=1 TO N : PRINT "ANSWER #"; K; ":"; C(K) : NEXT K
```

Note: DATA statements are omitted here.

There are many ways you could have done this. Another way is shown below, where line 210 has been "broken up" into single statements.

```
210 READ V
220 IF V = -1 THEN 310
230 C(V)=C(V)+1
240 GOTO 210
```

36. The problems in frames 26–35 dealt with counting votes. Each time through the loop that reads data (a data loop) you added one (1) to an array element [LET C(V) = C(V)+1]. Almost any vote counting application you might want to try is going to be similar to the solutions in frame 35. Now you can volunteer to be the official ballot counter for all the elections in your community—PTA, computer club, school class offices, church groups, ad infinitum.

On to more serious business. A similar, but not identical application of simple one-dimensional arrays deals with counting things or money, instead of votes.

Let's set the stage. You are the sponsor for the neighborhood computer club for eight local kids. The kids want to buy a new superduper color graphics terminal for the neighborhood computer system. It's only $1200 in kit form. Raising funds is the problem. The kids agree to sell milk chocolate candy bars for $1.00 each to raise money. (The club makes 55¢ profit per sale—not bad!) But you must do the recordkeeping. You assign each kid a number. Whenever a kid comes by for candy bars, you identify the kid by number, and note how many bars were taken. The money will be turned in later.

Here are the ID numbers assigned to each club member.

1. Jerry
2. Bobby
3. Mary
4. Danny
5. Karl
6. Mimi
7. Doug
8. Scott

When Danny first takes 6 bars you note it as 4,6. The 4 is Danny's ID number for the computer, and 6 is the number of candy bars he took. When Doug takes 12 bars, your note is ___, ___. When Mary takes 6, the note is ___, ___.

——————————

7,12; 3,6

37. After a few weeks of this, you've accumulated quite a pile of notes. It's time to tally and see how much money you've raised thus far. The information from your notes will be placed into DATA statements. (You could enter the information using INPUT, but it could take much too long!) Start at line 910 (a good place to put DATA assuming the rest of the program won't have line numbers past 900.)

```
900 REM **KID ID NUMBER FOLLOWED BY QUANTITY. FLAG:-1,-1
910 DATA 4,6,7,12,3,6,1,8,4,5,5,3,8,20
```

This shows that Danny took *another* 5 candy bars.

```
920 2,4,3,8,6,6,5,10,7,12,8,4,1,3
```

Mary took *another* 8.

```
930 DATA -1,-1
```

(a) Each item of data has (how many?) _____ numbers.

(b) DATA 6,6 means _____.

(c) The end-of-data flag has (how many?) _____ numbers.

Why? _____

——————————

(a) two
(b) Mimi took 6 bars
(c) Two. Each data element has two numbers. Two values will be read with one READ statement. An OUT OF DATA ERROR would result if there were only one (flag) value for the two variables in the READ statement.

38. Just as you complete entering the DATA, Bobby shows up to take another 6 bars. Show how you could add this data without changing any of the existing DATA statements. Use the highest line number permissible and still have the end-of-data flags as the last values read by the program. _____

```
929 DATA 2,6
```

The line number cannot be larger than 929, or the flags in line 930 will not be the *last* data item read by the program. Moral: Be careful *where* you add DATA into an existing program.

39. We need an array with eight elements. That means we need a subscripted variable with subscripts from 1 to 8 to represent the eight members of the club. The *value* added to each element (or subscripted variable) in the array will be the number of candy bars each kid took. But first, initialize the array by writing one multiple-statement line that will dimension the array and assign a zero to each element. We will call this the A array and use A(X) for the subscripted variable.

```
100 REM **CANDY BAR COUNTER
110 REM **INITIALIZE

120_____
```

```
120 DIM A(8) : FOR X=1 TO 8 : LET A(X)=0 : NEXT X
```

You could omit the LET, and the X after NEXT. You could omit the DIM statement since BASIC allows up to 10 elements in an array automatically, but we consider that a poor programming practice. For that matter, you could omit the whole line in Applesoft BASIC and many other versions of BASIC, as the computer will consider *any* variable it comes upon to have a value of zero if it has not been assigned a value earlier in the program.

40. Now let's read the *data in pairs* (two items at a time). Use K for kid and Q for quantity of candy bars, and test for end of DATA, all on one line. If we run out of data, have the program branch to line 310.

```
220 REM **READ DATA, TEST FOR FLAG, AND ACCUMULATE (TALLY)

210_____
```

```
210 READ K,Q : IF K=-1 THEN 310
```

41. Now the hard one! We must accumulate the number of bars in the correct array element corresponding to the kid who took them. Think of the subscript K in the subscripted variable A(K) as the kid's ID code.

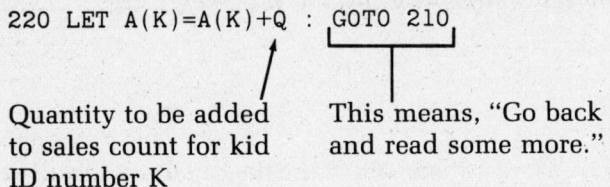

220 LET A(K)=A(K)+Q : GOTO 210

Quantity to be added to sales count for kid ID number K

This means, "Go back and read some more."

If K (for kid) is 2 and Q (quantity) is 4, then line 220 will cause array element A(__) to increase by _____.

— — — — — — — — —

A(2); 4

42. If the array elements look like those on the left *before*, how will they look *after* reading and adding the additional DATA given here?

920 DATA 4,6, 3,8, 6,6, 7,2, 4,3

	Before		After
A(1) =	8	A(1) =	
(2) =	4	(2) =	
(3) =	6	(3) =	
(4) =	4	(4) =	
(5) =	3	(5) =	
(6) =	2	(6) =	
(7) =	12	(7) =	
(8) =	7	(8) =	

A(1) =	8
(2) =	4
(3) =	14
(4) =	13
(5) =	5
(6) =	8
(7) =	14
(8) =	7

43. Here's our program so far.

```
100 REM **CANDY BAR COUNTER
110 REM **INITIALIZE
120 DIM A(8) : FOR X=1 TO 8 : LET A(X)=0 : NEXT X
200 REM **READ DATA, TEST FOR FLAG, AND ACCUMULATE (TALLY)
210 READ K,Q : IF K=-1 THEN 310
220 LET A(K)=A(K)+Q : GOTO 210
900 REM **KID ID NO. FOLLOWED BY QUANTITY. FLAG:-1,-1
910 DATA 4,6,7,12,3,6,1,8,4,5,5,3,8,20
920 DATA 2,4,3,8,6,6,5,10,7,12,8,4,1,3
929 DATA 1,6
930 DATA -1,-1
```

It starts and it accumulates. Before it stops, we must have it print our report. Let's start the report with a heading.

```
300 REM **PRINT THE REPORT
310 PRINT "KID ID NO.", "QUANTITY"
```

Now we print the results using a FOR-NEXT loop.

```
320 FOR X=1 TO 8
330 PRINT X, A(X)
340 NEXT X
```

or

```
320 FOR X=1 TO 8 : PRINT X, A(X) : NEXT X
```

Using the data in the DATA statement, show below how the report will look after running our program.

―――――――――

```
RUN
KID ID NO.    QUANTITY
1             17
2              4
3             14
4             11
5             13
6              6
7             24
8             24
```

44. So far our report shows us who has what, but it doesn't give us names or totals or profits. With some help, the computer can do all those things.

Let's start with the total. In Applesoft BASIC and most other BASICs, each array has an element we haven't used yet. It's the zero (0) element. Remember, when you DIMension an array of eight elements with a DIM statement, DIM A(8), you really get 9: 0, 1, 2, 3, 4, 5, 6, 7, and 8.

Since we haven't assigned any kid the ID number 0 (zero), the "A array" element with the subscript 0 has not been used or assigned a value. So the A(0) element can be used for accumulating totals, although we could use some other variable. Look at statement 410, which accumulates the total number of bars sold in A(0).

```
400 REM **ACCUMULATE TOTAL AND PRINT RESULT
410 FOR X=1 TO 8 : LET A(0)=A(0)+A(X) : NEXT X
```

If the A array starts at zero, we must remember to change the FOR statement in the initializing routine to start assigning zeros at A(0). Replace (rewrite) the initializing line for this program so that all the array elements are given the initial value of zero.

120_____

— — — — — — — — —

```
120 DIM A(8) : FOR X=0 TO 8: A(X)=0 : NEXT X
```

45. The statement that tallies up all the candy sold by the club uses the A(0) element in the A array to accumulate the value stored in A(1) through A(8).
   If the array looks as it did in frame 42 (after reading data), then what value will be stored in A(0) after one time through the loop in line 410? _____
After three times through the loop in 410? _____

— — — — — — — — —

8; 26

46. Write a line 420 to print the total and the profit (55¢ on each bar). Here is what we want line 420 to print:

```
TOTAL IS 113
PROFIT IS 62.15
```

420_____

— — — — — — — — —

```
420 PRINT "TOTAL IS "; A(0) : PRINT "PROFIT IS "; A(0)*.55
```

47. Here is a complete list and run so far.

```
100 REM **CANDY BAR COUNTER
110 REM **INITIALIZE
120 DIM A(8) : FOR X=0 TO 8 : A(X)=0 : NEXT X
200 REM **READ DATA, TEST FOR FLAG, AND ACCUMULATE (TALLY)
210 READ K,Q : IF K=-1 THEN 310
220 LET A(K)=A(K)+Q : GOTO 210
300 REM **PRINT THE REPORT
310 PRINT "KID ID NO.", "QUANTITY"
320 FOR X=1 TO 8 : PRINT X, A(X) : NEXT X
400 REM **ACCUMULATE TOTAL AND PRINT RESULT
410 FOR X=1 TO 8 : LET A(0)=A(0)+A(X) : NEXT
420 PRINT "TOTAL IS "; A(0) : PRINT "PROFIT IS "; A(0)*.55
900 REM **KID ID NO. FOLLOWED BY QUANTITY. FLAG:-1,-1
910 DATA 4,6,7,12,3,6,1,8,4,5,5,3,8,20
920 DATA 2,4,3,8,6,6,5,10,7,12,8,4,1,3
929 DATA 1,6
930 DATA -1,-1

RUN
KID ID NO.    QUANTITY
1             17
2             4
3             14
4             11
5             13
6             6
7             24
8             24
TOTAL IS 113
PROFIT IS 62.15
```

That's a nice report . . . but wait! In this day of impersonalization, wouldn't it be nice to print each kid's name instead of a number? How can we do it? Easily. We can have the computer READ the names from DATA statements into another array, and then print elements from that array in the appropriate places. To do this, we use the subscripted *string* variable.

Arrays that store strings follow all the same rules as arrays that store numerical values. As before, the subscript identifies a particular element or box in the array, and the subscripted string variable can be used like any other variable in READ, LET, INPUT, and PRINT statements.

Subscripted string variables must be DIMensioned, just as an array storing numerical values instead of strings. You can use one DIM statement to dimension all the arrays in your program, whether numerical or string. Just don't forget the properly placed $ that identifies a string variable. You may prefer to DIMension each array in the same multiple-statement line where the array is first used or initialized.

Write a DIM statement to initialize N$(X) for string array N$ that will be enough to store the names of the members of the computer club.

    130 _____

———————————

    130 DIM N$(8)

We would accept DIM N$(7) as an answer, since many versions of BASIC allow string array elements to start numbering at zero, just as we showed for numeric arrays.

48. Let's say that we have placed the club members' names in a DATA statement, in the same order as their ID numbers.

    DATA JERRY,BOBBY,MARY,DANNY,KARL,MIMI,DOUG,SCOTT

Write a FOR-NEXT loop on the same line as the DIM statement that will read the names in the DATA statement into the elements or "boxes" in array N$.

    130 DIM N$(8) :_____

———————————

    130 DIM N$(9) : FOR X=1 TO 8 : READ N$(X) : NEXT X

49. After executing line 130, what will we find stored in N$(1)?_____ In N$(4)?_____

———————————

    JERRY, DANNY

294 BASIC FOR THE APPLE II

50. Here is a listing of the program.

```
100 REM **CANDY BAR COUNTER
110 REM **INITIALIZE
120 DIM A(8) : FOR X=0 TO 8 : A(X)=0 : NEXT X
130 DIM N$(8) : FOR X=1 TO 8 : READ N$(X) : NEXT X
200 REM **READ DATA, TEST FOR FLAG, AND ACCUMULATE (TALLY)
210 READ K,Q : IF K=-1 THEN 310
220 LET A(K)=A(K)+Q : GOTO 210
300 REM **PRINT THE REPORT
310 PRINT "KID ID NO.", "QUANTITY"
320 FOR X=1 TO 8 : PRINT X, A(X) : NEXT X
400 REM **ACCUMULATE TOTAL AND PRINT RESULT
410 FOR X=1 TO 8 : LET A(0)=A(0)+A(X) : NEXT X
420 PRINT "TOTAL IS " ; A(0) : PRINT "PROFIT IS "; A(0)*.55
900 REM **KID ID NO. FOLLOWED BY QUANTITY. FLAG:-1,-1
910 DATA 4,6,7,12,3,6,1,8,4,5,5,3,8,20
920 DATA 2,4,3,8,6,6,5,10,7,12,8,4,1,3
929 DATA 1,6
930 DATA -1,-1
```

There is now the touchy problem of *where* to place the DATA statement that contains the club members' names. Keep in mind that we want to avoid an error message just because a READ statement with a numeric variable came upon a DATA statement containing strings!

What line numbers in the program could the DATA statement have?

_____

_ _ _ _ _ _ _ _ _ _

901 to 909 (or any place *before* line 910)

51. One final change is needed in line 320 in the report printing section. Line 320 looks like this.

```
320 FOR X=1 TO 8 : PRINT X, A(X) : NEXT X
```

Change the line so it will cause the name to be printed instead of the kid number. While you're at it, change the heading line (310) to print NAME and QUANTITY

310_____

320_____

_ _ _ _ _ _ _ _ _ _

```
310 PRINT "NAME", "QUANTITY"
320 FOR X=1 TO 8 : PRINT N$(X), A(X) : NEXT X
```

```
NAME          QUANTITY
JERRY          17
BOBBY          4
MARY           14
DANNY          11
KARL           13
MIMI           6
DOUG           24
SCOTT          24
TOTAL IS  113
PROFIT IS  62.15
```

```
RUN
NAME            QUANTITY
JERRY           17
BOBBY           4
MARY            14
DANNY           11
KARL            13
MIMI            6
DOUG            24
SCOTT           24
TOTAL IS 113
PROFIT IS 62.15
```

53. Let's look at one other application of singly subscripted variables. This one neither counts votes nor accumulates anything.

No doubt you've read about computer dating. Ever wonder how it works? You answer a series of questions that are then stored in the computer; other people who wish to be matched do likewise. Then the responses are compared to test for "compatability." Let's do a simplified version of a computer dating program which you can alter for your own uses.

We'll use a multiple-choice questionnaire with only five questions. (Ask anything you'd like!) Responses will be stored in DATA statements, with the name first, and the five responses following. My responses appear in line 910 below.

```
900 REM **QUESTIONNAIRE RESPONSES. NAME THEN ANSWERS.
909 REM **LINE 910: 'HIS' RESPONSES
910 DATA LEROY,3,3,4,2,1
```

Now, you create DATA statements in lines 920–970 for these respondents, plus an end-of-data flag.

	Q1	Q2	Q3	Q4	Q5
JOAN	1	4	2	2	1
TONI	2	2	2	3	3
LAURA	2	3	3	1	2
MARY	3	3	4	2	1
IRENE	3	1	4	2	1

920 _____

930 _____

940 _____

950 _____

960 _____

970 _____

```
920 DATA JOAN,1,4,2,2,1
930 DATA TONI,2,2,2,3,3
940 DATA LAURA,2,3,3,1,2
950 DATA MARY,3,3,4,2,1
960 DATA IRENE,3,1,4,2,1
970 DATA END
```

54. Now, you write the rest of the program with some gentle supervision. First, you will need a DIM statement that will allow the program to compare "his" responses (stored in array C) with "her" responses (stored in array A).

Note: You can DIMension more than one array in one DIM statement.

```
100 REM **COMPUTER DATING SIMULATION
105 REM **INITIALIZE

110_____
```

```
110 DIM C(5), A(5)
```

55. Next, READ the first data statement which contains "his" name, and READ "his" five responses. The responses should be read directly into array C. Then print "his" name and responses all on one line, so that later you can compare them with "hers."

```
220 REM **READ AND PRINT 'HIS' NAME & RESPONSES

210_____
220_____
```

```
210 READ N$ : FOR X=1 TO 5 : READ C(X) : NEXT
220 PRINT N$, : FOR X=1 TO 5 : PRINT C(X); " "; : NEXT X : PRINT
```

Did you remember this PRINT statement?

56. Next, READ *one* set of "her" names and responses into array A, and print "her" responses so you can visually compare the "his" responses with "her" responses. After you read "her" name in line 310, check to see if it is the end-of-data flag (the word END). Use the string comparison IF H$ = "END" THEN END. The output we want so far should look like this.

```
RUN
LEROY      3 3 4 2 1
JOAN       1 4 2 2 1
```

Complete the program segment to produce this output or printout.

```
300 REM **READ AND PRINT 'HER' NAMES AND RESPONSES
310_____
320_____
330_____
```

— — — — — — — — —

```
310 READ H$ : IF H$="END" THEN END
320 FOR X=1 TO 5 : READ A(X) : NEXT X
330 PRINT H$, : FOR X=1 TO 5 : PRINT A(X); " "; : NEXT X : PRINT
```

57. Now comes the crucial part. This is where you compare the contents of array C with the contents of array A and add the number of matches into variable M. Think about that and complete the program below, so that a RUN of the complete program looks like the one here.

```
RUN
LEROY        3 3 4 2 1
JOAN         1 4 2 2 1
2 MATCHES

TONI         2 2 2 3 3
0 MATCHES

LAURA        2 3 3 1 2
1 MATCHES

MARY         3 3 4 2 1
5 MATCHES

IRENE        3 1 4 2 1
4 MATCHES
```

Fill in the spaces.

```
400 REM **COMPARE RESPONSES & PRINT NUMBER OF 'MATCHES'
410 M=0
420 FOR X=1 TO 5
430 IF_____ THEN 450    ← Compare.
440 LET M=_____  ←————————————  Add matches.
450 _____  ←————————————  Close the loop to compare another.
460 PRINT_____" MATCHES"
470 PRINT
480 GOTO_____  ←————————————  Read another set of responses.
```

— — — — — — — — — —

```
400 REM **COMPARE RESPONSES & PRINT NUMBER OF 'MATCHES'
410 M=0
420 FOR X=1 TO 5
430 IF C(X)<>A(X) THEN 450
440 LET M=M+1
450 NEXT X
460 PRINT M; " MATCHES"
470 PRINT
480 GOTO 310
```

Following is a complete listing and RUN of our computer dating program.

```
100 REM **COMPUTER DATING SIMULATION
105 REM **INITIALIZE
110 DIM C(5), A(5)
200 REM **READ AND PRINT 'HIS' NAME & RESPONSES
210 READ N$, : FOR X=1 TO 5 : READ C(X); : NEXT
220 PRINT N$, : FOR X=1 TO 5 : PRINT C(X); : NEXT X : PRINT
300 REM **READ AND PRINT 'HER' NAMES AND RESPONSES
310 READ H$ : IF H$="END" THEN END
320 FOR X=1 TO 5 : READ A(X) : NEXT X
330 PRINT H$, : FOR X=1 TO 5 : PRINT A(X); " "; : NEXT X : PRINT
400 REM **COMPARE RESPONSES & PRINT NUMBER OF 'MATCHES'
410 M=0
420 FOR X=1 TO 5
430 IF C(X)<>A(X) THEN 450
440 LET M=M+1
450 NEXT X
460 PRINT M: " MATCHES"
470 PRINT
480 GOTO 310
900 REM **QUESTIONNAIRE RESPONSES. NAME THEN ANSWERS.
909 REM **LINE 910 : 'HIS' RESPONSES
910 DATA LEROY,3,3,4,2,1
920 DATA JOAN,1,4,2,2,1
930 DATA TONI,2,2,2,3,3
940 DATA LAURA,2,3,3,1,2
950 DATA MARY,3,3,4,2,1
960 DATA IRENE,3,1,4,2,1
970 DATA END

RUN
LEROY       3 3 4 2 1
JOAN        1 4 2 2 1
2 MATCHES


TONI        2 2 2 3 3
0 MATCHES


LAURA       2 3 3 1 2
1 MATCHES


MARY        3 3 4 2 1
5 MATCHES


IRENE       3 1 4 2 1
4 MATCHES
```

Self-Test

If you can complete the Self-Test on subscripted variables, you will be ready for the next chapter, which will expand your programming ability to include the use of more complex subscripted variables. Therefore, it is important that you have the information in this chapter well in hand.

1. Indicate which of the following are legal BASIC subscripted variables.
   ____(a) X   ____(b) X2   ____(c) X(2)
   ____(d) 2(X)   ____(e) XX(2)   ____(f) X(K)
   ____(g) X_2 ____(h) X(I–J)

2. Assume that values have been assigned to variables as shown below. Note that both simple and subscripte variables are shown.

Q	2	A(1)	37
A	3	A(2)	4
A1	1	A(3)	23
		A(4)	19

   Remember, A, A1, and A(1) are distinct variables. Write the value of each variable below.

   (a) A(Q)_____
   (b) A(A)_____
   (c) A(A1)_____
   (d) A(A(2))_____
   (e) A(A(Q))_____
   (f) A(A–Q)_____
   (g) A(A+A1)_____
   (h) A(2*Q)_____

3. What will be printed if we RUN the following program?

```
100 REM **MYSTERY PROGRAM
110 READ N
120 FOR K=1 TO N
130 READ X(K)
140 NEXT K
150 FOR K=1 TO N
160 IF X(K)<0 THEN 180
170 PRINT X(K); " ";
180 NEXT K
900 REMARK VALUES OF N AND X(1) THRU X(N)
910 DATA 7
920 DATA 23,-44,37,0,-12,-58,87
RUN
```

_____

4. There is no DIM statement in the preceding program of question 3. Therefore, what is the largest value of N for which the program can be used? _____ What would happen if we tried to RUN the program using the following DATA? _____

_____

```
910 DATA 12
920 DATA 3,6,-2,0,9,0,7,3,-5,4,-1,7
```

5. Modify the vote-counting program of frame 28 so that the total votes (for both candidates) are also printed. The printout might look like this.

   RUN

   SAM SMOOTHE: 19
   GABBY GRUFF: 16

   TOTAL VOTES: 35

6. Modify the vote-counting program of frame 28 so that the printout is percent of total votes, rounded to the nearest *whole-number* percent.

   RUN

   SAM SMOOTHE: 54%
   GABBY GRUFF: 46%

310 _____
320 _____
330 _____
340 _____
350 _____

7. You are selected chairman of the United Collection in your neighborhood. You have five people who collect money door-to-door and turn in the money to you at the end of each day. You record their names and dollar amounts collected on a form. This data is then entered into your computer for further processing. Write a BASIC program that will accumulate the current amount each person has collected and the total amount collected by all five people. Your report should show the names of each collector with the amounts collected.

```
RUN

NAME                    AMOUNT COLLECTED
FRED                    125
JOANN                   205
MARYJO                  100
JERRY                   100
BOB                     200
TOTAL 730
```

8. Your computer club kids decide they want to find out who is the best programmer in their group. As club sponsor, you decide to give them a multiple-choice test on programming concepts and correct the test using the computer. The multiple choice answers will be the numbers 1,2,3,4, or 5. There are 10 questions on the test. You enter the 10 *correct* answers in the first DATA statement in the program. These are read into array K. In subsequent DATA statements, you first enter the name of the club member, followed by the 10 answers that person gave for the test. (Enter in array R.) Your task is to write a BASIC program that will correct the tests and print a report that looks similar to the one below. The technique is similar to the matching process in the "computer-dating" program.

```
RUN
NAME                    SCORE
DANNY                   5
KARL                    5
MIRIAM                  4
SCOTT                   7
```

Here are the DATA statements for the above RUN.

```
90  REM TEST ANSWERS
100 DATA 3,4,3,3,5,1,2,3,2,1
110 REM TEST RESPONSES
120 DATA DANNY,1,2,3,4,5,1,2,3,4,5
130 DATA KARL,1,3,2,4,4,1,2,3,2,1
140 DATA MIRIAM,3,2,2,1,4,1,2,3,1,2
150 DATA SCOTT,1,2,3,3,5,1,2,3,2,2
160 DATA END
```

9. Are you curious about your chances of winning at any game using dice? If you developed a program to simulate the rolling of one die and counted how many times each side appeared, you would get a better idea of your chances of winning.

Write a BASIC program to simulate the roll of one die 1000 times (or make that an input variable). After each simulated roll, accumulate or add to the correct array element one appearance or "vote." After 1000 rolls, print the contents of your array in report form showing how many times each die side appeared during the computer simulation. Your report should look like the one following. Write your program following the sample program.

```
RUN
HOW MANY SIMULATED ROLLS? 1000
DICE ROLL              NO. OF OCCURENCES
1                      159
2                      152
3                      173
4                      142
5                      189
6                      185
```

Answers to Self-Test

The frame numbers in parentheses refer to the frames in the chapter where the topic is discussed. You may wish to refer back to these for quick review.

1. (c), (e), (f), and (h) are legal subscripted variables.

    (frame 1)

2. (a) 4
    (b) 23
    (c) 37
    (d) 19 $A(A(2)) = A(4) = 19$
    (e) 19 $A(A(Q)) = A(A(2)) = A(4) = 19$
    (f) 37 $A(3-2) = A(1) = 37$
    (g) 19 $A(3+1) = A(4) = 19$
    (h) 19 $A(2+2) = A(4) = 19$

    (frame 4)

3. RUN

   23 37 0 87

   (frames 7, 8)

4. 10. The computer would print an error message. Our computer printed:

   ?BAD SUBSCRIPT ERROR AT LINE 130

   (frames 11,12)

5. Add the following statements.

   ```
   330 PRINT
   340 PRINT "TOTAL VOTES: ";C(1)+C(2)
   ```

   (frames 45, 46)

6. Beginning at line 310, make these changes.

   ```
   310 LET T=C(1)+C(2)
   320 LET S=INT(100*C(1)/T + .5)
   330 LET G=INT(100*C(2)/T + .5)
   340 PRINT "SAM SMOOTHE: ";S;"%"
   350 PRINT "GABBY GRUFF: ";G;"%"
   ```

   (frame 28 and Chapter 4)

7.
   ```
   10 REM **UNITED COLLECTION ANALYSIS
   15 REM **INITIALIZE
   20 DIM N$(5),T(5) : G=0 : FOR X=1 TO 5 : LET T(X)=0 : NEXT X
   25 REM **READ NAMES
   30 FOR N=1 TO 5 : READ N$(N) : NEXT N
   35 REM **READ AND ACCUMULATE DATA
   40 READ P,D : IF P=-1 THEN 60
   50 LET T(P)=T(P)+D : G=G+D : GOTO 40
   55 REM **PRINT REPORT
   60 PRINT"NAME", "AMOUNT COLLECTED"
   70 FOR P=1 TO 5 : PRINT N$(P),T(P) : NEXT P
   80 PRINT "TOTAL ";G
   90 REM **NAMES OF COLLECTORS
   100 DATA FRED, JOANN, MARYJO, JERRY, BOB
   110 REM DATA BY PERSON BY AMOUNT
   120 DATA 2,45,1,75,3,25,4,100,3,25,5,125
   130 DATA 3,50,1,50,2,120,2,40,5,75,-1,-1
   ```

   (frames 36-52)

8.
```
10 REM **TEST CORRECTOR
15 REM **INITIALIZE
20 DIM K(10),R(10) : PRINT"NAME", "SCORE"
25 REM **READ CORRECT ANSWERS
30 FOR X=1 TO 10 : READ K(X) : NEXT X :
35 REM **READ STUDENT RESPONSE
40 READ N$ : IF N$="END"THEN END
50 FOR X=1 TO 10 : READ R(X) : NEXT X : LET S=0
55 REM **CORRECT TESTS
60 FOR X=1 TO 10 : IF K(X)<>R(X) THEN 70
65 LET S=S+1
70 NEXT X : PRINT N$,S : GO TO 40
90 REM **TEST ANSWERS
100 DATA 3,4,3,3,5,1,2,3,2,1
110 REM TEST RESPONSES
120 DATA DANNY,1,2,3,4,5,1,2,3,4,5
130 DATA KARL,1,3,2,4,4,1,2,3,2,1
140 DATA MIRIAM,3,2,2,1,4,1,2,3,1,2
150 DATA SCOTT,1,2,3,3,5,1,2,3,2,2
160 DATA END
```

(frames 53–57)

9.
```
10 REM **DICE SIMULATION
20 DIM D(6) : FOR X=1 TO 6 : LET D(X)=0 : NEXT X
30 INPUT "HOW MANY SIMULATED ROLLS";R
40 FOR X=1 TO R : LET N=INT(6*RND(1))+1 : LET D(N)=D(N)+1 : NEXT X
50 PRINT"DICE ROLL", "NO. OF OCCURENCES"
55 REM **PRINT REPORT
60 FOR X=1 TO 6 : PRINT X,D(X) : NEXT X
```

(frames 26–31)

CHAPTER TEN

Double Subscripts

In Chapter 9 you were introduced to singly subscripted variables and their many applications. The only *new* statement was DIM. There is one new function (TAB) in this chapter, as well as some new uses and variations of what you already know.

In this chapter we'll extend your use of Applesoft BASIC to variables with *two* subscripts, which we call doubly subscripted variables. Doubly subscripted variables are used with arrays of numbers which might require several columns and rows, such as in complex voter analysis problems, detailed dollar analysis problems, and a whole host of board game applications. When you complete this chapter, you will be able to:

- Use variables with two subscripts
- Assign values to doubly subscripted variables in a two-dimensional array (also called a table or matrix)
- Use the DIM statement to tell the computer the dimensions of two-dimensional arrays.
- Use the TAB function to position PRINT statement output in other than standard print positions

1. In Chapter 9, we described subscripted variables such as X(7) and T(K). These are *singly subscripted* variables. That is, each variable has exactly *one* subscript.

$$X(7) \qquad T(K) \qquad A\$(X)$$
$$\uparrow \qquad \quad \uparrow \qquad \quad \uparrow$$
One subscript One subscript One subscript

In this chapter, we will use *doubly subscripted* variables, variables that have *two* subscripts.

$$T(2,3)$$
$$\;\uparrow\uparrow$$
Two subscripts, separated by a comma

T(3) is a subscripted variable with how many subscripts? _____

T(7,5) is a subscripted variable with how many subscripts? _____

—————————

1; 2

2. It is convenient to think of doubly subscripted variables arranged in an *array* of *rows* and *columns*, as shown below.

	Column 1	Column 2	Column 3	Column 4
Row 1	A(1,1) ☐	A(1,2) ☐	A(1,3) ☐	A(1,4) ☐
Row 2	A(2,1) ☐	A(2,2) ☐	A(2,3) ☐	A(2,4) ☐
Row 3	A(3,1) ☐	A(3,2) ☐	A(3,3) ☐	A(3,4) ☐

The above array has ____ rows and ____ columns.

—————————

3; 4

3. With the arrangement shown in frame 2, we can relate subscripts to particular places (locations, or "boxes" for values) in rows and columns. These are called the *elements* in the array. For example:

```
    A(2,3)
     ↑ ↑
   Row  \
   Column
```

A(1,1) is in row 1, column 1. A (1,2) is in row 1, column 2. What subscripted variable is in row 3, column 2? _____

—————————

A(3,2)

DOUBLE SUBSCRIPTS   311

4. The rectangular arrangement of doubly subscripted variables shown in frame 2 is called a *table*, *matrix*, or *two-dimensional array*.

In Chapter 9 we described arrays of singly subscripted variables which are also called *lists*, *vectors*, or *one-dimensional arrays*.

This is a *list*:   X(1)   X(2)   X(3)

This is a *table*:   C(1,1)   C(1,2)   C(1,3)
                      C(2,1)   C(2,2)   C(2,3)
                      C(3,1)   C(3,2)   C(3,3)

(a) A list is also called a _____ or a _____ .

(b) A table is also called a _____ or a _____ .

_ _ _ _ _ _ _ _ _ _

(a) vector, one-dimensional array (one subscript)
(b) matrix, two-dimensional array (two subscripts)

5. A doubly subscripted variable is simply the name of a location in the computer. As with any other variable, you can think of it as the name for a box, a place to store a number. Here is a table of doubly subscripted variables.

B(1,1) [ ]   B(1,2) [ ]   B(1,3) [ ]

B(2,1) [ ]   B(2,2) [ ]   B(2,3) [ ]

Pretend you are the computer and assign the value of 73 to variable B(2,1). In other words, take pencil in hand and write the number 73 in the box labeled B(2,1). Then do the same for the following.

```
LET B(1,3)=0
LET B(1,1)=49
LET B(2,3)=B(2,1) - B(1,1)
LET B(1,2)=2*B(2,1)
LET B(2,2)=INT(B(2,1)/B(2,3))
```

_ _ _ _ _ _ _ _ _ _

B(1,1) [49]   B(1,2) [146]   B(1,3) [0]

B(2,1) [73]   B(2,2) [3]   B(2,3) [24]

6. As we learned in Chapter 9, subscripts can be variables. The subscripted variable P(R,C) has variable subscripts.
If R = 1 and C = 2, then P(R,C) is P(1,2).
If R = 4 and C = 3, then P(R,C) is P(4,3).
If R = 7 and C = 5, then P(R,C) is _____.

— — — — — — — —

P(7,5)

7. Let's assume that the following values (in the boxes) have been assigned to the corresponding variables. Note that there are both simple and subscripted variables.

R	2	T(1,1)	7	T(1,2)	0	T(1,3)	−12
C	3	T(2,1)	9	T(2,2)	5	T(2,3)	8
A	1	T(3,1)	16	T(3,2)	13	T(3,3)	10
B	2						

	Value of Subscripted Variable	Subscript Values
(a) T (2, 3) =	_____	_____, _____
(b) R=	_____	_____, _____
(c) C =	_____	_____, _____
(d) T (R, C) =	_____	_____, _____
(e) T (A, B) =	_____	_____, _____
(f) T (1, 1) =	_____	_____, _____
(g) A =	_____	_____, _____
(h) T (A, A) =	_____	_____, _____
(i) T (B, R) =	_____	_____, _____
(j) T (R, A) =	_____	_____, _____
(k) T (R + 1, C − 2) =	_____	_____, _____

(a) 8; 2, 3
(b) 2; none
(c) 3; none
(d) 8; 2, 3
(e) 0; 1, 2
(f) 7; 1, 1
(g) 1; none
(h) 7; 1, 1
(i) 5; 2, 2
(j) 9; 2, 1
(k) 16; 3, 1 because T (R + 1, C − 2) = T (2 + 1, 3 − 2) = T (3, 1)

8. Election time again. (Before starting on this, you may wish to review the vote-counting application in Chapter 9.) The questionnaire below requires two answers.

> Q1. Who will you vote for in the coming election? Circle the number to the left of your choice.
>   1. Sam Smoothe
>   2. Gabby Gruff
>   3. No opinion
> Q2. What age group are you in? Circle the number to the left of your age group.
>   1. Under 30
>   2. 30 or over

Since there are two questions, each reply consists of two numbers: the answer to question 1 and the answer to question 2. We will use V (for vote) to represent the answer to question 1 and A (for age) to represent the answer to question 2.

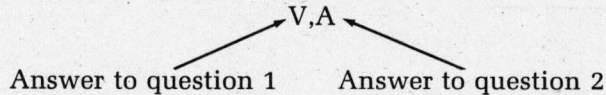

Answer to question 1   Answer to question 2

The possible values of V are 1, 2, or 3. What are the possible values of A?

_____

_ _ _ _ _ _ _ _ _

1 or 2

9. We sent out some questionnaires. Some typical replies are shown below.

Reply	Meaning
1,1	One vote for Sam Smoothe, voter is under 30
1,2	One vote for Sam Smoothe, voter 30 or over
3,1	No opinion, voter is under 30

What does the reply 2,2 mean? _____

__ __ __ __ __ __ __ __ __ __

One vote for Gabby Gruff, voter is 30 or over

10. We want to write a program to summarize data for a two-question questionnaire. We will use subscripted variables to count votes as follows.

		Under 30	30 or over
Sam Smoothe	C(1,1)	☐	C(1,2) ☐
Gabby Gruff	C(2,1)	☐	C(2,2) ☐
No opinion	C(3,1)	☐	C(3,2) ☐

In other words, C(1,1) will hold the count for Sam Smoothe by people under 30. C(1,2) will hold the total for Sam Smoothe by people 30 or over. C(2,1) will hold the total for _____ by people _____.

What subscripted variable will hold the No opinion count for people 30 or over? _____

__ __ __ __ __ __ __ __ __ __

Gabby Gruff; under 30; C(3,2)

11. Here are 29 replies to our questionnaire. Remember, each reply is a *pair* of numbers and represents *one* vote. The first number of each pair is the answer to question 1. The second number of each pair is the answer to question 2.

```
3,1   2,2   3,2   1,2   1,2   2,1
2,2   1,1   1,2   3,1   3,2   2,2
3,1   2,1   2,2   1,1   1,1   1,2
1,1   2,1   2,1   1,2   2,1   3,1
2,1   3,1   2,1   3,1   2,2
```

Write the appropriate count in each box below.

		Under 30		30 or over
Sam Smoothe	C(1,1)		C(1,2)	
Gabby Gruff	C(2,1)		C(2,2)	
No opinion	C(3,1)		C(3,2)	

- - - - - - - - - - -

C(1,1)	4	C(1,2)	5
C(2,1)	7	C(2,2)	5
C(3,1)	6	C(3,2)	2

12. Naturally, we want the computer to do the counting. Below is the beginning of our program.

```
100 REM **VOTE COUNTING, TWO QUESTIONS
110 DIM C(3,2)
```

The DIM statement (line 110) defines an array with at most 3 rows and 2 columns. That is, the DIM statement defines an array of doubly subscripted variables in which the maximum value of the first subscript is 3 and the maximum value of the second subscript is 2. You must *always* DIM doubly subscripted arrays or you'll get an error message.

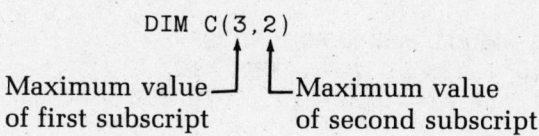

DIM C(3,2)

Maximum value ⏌ ⏌ Maximum value
of first subscript   of second subscript

Next, we want to set all counts to zero. That is, we want to assign zero to C(1,1), C(1,2), and so on up to C(3,2). Even though other versions of BASIC might do this automatically, it is good programming practice to initialize every program. You complete this part of the program.

```
200 REM **INITIALIZE: SET ALL COUNTS TO ZERO
```

Here are four ways to do it!

Method 1
```
210 LET C(1,1)=0
220 LET C(1,2)=0
230 LET C(2,1)=0
240 LET C(2,2)=0
250 LET C(3,1)=0
260 LET C(3,2)=0
```

Method 2
```
210 FOR K=1 TO 3
220 LET C(K,1)=0
230 LET C(K,2)=0
240 NEXT K
```

Method 3
```
210 FOR K=1 TO 3
220 FOR L=1 TO 2
230 LET C(K,L)=0
240 NEXT L
250 NEXT K
```

Method 4
```
210 FOR K=1 TO 3 : FOR L=1 TO 2 : LET C(K,L)=0 : NEXT L,K
```

We will use methods 3 and 4 because they are easily generalized to arrays of different sizes. Using method 3, we can add more rows by changing line 210, more columns by changing line 220. (Of course, we would also have to change the DIM statement.)

13. The array is now set up. Let's READ and count the votes.

```
300 REM **READ AND COUNT VOTES
310 READ V,A : IF V=-1 THEN 410
320 LET C(V,A)=C(V,A)+1 : GOTO 310
```

Line 320 is the crucial vote-counting statement. It adds 1 (vote) to the array element specified by V and A. Suppose this is the array before executing lines 310 and 320.

C(1,1)	0		C(1,2)	4
C(2,1)	2		C(2,2)	7
C(3,1)	5		C(3,2)	0

Show how the array would look after this additional data was processed.

910 DATA 3, 1, 2, 2, 3, 2, 1, 2

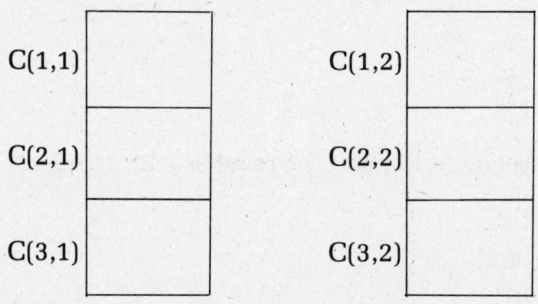

- - - - - - - - - - - -

C(1,1)	0		C(1,2)	5
C(2,1)	2		C(2,2)	8
C(3,1)	6		C(3,2)	1

14. Since line 310 is a READ statement, some DATA statements must be given somewhere. Here they are, featuring the data from frame 11.

```
900 REM **VOTE AND AGE GROUP DATA IN PAIRS. FLAGS=-1,-1
910 DATA 3,1, 2,2, 3,2, 1,2, 1,2, 2,1
920 DATA 2,2, 1,1, 1,2, 3,1, 3,2, 2,2
930 DATA 3,1, 2,1, 2,2, 1,1, 1,1, 1,2
940 DATA 1,1, 2,1, 2,1, 1,2, 2,1, 3,1
950 DATA 2,1, 3,1, 2,1, 3,1, 2,2, -1,-1
```

Remember, each reply is a *pair* of numbers representing *one* vote. To emphasize this, we have typed a space after each reply (pair of values) in the DATA statements above. Why is the flag −1,−1 instead of just −1? _____

_____

——————————

If the computer could not find a value for READ variable A as well as variable V in line 310, it would print a data error message and stop.

15. Only one task remains—print the results! For the data shown in frame 14, the results should look like the one following when the program is RUN.

```
]RUN
CANDIDATE     18 − 29     30 PLUS

SAM SMOOTHE   4           5
GABBY GRUFF   7           5
NO OPINION    6           2
```

You do it. Complete the program segment to print the results—C(1,1), C(1,2), and so on—as shown above.

```
400 REM **PRINT THE RESULTS
410 _____
420 _____
430 _____
440 _____
450 _____
```

——————————

We did it like this.

```
400 REM **PRINT THE RESULTS
410 PRINT "CANDIDATE","18 − 29","30 PLUS"
420 PRINT
430 PRINT "SAM SMOOTHE", C(1,1), C(1,2)
440 PRINT "GABBY GRUFF", C(2,1), C(2,2)
450 PRINT "NO OPINION", C(3,1), C(3,2)
```

Here is a listing of the complete vote-counting program.

```
100 REM **VOTE COUNTING, TWO QUESTIONS
110 DIM C(3,2)
200 REM **INITIALIZE: SET ALL COUNTS TO ZERO
210 FOR K=1 TO 3 : FOR L=1 TO 2 : LET C(K,L)=0 : NEXT L,K
300 REM **READ AND COUNT VOTES
310 READ V,A : IF V=-1 THEN 410
320 LET C(V,A)=C(V,A)+1 : GOTO 310
400 REM **PRINT THE RESULTS
410 PRINT "CANDIDATE","18 - 29","30 PLUS"
420 PRINT
430 PRINT "SAM SMOOTHE",C(1,1),C(1,2)
440 PRINT "GABBY GRUFF",C(2,1),C(2,2)
450 PRINT "NO OPINION",C(3,1),C(3,2)
900 REM ***VOTE AND AGE GROUP DATA IN PAIRS. FLAGS=-1,-1
910 DATA 3,1, 2,2, 3,2, 1,2, 1,2, 2,1
920 DATA 2,2, 1,1, 1,2, 3,1, 3,2, 2,2
930 DATA 3,1, 2,1, 2,2, 1,1, 1,1, 1,2
940 DATA 1,1, 2,1, 2,1, 1,2, 2,1, 3,1
950 DATA 2,1, 3,1, 2,1, 3,1, 2,2, -1,-1
```

16. Until now we have depended on the print positions built into Applesoft BASIC for 40-column displays. By using either the comma or semicolon in PRINT statements, we have been able to get a reasonable amount of information across the display screen.

However, for displays where three columns of information are not desirable, BASIC provides the TAB function to tell the computer exactly where across a display line to place the next PRINT statement output.

The TAB function is so called because it is similar to setting tabs on a typewriter. TAB is only used in PRINT statements. For example,

```
150 PRINT TAB(23)"HELLO"
```

tells the computer to display the first character in the string HELLO at character position 23. We find TAB extremely useful when setting up displays of tables and charts that have more than three columns of information.

Examine this statement:

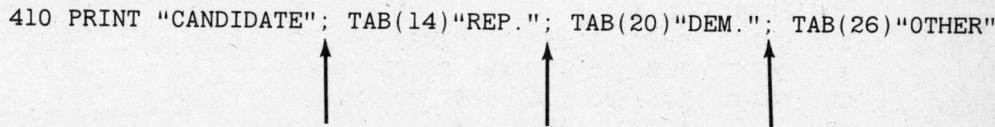

```
410 PRINT "CANDIDATE"; TAB(14)"REP."; TAB(20)"DEM."; TAB(26)"OTHER"
```

(The semicolons following CANDIDATE, REP., and DEM. are optional; we put them in for your ease in reading the statements.)

Give the character positions in a display line that each string in line 410 will occupy.

(a) CANDIDATE   positions ____ to ____
(b) REP.   positions ____ to ____
(c) DEM.   positions ____ to ____
(d) OTHER   positions ____ to ____

(a) 1, 9
(b) 14, 17
(c) 20, 23
(d) 26, 30

17. There several restrictions on the use of TAB.

   1. You cannot TAB backward. If the cursor is at character position 25, you cannot TAB(20) on the same display line.
   2. Negative values for TAB are not allowed.
   3. TAB values range from TAB(0) to TAB(255). Since a display line is usually 40 characters, a TAB(55) actually places the next PRINT output at character position 15 in the second line down. TAB(0) acts like TAB(256). Values larger than 255 in the TAB argument will result in an error.
   4. The value for the TAB argument can be a variable or a calculated expression. As you will see, this conveniently allows you to automate the TAB function for placing output from an array at evenly spaced positions across a display line and under chart or table headings. This is accomplished by calculating increasing TAB values for output from a PRINT statement located inside a FOR-NEXT loop.

Now examine this program, and predict the display position(s) for the output from each PRINT statement.

```
10  PRINT 1;2;3
20  PRINT 1,2,3
30  PRINT "ONE"; TAB( 10);"TEN"
40  PRINT    TAB( 15)15 TAB( 20)20
50  PRINT    TAB( 15);15; TAB( 20);20
60  A = 20:  PRINT   TAB( A);A
70  B = 6:   PRINT   TAB( A - B);A - B
80  PRINT    TAB( A / B);A / B
90  PRINT    TAB( B - A);B - A
```

DOUBLE SUBSCRIPTS **321**

Output for:
(a) line 10:   positions ____ to ____
(b) line 20:   positions ____ , ____, and ____
(c) line 30:   positions ____ to ____, and ____ to ____
(d) line 40:   positions ____ to ____, and ____ to ____
(e) line 50:   positions ____ to ____, and ____ to ____
(f) line 60:   positions ____ to ____
(g) line 70:   positions ____ to ____
(h) line 80:   positions ____ to ____
(i) line 90:   position _____

— — — — — — — — —

(a) 1, 3
(b) 1, 17, and 33 (standard print positions)
(c) 10, 12
(d) 15, 16; 20, 21
(e) same as (d) because omitting semicolons has no effect in PRINT statements except at the end of a PRINT statement
(f) 20, 21
(g) 14, 15
(h) starts in print position 3, and goes to 12 [20/6 is displayed as 3.33333333, but only the integer part (the 3 before the decimal point) is used by TAB]
(i) illegal quantity error in line 90, because negative values are not allowed for TAB.

A RUN of the program looks like this:

```
]RUN
123
1               2               3
ONE     TEN
                15      20
                15      20
                        20
            14
     3.33333333

?ILLEGAL QUANTITY ERROR IN 90
```

18. Return with us now to the thrilling concept of vote counting using arrays. Suppose the questionnaire had been the following.

> Q1. Who will you vote for in the coming election? Circle the number to the left of your choice.
>   1. Sam Smoothe
>   2. Gabby Gruff
>   3. No opinion
>
> Q2. What is your political affiliation? Circle the number to the left of your answer.
>   1. Democrat
>   2. Republican
>   3. Other

Modify the vote-counting program on page 319 so that answers are counted as follows.

	Democrat	Republican	Other
Sam Smoothe	C(1,1)	C(1,2)	C(1,3)
Gabby Gruff	C(2,1)	C(2,2)	C(2,3)
No opinion	C(3,1)	C(3,2)	C(3,3)

You will have to change lines 110, 210, 410, 430, 440, and 450.

```
110 HOME: DIM _____

210 _____
410 PRINT "CANDIDATE"; TAB( 14)"DEM."; TAB( 20)"REP."; TAB( 26)"OTHER"
420 PRINT

430 _____

440 _____

450 _____
```

```
110 HOME : DIM C(3,3)
210 FOR K = 1 TO 3: FOR L = 1 TO 2: LET C(K,L) = 0: NEXT L,K
410 PRINT "CANDIDATE"; TAB( 14)"DEM."; TAB( 20)"REP."; TAB( 26)"OTHER"
420 PRINT
430 PRINT "SAM SMOOTHE"; TAB( 14);C(1,1); TAB( 20);C(1,2);
    TAB( 26);C(1,3)
440 PRINT "GABBY GRUFF"; TAB( 14);C(2,1); TAB( 20);C(2,2);
    TAB( 26);C(2,3)
450 PRINT "NO OPINION"; TAB( 14);C(3,1); TAB( 20);C(3,2);
    TAB( 26);C(3,3)
```

Note: Even though we changed the questionnaire, we didn't have to change the crucial vote-counting statement in line 320.

19. Following is a LISTing of the modified program and new DATA statements for the questionnaire in frame 18. You be the computer and print the output for the program when it is RUN.

```
100 REM ***VOTE COUNTING, TWO QUESTIONS
110 HOME : DIM C(3,3)
200 REM ***INITIALIZE: SET ALL COUNTS TO ZERO
210 FOR K = 1 TO 3: FOR L = 1 TO 2: LET C(K,L) = 0: NEXT L,K
300 REM ***READ AND COUNT VOTES
310 READ V,A: IF V = - 1 THEN 410
320 LET C(V,A) = C(V,A) + 1: GOTO 310
400 REM ***PRINT THE RESULTS
410 PRINT "CANDIDATE"; TAB( 14)"DEM."; TAB( 20)"REP."; TAB( 26)"OTHER"
420 PRINT
430 PRINT "SAM SMOOTHE"; TAB( 14);C(1,1); TAB( 20);C(1,2);
    TAB( 26);C(1,3)
440 PRINT "GABBY GRUFF"; TAB( 14);C(2,1); TAB( 20);C(2,2);
    TAB( 26);C(2,3)
450 PRINT "NO OPINION"; TAB( 14);C(3,1); TAB( 20);C(3,2);
    TAB( 26);C(3,3)
900 REM ** VOTE AND POLITICAL AFFILIATION DATA IN PAIRS.
    FLAGS = -1,-1
910 DATA  1,3, 1,2, 2,1, 2,3, 3,3, 3,3, 3,2, 3,3, 1,3
920 DATA  2,1, 3,1, 1,3, 2,2, 3,1, 3,1, 2,1, 2,3, 3,2
930 DATA  1,3, 1,1, 1,1, 2,3, 3,2, 3,2, 2,2, 2,1, 1,3
940 DATA  3,3, 3,1, 2,3, 1,2, 2,1, 1,2, 1,2, 3,1, 1,1
950 DATA  3,1, 2,3, 3,3, 1,2, 1,1, 2,2, 2,1, 3,2, -1,-1
RUN
```

_____
_____
_____
_____

__ __ __ __ __ __ __

```
]RUN
CANDIDATE     DEM.  REP.  OTHER

SAM SMOOTHE    4     5     5
GABBY GRUFF    6     3     5
NO OPINION     6     5     5
```

20. Look at this section of the program.

```
430 PRINT "SAM SMOOTHE"; TAB( 14);C(1,1); TAB( 20);C(1,2);
    TAB( 26);C(1,3)
440 PRINT "GABBY GRUFF"; TAB( 14);C(2,1); TAB( 20);C(2,2);
    TAB( 26);C(2,3)
450 PRINT "NO OPINION"; TAB( 14);C(3,1); TAB( 20);C(3,2);
    TAB( 26);C(3,3)
```

We have used the subscripted variables with the actual numerical values for the subscripts. Instead, we could have used a FOR-NEXT loop to print the results for each candidate and no opinion, and could do this using just three multiple-statement lines.

If our display screen had more than 40 character positions across a line and also allowed more than 3 automatic print positions for PRINT statement output with comma spacing, the program could look like this:

```
430 PRINT "SAM SMOOTHE",  : FOR X=1 TO 3 : PRINT C(1,X),  : NEXT: PRINT
440 PRINT "GABBY GRUFF",  : FOR X=1 TO 3 : PRINT C(2,X),  : NEXT: PRINT
450 PRINT "NO OPINION",   : FOR X=1 TO 3 : PRINT C(3,X),  : NEXT
```

However, since we have 4 columns in the display (with headings CANDIDATE, DEM., REP., OTHER), we also must find a way to have the spacing of the numbers across the line match up with the headings. The first C array value [C(1,1), which is 4] should line up with DEM. at TAB(14). The second value [C(1,2), which is 5] should line up with REP. at TAB(20). The next value should line up under OTHER at TAB(26). After TAB(14), notice that each of these columns is 6 character positions past the previous one. The FOR variable X can be used not only to select the proper C array value to display, but also to select the proper TAB position to display it. Look at the TAB function in line 432.

```
430 PRINT "SAM SMOOTHE";
431 FOR X = 1 TO 3
432 PRINT   TAB( 14 + 6 * (X − 1));C(1,X);
433 NEXT
434 PRINT
```

Where will the TAB function cause the value of C(1,X) to be displayed for the following?
(a) X = 1: position _____
(b) X = 2: position _____
(c) X = 3: position _____

(a) 14
(b) 20
(c) 26

21. In the program segment in the previous frame, notice the semicolon at the end of lines 430 and 432. This is one place where the semicolon is essential. You have seen it used previously in "counting" loop programs:

    30 PRINT N; " ";

This tells the computer to display the next PRINT statement output on the same line. The same principle applies here. After the three values of C(1,X) have been displayed, then a blank PRINT statement (line 434) "cancels" the semicolon, and the next PRINT output is displayed on the next line.

Now write a multiple-statement line that will cause the vote breakdown for GABBY GRUFF to be properly displayed under the political affiliation headings in this vote-counting program.

440 PRINT "GABBY GRUFF";

441 _____

— — — — — — — — —

441 FOR X = 1 TO 3: PRINT TAB(14 + 6 * (X − 1));C(2,X);:NEXT X: PRINT

22. Complete the program lines for NO OPINION in the vote-counting program, using automated TAB.

450 _____

451 _____

— — — — — — — — —

450 PRINT "NO OPINION";
451 FOR X = 1 TO 3: PRINT TAB(14 + 6 * (X − 1));C(3,X);:NEXT X: PRINT

Here is a listing of the program (with the DATA statements omitted) with all the changes you have accumulated. Try it out.

```
100 REM ** VOTE COUNT, TWO QUESTIONS
110 HOME : DIM C(3,3)
200 REM ** INITIALIZE: SET ALL COUNTS TO ZERO
210 FOR K = 1 TO 3: FOR L = 1 TO 3: LET C(K,L) = 0: NEXT L,K
300 REM ** READ AND COUNT VOTES
310 READ V,A: IF V = -1 THEN 410
320 LET C(V,A) = C(V,A) + 1: GOTO 310
400 REM **PRINT THE RESULTS
410 PRINT "CANDIDATE"; TAB( 14)"REP."; TAB( 20)"DEM."; TAB( 26)"OTHER"
420 PRINT
430 PRINT "SAM SMOOTHE";
431 FOR X = 1 TO 3
432 PRINT  TAB( 14 + 6 * (X - 1));C(1,X);
433 NEXT
434 PRINT
440 PRINT "GABBY GRUFF";
441 FOR X = 1 TO 3: PRINT  TAB( 14 + 6 * (X - 1));C(2,X);: NEXT : PRINT
450 PRINT "NO OPINION";
451 FOR X = 1 TO 3: PRINT  TAB( 14 + 6 * (X - 1));C(3,X);: NEXT : PRINT
```

23. Just as for one-dimensional arrays, the *subscripts* for variables that identify elements in a two-dimensional array *can start at zero*. Our current version of the program has four headings. Let's add another column to the report that gives the total number of votes for each candidate, as well as the breakdown by party affiliation. These totals should be accumulated in C(1,0), C(2,0), and C(3,0).

To display the values stored in the C array, now the report section of the program will use FOR statements that go from 0 to 3. This will also simplify the "automated" TAB function slightly:

```
TAB(14 + X * 6)
```

Make the changes to the previous program to create the display shown in the following RUN, including the addition of totals accumulation, chart headings, etc. You should look carefully through the program to be sure you make all changes necessary to accomplish this. (*Hints:* Initialize all elements of the array, accumulate the votes for each candidate regardless of political affiliation in the section or subroutine called READ AND COUNT VOTES, and make the necessary changes in the routine that prints the report.)

```
]RUN
CANDIDATE       TOTAL   REP.   DEM.   OTHER

SAM SMOOTHE     14      4      5      5
GABBY GRUFF     14      6      3      5
NO OPINION      16      6      5      5
```

The following listing (DATA statements omitted) has the modified or added lines checkmarked.

```
100 REM ** VOTE COUNT, TWO QUESTIONS
110 HOME : DIM C(3,3)
200 REM ** INITIALIZE: SET ALL COUNTS TO ZERO
✓210 FOR K = 0 TO 3: FOR L = 0 TO 3: LET C(K,L) = 0: NEXT L,K
300 REM ** READ AND COUNT VOTES
✓310 READ V,A: IF V = -1 THEN 330
320 LET C(V,A) = C(V,A) + 1: GOTO 310
✓330 FOR K = 1 TO 3: FOR L = 1 TO 3: LET C(K,0) = C(K,0) + C(K,L):
    NEXT L,K
400 REM ::PRINT THE RESULTS
✓410 PRINT "CANDIDATE";
✓411 PRINT  TAB( 14)"TOTAL"; TAB( 20)"REP."; TAB( 26)"DEM.";
    TAB( 32)"OTHER"
420 PRINT
✓430 PRINT "SAM SMOOTHE";
✓431 FOR X = 0 TO 3
✓432 PRINT  TAB( 14 + 6 * X);C(1,X);
433 NEXT
434 PRINT
✓440 PRINT "GABBY GRUFF";
✓441 FOR X = 0 TO 3: PRINT  TAB( 14 + 6 * X);C(2,X);: NEXT : PRINT
✓450 PRINT "NO OPINION";
✓451 FOR X = 0 TO 3: PRINT  TAB( 14 + 6 * X);C(3,X);: NEXT : PRINT
```

24. Do you remember the problem on counting candy bars? You might want to review it in Chapter 9, frames 36 to 52, before we go on.

Before, we were selling one chocolate candy bar for $1.00, on which the profit was 55¢. Now let's add another product—a bag of jelly beans which sells for 50¢, on which we profit 30¢. Our job is to reprogram our computer to tabulate individual sales and overall profits. Here's the report we'd like to produce.

```
]RUN
KID ID#      TOTAL $    CHOCOLATE   JEL.BEANS
1            0          0           0
2            3          3           0
3            0          0           0
4            6          3           6
5            10         6           8
6            0          0           0
7            0          0           0
8            12         6           12

TOTALS:      31         18          26

PROFITS:     17.7       9.9         7.8
```

(a) From the report above, who had the greatest overall dollar sales? _____

(b) Who sold the most chocolate bars? _____

(c) The most jelly beans? _____

(d) Can you tell who made us the most profit? _____

— — — — — — — — — —

(a) 8
(b) 5 and 8
(c) 8
(d) not directly from the report   (It's number 8.)

25. For recordkeeping purposes we will prepare some preprinted forms to keep track of who takes what. Now, when one of the kids asks for candy we fill in a form like the one following.

Name	Danny
ID no.	4
1. Milk chocolate	3
2. Jelly beans	6

This shows that Danny (number 4) took 3 chocolate bars and 6 bags of jelly beans. When we convert that into computer data we use the following format.

    kid number, candy number (1 or 2), quantity

Thus, to show the data on this one slip requires 6 data items.

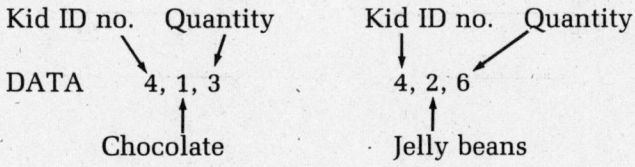

(Notice how we designed the form to conform to our system of data entry!)

From the three forms below, complete the DATA statements. Include end-of-data flags.

ID no. 5	ID no. 2	ID no. 8
1. 5	1. 3	1. 6
2. 8	2. 0	2. 12

```
900 REM **KID ID NUMBER, CANDY ID NUMBER, QUANTITY
910 DATA 4,1,3, 4,2,6
920 _____
930 _____
```

These data are not even necessary, since this kid didn't take any jelly beans to sell.

```
920 DATA 5,1,6, 5,2,8, 2,1,3, 2,2,0, 8,1,6, 8,2,12
930 DATA −1,−1,−1
```

End-of-data flag

26. Our array will look like this.

Array A.   1 = Chocolate   2 = Jelly beans

1 = Jerry

2 = Bobby

3 = Mary

4 = Danny

5 = Karl

6 = Mimi

7 = Doug

8 = Scott

Here is another way to visualize the same A-array.

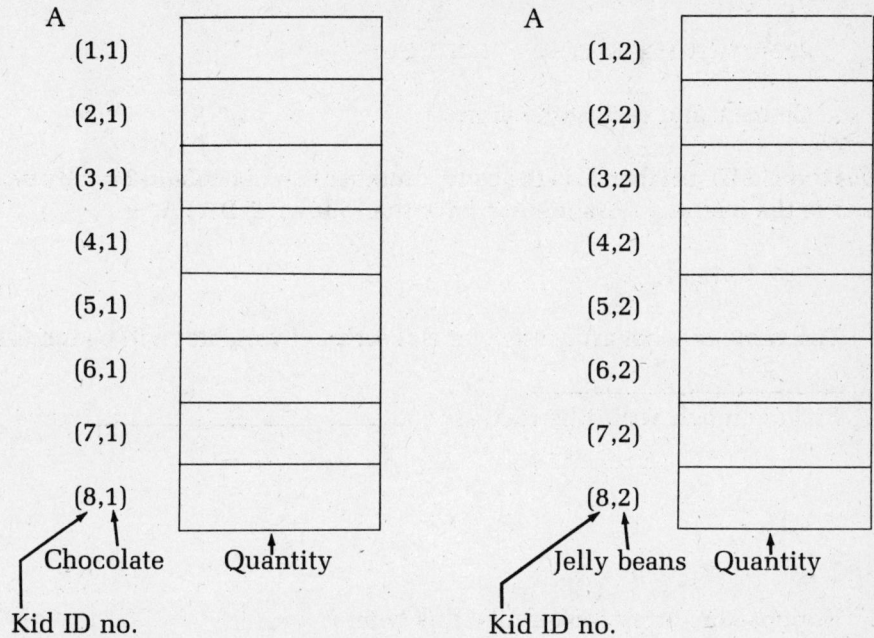

Your first task is to write the statement(s) to initialize the array and zero it out, that is, set the dimensions and set the values for all the variables to zero.

```
100 REM **CANDY BAR & JELLY BEAN COUNTER
110 REM **INITIALIZE

120 _____
```
— — — — — — — — — —
```
120 DIM A(8,2) : FOR X=1 TO 8 : FOR Y=1 TO 2 : A(X,Y)=0 :
    NEXT Y,X
```

27. Now READ a set of data (K,C,Q) and test for the end-of-data condition. When you encounter the end-of-data flag, jump to 410.

```
200 REM **READ DATA AND TEST FOR FLAG

210 _____
```
— — — — — — — — — —
```
210 READ K,C,Q : IF K=-1 THEN 410
```

28. The heart of this program is found in line 220, where the "accumulation" takes place.

```
220 A(K,C)=A(K,C)+Q : GOTO 210
                               ↑
                    Go back and read some more.
```

K is the kid ID number, C is the candy number (1 = chocolate, 2 = jelly beans), and Q is the quantity. Assume we have the following DATA.

```
910 DATA 4, 1, 3
```

(a) The value of what array element (subscripted variable) will be increased? _____

(b) By how much will it be increased? _____

_ _ _ _ _ _ _ _ _ _

(a) A(4,1)
(b) 3

29. Suppose the array looked like this before:

A			A	
(1,1)	7		(1,2)	10
(2,1)	0		(2,2)	0
(3,1)	6		(3,2)	8
(4,1)	5		(4,2)	12
(5,1)	3		(5,2)	0
(6,1)	6		(6,2)	8
(7,1)	8		(7,2)	9
(8,1)	3		(8,2)	10

Chocolate   Quantity   Jelly beans   Quantity
Kid ID no.   Kid ID no.

DOUBLE SUBSCRIPTS

How will it look *after* accumulating the data in these DATA statements?

```
910 DATA 4,1,3, 4,2,6
920 DATA 5,1,6, 5,2,8, 2,1,3, 2,2,0, 8,1,6, 8,2,12
```

A

(1,1)	
(2,1)	
(3,1)	
(4,1)	
(5,1)	
(6,1)	
(7,1)	
(8,1)	

A

(1,2)	
(2,2)	
(3,2)	
(4,2)	
(5,2)	
(6,2)	
(7,2)	
(8,2)	

A

(1,1)	7
(2,1)	3
(3,1)	6
(4,1)	8
(5,1)	9
(6,1)	6
(7,1)	8
(8,1)	9

A

(1,2)	10
(2,2)	0
(3,2)	8
(4,2)	18
(5,2)	8
(6,2)	8
(7,2)	9
(8,2)	22

30. Here is our program so far.

```
100 REM **CANDY BAR & JELLY BEAN COUNTER
110 REM **INITIALIZE
120 DIM A(8,2) : FOR X=1 TO 8 : FOR Y=1 TO 2 : A(X,Y)=0 : NEXT Y,X
200 REM **READ DATA AND TEST FOR FLAG
210 READ K,C,Q : IF K=-1 THEN 410
220 A(K,C)=A(K,C)+Q : GOTO 210
900 REM **KID ID NUMBER, CANDY ID NUMBER, QUANTITY
910 DATA 4,1,3, 4,2,6
920 DATA 5,1,6, 5,2,8, 2,1,3, 2,2,0, 8,1,6, 8,2,12
930 DATA -1,-1,-1
```

Now let's print a preliminary report like the one in frame 24; but without any totals. You fill in the blanks in the following program. This is how the report should look when the program is RUN.

```
RUN
KID ID NO.       CHOCOLATE      JELLY BEANS
1                0              0
2                3              0
3                0              0
4                3              6
5                6              8
6                0              0
7                0              0
8                6              12
```

400 REM **REPORT #1

410 PRINT "KID ID NO.", _____

420 FOR K=1 TO 8

430 PRINT K, ◄────────── The comma is important.

440 FOR C=1 TO _____

450 PRINT _____ , ◄────── The comma is important.

460 NEXT C

470 PRINT

480 NEXT _____

─ ─ ─ ─ ─ ─ ─ ─ ─ ─

```
410 PRINT  KID ID NO.", "CHOCOLATE", "JELLY BEANS"
440 FOR C=1 TO 2
450 PRINT A(K,C),
480 NEXT K  ◄────────── The K is optional, but not the NEXT.
```

31. In frame 30, why are the commas placed at the end of lines 430 and 450?

———————

to suppress the normal carriage return after the PRINT (that is, to keep the computer output on the same line)

32. Why did we include line 470 PRINT where we did? _____

———————

to force a carriage return (start a new line of printout), so the next KID ID no. will be printed in the correct place or position when line 420 is executed again

33. Running our program now gives these results.

```
RUN
KID ID NO.        CHOCOLATE         JELLY BEANS
1                 0                 0
2                 3                 0
3                 0                 0
4                 3                 6
5                 6                 8
6                 0                 0
7                 0                 0
8                 6                 12
```

Now, let's complete the program so it will print everything shown in frame 24. When we DIMensioned our array DIM (8,2) it included the 0,0 elements shown below. We are going to use these zero elements to accumulate totals.

Total units sold will go here

Total sales will go here

(0,0) (0,1) (0,2)
(1,0)
(2,0)
(3,0)
(4,0)
(5,0)
(6,0)
(7,0)
(8,0)

You fill in the blank lines in the following program. Line 120 is fixed to set all array elements (boxes) to zero, starting at the 0,0 element. Line 320 adds the total sales per kid (remember, jelly beans sell for 50¢ per bag). And line 350 adds units sold.

```
120 DIM A(8,2) : FOR X=0 TO 8 : FOR Y=0 TO 2 : A(X,Y)=0 : NEXT Y,X
210 READ K,C,Q : IF K=-1 THEN 310
220 LET A(K)=A(K)+Q : GOTO 210
300 REM **TOTAL OF UNITS SOLD AND TOTAL SALES IN DOLLARS

310 FOR K=1 TO _____
320 A(K,0)=A(K,1)*1.00+A(K,2)*.50
330 A(0,0)=A(0,0)+A(K,0)

340 FOR C= _____

350 A(0,C)=A(0,C)+A(K, _____ )
360 NEXT C

370 _____
380 REM **CALCULATE PROFITS

390 P1=A(0,1)*.55 : P2= _____ : P=P1+P2
```

```
310 FOR K=1 TO 8
340 FOR C=1 TO 2
350 A(0,C)=A(0,C)+A(K,C)
370 NEXT K
390 P1=A(0,1)*.55 : P2=A(0,2)*.30 : P = P1+P2
```

34. Did you understand what went on in lines 320, 330, and 350? If not, go back and review the problem a little more. These statements are *crucial* to your complete understanding of this type of problem.

Write the *line numbers* in the labeled boxes below to show which lines generate values for those boxes.

(0,0)		(0,1)		(0,2)	
(1,0)					
(2,0)					
(3,0)					
(4,0)					
(5,0)					
(6,0)					
(7,0)					
(8,0)					

(0,0)	330	(0,1)	350	(0,2)	350
(1,0)	320				
(2,0)	320				
(3,0)	320				
(4,0)	320				
(5,0)	320				
(6,0)	320				
(7,0)	320				
(8,0)	320				

35. In frame 33, what does line 330 do?

    330 A(0,0)=A(0,0)+A(K,0)

———————

It accumulates grand total sales in A(0,0).

36. In line 390, how would you describe what the statement P=P1+P2 accomplishes?

    390 P1=A(0,1)*.55 : P2=A(0,2)*.30 : P=P1+P2

———————

It computes total profits and assigns them to variable P.

37. Time to redo our report printing section to update *everything* shown in the following RUN (the same RUN as in frame 24). Fill in the blanks.

```
]RUN
KID ID#    TOTAL $     CHOCOLATE    JEL.BEANS
1          0           0            0
2          3           3            0
3          0           0            0
4          6           3            6
5          10          6            8
6          0           0            0
7          0           0            0
8          12          6            12

TOTALS:    31          18           26

PROFITS:   17.7        9.9          7.8
```

```
400 REM***REPORT VERSION #2

410 PRINT "KID ID NO." _____

411 _____

420 FOR K=1 TO 8

430 PRINT _____

440 FOR C= _____

450 PRINT A _____
460 NEXT C

470 _____

480 _____
490 PRINT

500 PRINT "TOTALS:", _____
510 PRINT

520 PRINT "PROFITS:" _____
```
———————————
```
400 REM ** REPORT VERSION #2
410 PRINT "KID ID#";
411 PRINT  TAB( 10);"TOTAL $"; TAB( 20);"CHOCOLATE"; TAB( 30);
    "JEL.BEANS"
420 FOR K = 1 TO 8
430 PRINT K;
440 FOR C = 0 TO 2
450 PRINT  TAB( 10 + 10 * C);A(K,C);
460 NEXT C
470 PRINT
480 NEXT K
490 PRINT
500 PRINT "TOTALS:"; TAB( 10)A(0,0); TAB( 20);A(0,1); TAB( 30);
    A(0,2)
510 PRINT
520 PRINT "PROFITS:"; TAB( 10);P; TAB( 20);P1; TAB( 30);P2
```

Now the program is done and the RUN should look just like the one above. Following is a complete listing of the program.

```
100 REM **CANDY BAR & JELLY COUNTER W/TOTAL $
110 HOME : REM ** INITIALIZE
120 DIM A(8,2): FOR X = 0 TO 8: FOR Y = 0 TO 2:A(X,Y) = 0: NEXT Y,X
200 REM ** READ DATA AND TEST FOR FLAG (-1)
210 READ K,C,Q: IF K = - 1 THEN 310
220 LET A(K,C) = A(K,C) + Q: GOTO 210
300 REM ** TOTAL OF UNITS SOLD AND OF SALES IN DOLLARS
310 FOR K = 1 TO 8
320 LET A(K,0) = A(K,1) * 1.00 + A(K,2) * .50
330 LET A(0,0) = A(0,0) + A(K,0)
340 FOR C = 1 TO 2
350 LET A(0,C) = A(0,C) + A(K,C)
360 NEXT C
370 NEXT K
380 REM ** CALCULATE PROFITS
390 LET P1 = A(0,1) * .55: LET P2 = A(0,2) * .30: LET P = P1 + P2
400 REM ** REPORT VERSION #2
410 PRINT "KID ID#";
411 PRINT  TAB( 10);"TOTAL $"; TAB( 20);"CHOCOLATE"; TAB( 30);"JEL.BEANS"
420 FOR K = 1 TO 8
430 PRINT K;
440 FOR C = 0 TO 2
450 PRINT  TAB( 10 + 10 * C);A(K,C);
460 NEXT C
470 PRINT
480 NEXT K
490 PRINT
500 PRINT "TOTALS:"; TAB( 10)A(0,0); TAB( 20);A(0,1); TAB( 30);A(0,2)
510 PRINT
520 PRINT "PROFITS:"; TAB( 10);P; TAB( 20);P1; TAB( 30);P2
900 REM ** KID ID# (1 TO 8), CANDY ID# (1=CHOC., 2=J.BEANS), QUANTITY
910 DATA 4,1,3,4,2,6
920 DATA 5,1,6,5,2,8,2,1,3,2,2,0,8,1,6,8,2,12
930 DATA -1,-1,-1
```

38. Here is one final double-array application. In a small class of 8 students, each student has taken 4 quizzes. The scores are shown below.

	Quiz 1	Quiz 2	Quiz 3	Quiz 4
Student 1	65	57	71	75
Student 2	80	90	91	88
Student 3	78	82	77	86
Student 4	45	38	44	46
Student 5	83	82	79	85
Student 6	70	68	83	59
Student 7	98	92	100	97
Student 8	85	73	80	77

Let S(B,J) be the score obtained by student B on quiz J. S(5,2) is the score obtained by student _____ on quiz _____. What is the value of S(5,2)? _____

— — — — — — — — —

5, 2; 82

39. Another class might have 30 students and 5 quizzes per student. Still another class might have 23 students and 7 quizzes per student, and so on. Let's begin a program to read scores for N students and Q quizzes per student.

```
100 REM **QUIZ-SCORE PROGRAM
110 DIM S(50,10)
```

The DIM statement permits up to _____ students and up to _____ quizzes.

— — — — — — — — —

50, 10

40. Next, we want to read the values of N and Q for a particular set of scores—in this case, the scores shown in frame 38. For this set of scores the value of N (number of students) is _____ and the value of Q (number of quizzes) is _____.

— — — — — — — — —

8, 4

41. We will put the values of N and Q and the scores in DATA statements. Now the program looks like this.

```
100 REM **QUIZ-SCORE PROGRAM
110 DIM S(50,10)

900 REM **VALUES OF N AND Q FOLLOWED BY SCORES
905 DATA 8,4  ←———————————————— Values of N,Q
911 DATA 65,57,71,75  ⎤
912 DATA 80,90,91,88  ⎥
913 DATA 78,82,77,86  ⎥
914 DATA 45,38,44,46  ⎬  N by Q array of quiz scores
915 DATA 83,82,79,85  ⎥  from frame 38
916 DATA 70,68,83,59  ⎥
917 DATA 98,92,100,97 ⎥
918 DATA 85,73,80,77  ⎦
```

Your turn. Complete line 120, below, to READ the values of N and Q.

    120 _____

— — — — — — — — — —

    120 READ N,Q (That's all there is to it!)

42. The values of N and Q read by line 120 (in frame 41) will be read from which DATA statement? Line _____.

— — — — — — — — — —

905

43. Now let's read the N by Q array of scores using FOR-NEXT loops. Fill in the blanks.

    130 FOR X=1 TO N: FOR Y=_____:READ_____NEXT Y:NEXT X

— — — — — — — — — —

    130 FOR X=1 TO N: FOR Y=1 TO Q:READ S(X,Y):NEXT Y:NEXT X

44. The numerical values read by line 130 are stored in the DATA statements, lines _____ through _____.

— — — — — — — — — —

911, 918

45. Now that we have the array in the computer, what shall we do with it? One thing someone might want is the average score for each student. Let's do it, beginning at line 200.

```
200 REM **COMPUTE AND PRINT AVERAGES FOR EACH STUDENT
210 PRINT "STUDENT #","AVERAGE"
220 FOR B=1 TO N  ⎫
230 LET T=0       ⎪
240 FOR J=1 TO Q  ⎬ ── Compute total of quiz scores for student B.
250 LET T=T+S(B,J)⎪
260 NEXT J        ⎭
270 LET A=T/Q  ◄──────── Compute average for student B.
280 PRINT B,A  ◄──────── Print student number and average.
290 NEXT B     ◄──────── Go back and compute scores for next stu-
                         dent.
```

Lines 230 through 280 are done for each student. That is, for B=1, then B=2, and so on up to B=N. For B=1, what is the value of T computed by lines 230 through 260? T=_____.

---

268. This is the sum of the 4 scores for student 1. Remember, Q=4. Therefore, line 250 will be done for J=1, J=2, J=3, and J=4.

46. For B=1, what is the value of A computed by line 270?

A = T/Q = _____.

---

67 (A = T/Q = 268/4 = 67)

47. Here is the complete program and a RUN.

```
100 REM **QUIZ-SCORE PROGRAM
110 DIM S(50,10)
120 READ N,Q
130 FOR X=1 TO N : FOR Y=1 TO Q : READS (X,Y) : NEXT Y : NEXT X
200 REM **COMPUTE AND PRINT AVERAGES FOR EACH STUDENT
210 PRINT "STUDENT #","AVERAGE"
220 FOR B=1 TO N
230 LET T=0
240 FOR J=1 TO Q
250 LET T=T+S(B,J)
260 NEXT J
270 LET A=T/Q
280 PRINT B,A
290 NEXT B
900 REM **VALUES OF N AND Q FOLLOWED BY SCORES
905 DATA 8,4
911 DATA 65,57,71,75
912 DATA 80,90,91,88
913 DATA 78,82,77,86
914 DATA 45,38,44,46
915 DATA 83,82,79,85
916 DATA 70,68,83,59
917 DATA 98,92,100,97
918 DATA 85,73,80,77

RUN

STUDENT #       AVERAGE
1               67
2               87.25
3               80.75
4               43.25
5               82.25
6               70
7               96.75
8               78.75
```

Your turn. Beginning with line 300, write a program segment to compute and print the average score for each quiz. For the data used in the program, the results might look like this.

```
RUN
QUIZ #          AVERAGE
1               75.5
2               72.75
3               78.125
4               76.625
```

- - - - - - - - - - -

```
300 REM **COMPUTE AND PRINT AVERAGE OF EACH QUIZ
310 PRINT "QUIZ #","AVERAGE"
320 FOR J=1 TO Q
330 LET T=0
340 FOR B=1 TO N
350 LET T=T+S(B,J)
360 NEXT B
370 LET A=T/N
380 PRINT J,A
390 NEXT J
```

48. Suppose some students take a multiple-choice quiz, 10 questions with 4 possible answers per question. We want to know how many students gave answer number 1 to question number 1, how many gave answer number 2 to question number 1, and so on.

Here are the answers given by 7 students. Each set of answers is in a DATA statement. The last DATA statement is a "fictitious student" and really means "end of data."

```
911 DATA 2,3,1,1,1,2,4,3,4,1     In each line of data, the first num-
912 DATA 2,3,2,4,1,2,4,2,1,1     ber is the answer to question 1, the
913 DATA 2,3,3,1,1,4,3,3,4,1     second number is the answer to
914 DATA 3,2,4,1,1,2,3,3,4,1     question 2, and so on.
915 DATA 2,3,4,1,1,3,4,3,4,1
916 DATA 2,1,2,3,1,2,4,3,4,2
917 DATA 3,4,1,1,1,4,3,1,4,2
918 DATA -1,0,0,0,0,0,0,0,0,0    "Fictitious student"
```

Student 1 (line 911) gave answer 1 to question 3. Student 5 (line 915) gave answer _____ to question 9. Student 7 (line 917) gave answer _____ to question 1.

——————————

4;3

49. Complete the following table showing the number of students giving each answer (1, 2, 3, or 4) to questions 1, 2, and 3.

	Answer 1	Answer 2	Answer 3	Answer 4
Question 1	0	5	2	0
Question 2	1	1	___	___
Question 3	___	___	___	___

——————————

       4 1
2 2 1 2

50. In frame 49, with your help, we have shown how the 7 students answered the first 3 questions. The totals look like a 3 by 4 array. If we had continued for all 10 questions the totals would have looked like a _____ -by-4 array.

——————————

10

51. Let's define an array T with 10 rows and 4 columns to hold the totals. Complete the following DIM statement.

    100 REM **QUIZ ANALYSIS PROGRAM

    110 DIM _____

——————————

    100 DIM T(10,4)

52. For each student there are 10 answers. Let's define a *list* of answers A(1) through A(10). Complete the following DIM statement.

    120 DIM _____

——————————

    120 DIM A(10)

53. We can save space by *combining* the two DIM statements into one DIM statement.

Note that a comma is used to separate T(10,4) and A(10).

```
110 DIM T(10,4),A(10)
```

The above DIM statement defines a _____ called T with at most 10 rows and 4 columns, and a _____ called A with at most 10 members.

— — — — — — — — —

two-dimensional array, matrix, or table
one-dimensional array, list, or vector

54. Here is the beginning of a program to read the students' answers and compute tht totals array.

```
100 REM **QUIZ ANALYSIS PROGRAM
110 DIM T(10,4),A(10)
```

Next, we want to initialize the totals array. That is, we want it to be a zero array. You do it.

```
120 REM **SET ALL TOTALS TO ZERO

130 _____
```

— — — — — — — — —

```
130 FOR X=1 TO 10:FOR Y=1 TO 4:LET T(X,Y)=0:NEXT X:NEXT Y
```

55. Write a statement to read the *list* A of answers for one student.

```
140 REM **READ ONE SET OF ANSWERS

150 _____
```

— — — — — — — — —

```
150 FOR X=1 TO 10:READ A(X):NEXT X
```

DOUBLE SUBSCRIPTS

56. Now, is this a real student or a fictitious student? Recall that a fictitious student signals the end of data. If this is the case, we want to print the answers, beginning with line 310. Complete the IF-THEN statement.

```
160 REM **CHECK FOR END OF DATA

170 IF _____ THEN 310
```
————————

  A(1)=−1

57. If the data are for a real student, we want to update the running tally in the T array. We did it this way.

```
180 REM **UPDATE THE TOTALS ARRAY
190 FOR Q=1 TO 10
200 LET T(Q,A(Q))=T(Q,A(Q))+1
210 NEXT Q
```

Here are the answers for one student. These are the values of A(1) through A(10).

  2,3,1,1,1,2,4,3,4,1

Suppose Q = 1. Then A(Q)=____ and T(Q,A(Q)) is T(____,____).

————————

2, T(1,2) (since Q=1 and A(Q)=2)

58. In the above case (frame 57), what happens when the computer obeys line 200? _____
————————

The total in T(1,2) is increased by 1. (It's just like counting votes!)

59. Since line 200 is in a FOR-NEXT loop, it will be done for each value of Q specified by the FOR statement. That is, it will be done for A = 1, 2, 3, 4, 5, 6, 7, 8, 9, and 10. When Q = 10, which element of the T matrix is increased by one? T(____,____).
————————

T(10,A(10)) or T(10,1) for the data in frame 48.

60. Let's move on. After tallying the answers for one student, we want the computer to return to line 150 and read another set of answers. (See frame 55.)

```
220 REM **GO BACK FOR ANOTHER SET OF ANSWERS
230 GOTO 150
```

Then the IF-THEN statement (frame 56) is encountered again. The IF-THEN statement causes the computer to go to line 310 if a fictitious student has been read. In that case, we want to print the headings and results, then stop. First, here is the report we want to produce.

```
     RUN
     QUESTION    NUMBER OF STUDENTS
     NUMBER:     CHOSING ANSWER #:
                 ONE   TWO    THREE  FOUR
     1           0     5      2      0
     2           1     1      4      1
     3           2     3      0      2
     4           4     0      1      2
     5           7     0      0      0
     6           0     5      1      1
     7           0     0      2      5
     8           1     2      4      0
     9           2     0      0      5
     10          5     2      0      0
```

Now complete the program segment below to generate the report.

```
300 REM ** PRINT THE TOTALS ARRAY
310 PRINT "QUESTION"; TAB( 15);"NUMBER OF STUDENTS"
311 PRINT "NUMBER:" TAB( 15);"CHOSING ANSWER #:"
320 PRINT   TAB( 15);"ONE"; TAB( 21);"TWO"; TAB( 27);"THREE;
    TAB( 33);"FOUR"

330 FOR X = _____

340 FOR Y = _____
350 NEXT Y: PRINT : NEXT X
```

———————

Here is a complete LIST and RUN, including lines 330 and 340.

]LIST

```
100 REM ** QUIZ ANALYSIS PROGRAM
110 HOME : DIM T(10,4)
120 REM ** SET ALL TOTALS TO ZERO
130 FOR X = 1 TO 10: FOR Y = 1 TO 4: LET T(X,Y) = 0: NEXT Y,X
140 REM ** READ ONE SET OF ANSWERS
150 FOR X = 1 TO 10: READ A(X): NEXT X
160 REM ** CHECK FOR END OF DATA
170 IF A(1) = - 1 THEN 310
180 REM ** UPDATE THE TOTALS ARRAY
190 FOR Q=1 TO 10
200 LET T(Q,A(Q))=T(Q,A(Q)) + 1
210 NEXT Q
220 REM **GO BACK FOR ANOTHER SET OF ANSWERS
230 GOTO 150
300 REM ** PRINT THE TOTALS ARRAY
310 PRINT "QUESTION"; TAB( 15);"NUMBER OF STUDENTS"
311 PRINT "NUMBER:" TAB( 15);"CHOSING ANSWER #:"
320 PRINT  TAB( 15);"ONE"; TAB( 21);"TWO"; TAB( 27);
    "THREE"; TAB( 33);"FOUR"
330 FOR X = 1 TO 10: PRINT  TAB( 6);X;
340 FOR Y = 1 TO 4: PRINT  TAB( 15 + 6 * (Y - 1));T(X,Y);
350 NEXT Y: PRINT : NEXT X
900 REM ** STUDENT ANSWERS TO MULTIPLE CHOICE QUESTIONS
911 DATA 2,3,1,1,1,2,4,3,4,1
912 DATA 2,3,2,4,1,2,4,2,1,1
913 DATA 2,3,2,4,1,2,4,2,1,1
914 DATA 3,2,4,1,1,2,3,3,4,1
915 DATA 2,3,4,1,1,3,4,3,4,1
916 DATA 2,1,2,3,1,2,4,3,4,2
917 DATA 3,4,1,1,1,4,3,1,4,2
918 DATA -1,0,0,0,0,0,0,0,0,0
```

]RUN

QUESTION NUMBER:	NUMBER OF STUDENTS CHOSING ANSWER #:			
	ONE	TWO	THREE	FOUR
1	0	5	2	0
2	1	1	4	1
3	2	3	0	2
4	4	0	1	2
5	7	0	0	0
6	0	5	1	1
7	0	0	2	5
8	1	2	4	0
9	2	0	0	5
10	5	2	0	0

Self-Test

Good for you! You have reached the Chapter 10 Self-Test. These problems will help you review the BASIC instructions you have learned for dealing with arrays of numbers, using variables with double subscripts.

As you have undoubtedly noticed, the programs are getting longer and more involved. Expect to spend some time working out the solutions to the programs in this Self-Test. However, you will find that as your understanding of arrays for storing and manipulating information becomes clearer, writing programs using arrays becomes easier and faster, and practice really helps.

1. Indicate which of the following are legal BASIC doubly-subscripted variables.

   ___(a) X(2+2)   ___(b) X(5,5)
   ___(c) X1(100,100)   ___(d) X(A+B,C)
   ___(e) X(X(1,2),X(2,1))   ___(f) X(A,A)

   Questions 2 through 7 refer to the following array, A.

	Column 1	Column 2
Row 1	1	2
Row 2	3	4
Row 3	5	6

2. What are the dimensions of A? ___,___
3. Write a DIMension statement for A, using line number 100.

   100 _____
4. What variable locates the "box" in row 3, column 2 of A? ___
5. What is the value of the following?

   (a) A(1,1) _____   (b) A(3,1) _____
6. Let X = 2, Y = 3. What is the value of the following?

   (a) A(X,X) _____   (b) A(X+1,Y−1) _____
7. What is the value of A(A(1,2),A(2,1)−1)? _____
8. Write a program which uses two FOR-NEXT loops to fill a 10-by-10 array (M) with zeros.
9. Your city officials seek to conduct a census of the citizenry. Among other things, they want to analyze the age and sex breakdown of the community. They ask you to program your home computer to take data from the form below and prepare a report like the RUN shown.

CITY CENSUS REPORT
DATA FORM
(check one box for each question)

Question one—age group
- [ ] 1. Less than 10
- [ ] 2. 10–15
- [ ] 3. 16–21
- [ ] 4. 22–30
- [ ] 5. 31–40
- [ ] 6. 41–50
- [ ] 7. 51–65
- [ ] 8. Over 65

Question two—sex
- [ ] 1. Male
- [ ] 2. Female

Use the following DATA statements in your program. When writing the report routine in the program, notice that the DATA in line 160 are strings, not values, and that they correspond to the part of the chart under the heading AGE.

```
100 REM DATA BY AGE GROUP, SEX GROUP
110 DATA 1,2,2,1,3,2,4,1,5,2,6,2,7,2,8,1
120 DATA 1,2,1,1,2,1,2,2,3,1,3,1,3,2,3,1,3,2,4,1,4,2
130 DATA 5,1,5,1,5,2,5,2,6,1,6,1,6,2,7,1,7,2,7,2,7,2
140 DATA 8,1,8,1,8,2,8,2,3,1,4,2,5,2,6,1,6,1,7,1,8,2
150 DATA -1,-1
160 DATA  <10,10-15,16-21,22-30,31-40,41-50,51-65,>65
]RUN
AGE        TOTAL      MALE      FEMALE

<10         3          1          2
10-15       3          2          1
16-21       7          4          3
22-30       4          2          2
31-40       6          2          4
41-50       6          4          2
51-65       6          2          4
>65         6          3          3
TOTALS:     41         20         21
```

10. Your brother-in-law owns the local jeans store. He carries a large inventory with tremendous variety but now finds he must cut back. The question is *which* items to cut back. He asks you to use your computer to analyze his sales and help him make the "which-item" decisions. He wants to analyze sales of children's pants first. He carries 10 styles in children's pants, each style with 3 colors. For your program, you should number the styles 1 through 10 and the colors 1 through 3, so that each piece of data will look like that below.

```
              DATA  1,   2,   12.50
```
            Style # Color # Sales price

Write a program to analyze the sales and prepare a report like the one below. Use the following DATA statements in your program.

```
100 REM DATA STYLE, COLOR, DOLLAR SALES
120 DATA 1,1,12,1,2,13,1,3,14,2,1,22,2,2,10,2,3,12
130 DATA 3,1,45,3,2,14,3,3,32,4,1,13,4,2,10,4,3,15
140 DATA 5,1,12,5,2,13,5,3,12,6,1,12,6,2,12,6,3,12
150 DATA 7,1,13,7,2,13,7,3,13,8,1,14,8,2,14,8,3,14
160 DATA 9,1,15,9,2,15,9,3,15,10,1,14,10,2,14,10,3,14
170 DATA 3,2,35,5,1,50,6,1,36,10,3,30,9,3,12,10,2,28
180 DATA 2,3,40,5,1,24,3,3,14,4,1,48,1,1,12,2,1,12,3,1,13
190 DATA -1,-1,-1
```

```
RUN
STYLE#    TOTAL    CLR#1    CLR#2    CLR#3

1         51       24       13       14
2         96       34       10       52
3         153      58       49       46
4         86       61       10       15
5         111      86       13       12
6         72       48       12       12
7         39       13       13       13
8         42       14       14       14
9         57       15       15       27
10        100      14       42       44

TOTALS:   $807     $367     $191     $249
```

11. In an effort to save some of your monthly budget dollars, you decide to shop around for some of the staple goods you use at home. There are four different stores nearby. You decide to shop the following six items in each store and then compare prices on your home computer: pepper, paper towels, paper napkins, laundry soap, flour, tissues.

Write a program that will prepare a report like the one shown below. The easiest way to enter your data is using DATA statements with the prices for all six items from one store in one DATA statement. (Be sure the six are in the same order for all four stores.)

```
]RUN
ITEM     STORE#1 STORE#2 STORE#3 STORE#4
PEPPER   .89     .95     .85     .83
TOWELS   .49     .55     .53     .47
NAPKINS  .85     .8      .79     .75
SOAP     .95     .93     .99     .9
FLOUR    .79     .85     .89     .75
TISSUES  .39     .45     .49     .39

TOTALS   $4.36   $4.53   $4.54   $4.09
```

Answers to Self-Test

The frame numbers in parentheses refer to the frames in the chapter where the topic is discussed. You may wish to refer back to these for quick review.

1. (b), (d), (e), and (f) are legal.
   (frames 5–7)
2. 3,2, meaning 3 rows, 2 columns. (frames 2–4)
3. 100 DIM A(3,2). (frame 12)
4. A(3,2). (frames 9–11)
5. (a) 1; (b) 5. (frame 11)
6. (a) 4; (b) 6. (frame 11)
7. 4. (frame 11)
8. ```
   10 DIM M(10,10)
   20 FOR R=1 TO 10
   30 FOR C=1 TO 10
   40 M(R,C)=0
   50 NEXT C
   60 NEXT R
   ```

   (frame 12)
   ```

9.  ```
    10 REM ** POPULATION AGE/SEX ANALYSIS
    15 REM ** INITIALIZE
    20 HOME : DIM V(8,2)
    25 FOR A = 0 TO 8: FOR S = 0 TO 2: LET V(A,S) = 0: NEXT S,A
    30 READ A,S: IF A = - 1 THEN 60
    40 LET V(A,S) = V(A,S) + 1: LET V(0,0) = V(0,0) + 1
    50 LET V(0,S) = V(0,S) + 1: LET V(A,0) = V(A,0) + 1: GOTO 30
    60 PRINT "AGE"; TAB( 10);"TOTAL"; TAB( 20);"MALE"; TAB( 30);
       "FEMALE": PRINT
    70 FOR A = 1 TO 8: READ A$: PRINT A$; TAB( 12);V(A,0);
    80 FOR S = 1 TO 2: PRINT  TAB( 12 + 10 * S);V(A,S);: NEXT S:
       PRINT
    90 NEXT A: PRINT
    95 PRINT "TOTALS:"; TAB( 12);V(0,0); TAB( 22);V(0,1);
       TAB( 32);V(0,2)
    100 REM ** DATA BY AGE GROUP, SEX GROUP
    110 DATA 1,2,2,1,3,2,4,1,5,2,6,2,7,2,8,1
    120 DATA 1,2,1,1,2,1,2,2,3,1,3,1,3,2,3,1,3,2,4,1,4,2
    130 DATA 5,1,5,1,5,2,5,2,6,1,6,1,6,2,7,1,7,2,7,2,7,2
    140 DATA 8,1,8,1,8,2,8,2,3,1,4,2,5,2,6,1,6,1,7,1,8,2
    150 DATA -1,-1
    160 DATA <10,10-15,16-21,22-30,31-40,41-50,51-65,>65
    ```
    (frames 8–23)

10. ```
    10 REM ** SALES ANALYSIS
    15 HOME : REM ** INITIALIZE
    20 DIM T(10,3): FOR S = 0 TO 10: FOR C = 0 TO 3:
       LET T(S,C) = 0: NEXT S
    25 REM ** READ, TEST FOR FLAG, ACCUMULATE DATA
    30 READ S,C,D: IF S = - 1 THEN 60
    40 LET T(S,C) = T(S,C) + D: LET T(0,0) = T(0,0) + D
    50 LET T(0,C) = T(0,C) + D: LET T(S,0) = T(S,0) + D: GOTO 30
    55 REM ** PRINT REPORT
    60 PRINT "STYLE#"; TAB( 9);"TOTAL";
    65 PRINT  TAB( 17);"CLR#1"; TAB( 26);"CLR#2";
       TAB( 35);"CLR#3"
    70 PRINT : FOR S = 1 TO 10: PRINT S; TAB( 9);T(S,0);
    80 FOR C = 1 TO 3: PRINT  TAB( 9 + 9 * C);T(S,C);:
       NEXT C: PRINT
    90 NEXT S: PRINT : PRINT "TOTALS:";
    95 FOR X = 0 TO 3: PRINT  TAB( 8 + 9 * X);"$";T(0,X);:
       NEXT X: PRINT
    100 REM ** DATA: STYLE#, COLOR#, DOLLAR SALES
    120 DATA 1,1,12,1,2,13,1,3,14,2,1,22,2,2,10,2,3,12
    130 DATA 3,1,45,3,2,14,3,3,32,4,1,13,4,2,10,4,3,15
    140 DATA 5,1,12,5,2,13,5,3,12,6,1,12,6,2,12,6,3,12
    150 DATA 7,1,13,7,2,13,7,3,13,8,1,14,8,2,14,8,3,14
    160 DATA 9,1,15,9,2,15,9,3,15,10,1,14,10,2,14,10,3,14
    170 DATA 3,2,35,5,1,50,6,1,36,10,3,30,9,3,12,10,2,28
    180 DATA 2,3,40,5,1,24,3,3,14,4,1,48,1,1,12,2,1,12,3,1,13
    190 DATA -1,-1,-1
    ```
    (frames 23–60)

11.

```
10 REM  ** STORE PRICE COMPARISON
15 REM ** INITIALIZE
20 HOME : DIM P(6,4)
25 REM ** READ DATA INTO THE ARRAY
30 FOR S = 1 TO 4: FOR I = 1 TO 6: READ P(I,S): NEXT I,S
35 REM ** ACCUMULATE AND STORE TOTALS
40 FOR S = 1 TO 4
50 FOR I = 1 TO 6: LET P(0,S) = P(0,S) + P(I,S): NEXT I
55 NEXT S
60 REM ** PRINT THE REPORT
65 PRINT "ITEM"; TAB( 8)"STORE#1"; TAB( 16)"STORE#2";
70 PRINT  TAB( 24)"STORE#3"; TAB( 32)"STORE#4"
80 FOR I = 1 TO 6: READ I$: PRINT I$;
90 FOR S = 1 TO 4: PRINT  TAB( 8 + 8 * (S - 1));P(I,S);:
   NEXT S: PRINT
100 NEXT I: PRINT : PRINT "TOTALS";
110 FOR S = 1 TO 4: PRINT  TAB( 8 + 8 * (S - 1));"$";P(0,S);:
    NEXT S: PRINT
120 REM ** PRICES IN EACH DATA STATEMENT FOR ONE STORE
130 DATA .89, .49, .85, .95, .79, .39
140 DATA .95, .55, .80, .93, .85, .45
150 DATA .85, .53, .79, .99, .89, .49
160 DATA .83, .47, .75, .90, .75, .39
170 DATA PEPPER, TOWELS, NAPKINS, SOAP, FLOUR, TISSUES
```

(frames 23–37)

CHAPTER ELEVEN

Subroutines

We're heading down the home stretch. This chapter deals with things that you can live without but are sure nice to have when you need them. We're about to enter the realm of programs within programs, called *subroutines*. Subroutines let you organize computer programs for easy use by breaking them down into functional parts that may be reused in other programs when needed.

When you complete this chapter, you will be able to design programs in subroutine format, write appropriate main programs to access subroutines, and be able to use the following BASIC statements.

    GOSUB
    RETURN
    STOP
    END

1. In this book we have worked with two-computer-program-building processes. The first method was analogous to remodeling: the modification of an existing program. The second was building a program from the ground up. Now let us try building with prefabricated parts. This technique is handy for organizing a program according to the function performed by a group of one or more statements.

    The prefabricated sections, or groups of statements, are called *subroutines*. The statement that tells a computer to go to a subroutine is, appropriately enough, the GOSUB statement. Like the GOTO statement, it is followed by a line number that corresponds to the first statement in the subroutine.

    20 GOSUB 100 means skip to the subroutine in this program that has
    100 as the line number of its first statement

    The last statement in a subroutine is the RETURN statement. It automatically causes the computer to RETURN to the main program, that is, to the line number immediately following the GOSUB statement that originally "called up" the subroutine. For example, the subroutine at line 100 in the following program was "called" by line 20. After executing the subroutine, the last statement the computer encounters is 130 RETURN. This tells the computer to return to line 30, the line after the statement that originally called the subroutine. Look at this demonstration program to see how GOSUB and RETURN statements work.

```
5 REM **HOW GOSUB AND RETURN WORK
10 REMARK MAIN PROGRAM
20 GOSUB 100
30 GOSUB 200
40 GOSUB 300
50 PRINT "THIS IS THE END OF THE MAIN PROGRAM."
60 STOP

100 REM **SUBROUTINE #1 STARTS HERE
110 PRINT "THIS IS SUBROUTINE #1 (OR 100)."
120 PRINT
130 RETURN

200 REM **SUBROUTINE #2 STARTS HERE
210 PRINT "THIS LINE COURTESY OF SUBROUTINE #2 (OR 200)."
220 PRINT
230 RETURN

300 REM **SUBROUTINE #3 STARTS HERE
310 PRINT "SUBROUTINE #3 (OR 300 IF YOU PREFER) AT YOUR SERVICE."
320 PRINT
330 RETURN

RUN
THIS IS SUBROUTINE #1 (OR 100).

THIS LINE COURTESY OF SUBROUTINE #2 (OR 200).

SUBROUTINE #3 (OR 300 IF YOU PREFER) AT YOUR SERVICE.

THIS IS THE END OF THE MAIN PROGRAM.
```

Examine the program and the RUN. To demonstrate your understanding of how the computer goes from the main program (lines 5 to 60) to the subroutine and back again to the main program, list the line numbers in the order in which the computer executes them in running this program.

_____

_____

_____

5, 10, 20, 100, 110, 120, 130, 30, 200, 210, 220, 230, 40, 300, 310, 320, 330, 50, 60

2. There are two helpful statements that may be used in conjunction with GOSUB and RETURN. These are the STOP and END statements. Either may be used at the end of a main program. If you use STOP in our version of BASIC, the computer tells you the line number where it encountered the STOP with the message BREAK IN 60. If you use END, the computer merely gives you the "bracket]" to indicate that it has finished the RUN.

If we did not have a STOP or END statement as the last statement in the main program in frame 1, what would the computer execute next after RETURNing from the last subroutine called? _____

_____

— — — — — — — — —

The computer would execute line 100 and the rest of the subroutine in line number order on through the program, or terminate with an error message when it encountered a RETURN and did not know where to RETURN to.

3. Below, we have modified a portion of just the main program of the program in frame 1. (No subroutines are changed.) Notice how these modifications change the printout of the RUN.

```
20 GOSUB 300
30 GOSUB 100
40 GOSUB 200

RUN
SUBROUTINE #3 (OR 300 IF YOU PREFER) AT YOUR SERVICE.

THIS IS SUBROUTINE #1 (OR 100).

THIS LINE COURTESY OF SUBROUTINE #2 (OR 200).

THIS IS THE END OF THE MAIN PROGRAM.
```

Here is another modification of the main program. (Subroutines remain as they were in frame 1.) What will the computer type when the program is RUN?

```
5 REM **HOW GOSUB AND RETURN WORK
10 REM **MAIN PROGRAM
20 GOSUB 100
50 PRINT "THIS IS THE END OF THE MAIN PROGRAM"
60 STOP

RUN
```

RUN
THIS IS SUBROUTINE #1 (OR 100).

THIS IS THE END OF THE MAIN PROGRAM.

4. Now try this one. What will the computer print when the program is RUN? (Subroutines remain as they were in frame 1.)

```
5 REM **HOW GOSUB AND RETURN WORK
10 REMARK MAIN PROGRAM
20 GOSUB 100
30 GOSUB 100
40 GOSUB 100
50 PRINT "THIS IS THE END OF THE MAIN PROGRAM."
60 STOP
```

RUN

RUN
THIS IS SUBROUTINE #1 (OR 100).

THIS IS SUBROUTINE #1 (OR 100).

THIS IS SUBROUTINE #1 (OR 100).

THIS IS THE END OF THE MAIN PROGRAM.

5. Below is a listing of the CANDY BAR & JELLY BEAN COUNTER program which you developed in Chapters 9 and 10.

```
100 REM **CANDY BAR & JELLY COUNTER W/TOTAL $
110 HOME : REM ** INITIALIZE
120 DIM A(8,2): FOR X = 0 TO 8: FOR Y = 0 TO 2:A(X,Y) = 0: NEXT Y,X
200 REM ** READ DATA AND TEST FOR FLAG (-1)
210 READ K,C,Q: IF K = - 1 THEN 310
220 LET A(K,C) = A(K,C) + Q: GOTO 210
300 REM ** TOTAL OF UNITS SOLD AND OF SALES IN DOLLARS
310 FOR K = 1 TO 8
320 LET A(K,0) = A(K,1) * 1.00 + A(K,2) * .50
330 LET A(0,0) = A(0,0) + A(K,0)
340 FOR C = 1 TO 2
350 LET A(0,C) = A(0,C) + A(K,C)
360 NEXT C
370 NEXT K
380 REM ** CALCULATE PROFITS
390 LET P1 = A(0,1) * .55: LET P2 = A(0,2) * .30: LET P = P1 + P2
400 REM ** REPORT VERSION 2
410 PRINT "KID ID#";
411 TAB( 10);"TOTAL $"; TAB( 20);"CHOCOLATE"; TAB( 30);"JEL.BEANS"
420 FOR K = 1 TO 8
430 PRINT K;
440 FOR C = 0 TO 2
450 PRINT  TAB( 10 + 10 * C);A(K,C);
460 NEXT C
470 PRINT
480 NEXT K
490 PRINT
500 PRINT "TOTALS:"; TAB( 10)A(0,0); TAB( 20);A(0,1); TAB( 30);A(0,2)
510 PRINT
520 PRINT "PROFITS:"; TAB( 10);P; TAB( 20);P1; TAB( 30);P2
900 REM ** KID ID# (1 TO 8), CANDY ID# (1 OR 2), QUANTITY
910 DATA 4,1,3,4,2,6
920 DATA 5,1,6,5,2,8,2,1,3,2,2,0,8,1,6,8,2,12
930 DATA -1, -1, -1
```

(a) How many times is the section beginning at line 200 processed when the program is RUN? _____

(b) How many times are the sections beginning at line 300 and 400 processed when the program is RUN? _____

(a) Nine times, once for each set of data. However, once the computer has finished reading all the data, it does not return to this section of the program again during the same RUN.

(b) once each

6. As an exercise in the use of GOSUBs, modify the program in frame 5 to subroutine format. All subroutines should be "called up" by statements in the *main program only*. Show your modifications.

Note: Checkmarks indicate added or modified lines. A RUN is included just to convince you that the program functions properly.

```
✓100 REM ***CANDY BAR & JELLY BEAN COUNTER W/TOTAL $ USING SUBROUTINES
✓101 GOSUB 110
✓102 GOSUB 200
✓103 GOSUB 300
✓104 GOSUB 400
✓105 END
 110 HOME : REM ***INITIALIZE
 120 DIM A(8,2): FOR X = 0 TO 8: FOR Y = 0 TO 2:A(X,Y) = 0: NEXT Y,X
✓130 RETURN
 200 REM ***READ DATA AND TEST FOR FLAG (-1)
✓210 READ K,C,Q: IF K = - 1 THEN RETURN
 220 LET A(K,C) = A(K,C) + Q: GOTO 210
 300 REM ***TOTAL OF UNITS SOLD AND OF SALES IN DOLLARS
 310 FOR K = 1 TO 8
 320 LET A(K,0) = A(K,1) * 1.00 + A(K,2) * .50
 330 LET A(0,0) = A(0,0) + A(K,0)
 340 FOR C = 1 TO 2
 350 LET A(0,C) = A(0,C) + A(K,C)
 360 NEXT C
 370 NEXT K
 380 REM ***CALCULATE PROFITS
✓390 LET P1 = A(0,1) * .55: LET P2 = A(0,2) * .30:
     LET P = P1 + P2: RETURN
 400 REM ***REPORT VERSION #2
 410 PRINT "KID ID#";
 411 PRINT  TAB( 10);"TOTAL $"; TAB( 20);"CHOCOLATE";
     TAB( 30);"JEL.BEANS"
 420 FOR K = 1 TO 8
 430 PRINT K;
 440 FOR C = 0 TO 2
 450 PRINT  TAB( 10 + 10 * C);A(K,C);
 460 NEXT C
 470 PRINT
 480 NEXT K
 490 PRINT
 500 PRINT "TOTALS:"; TAB( 10)A(0,0); TAB( 20);A(0,1);
     TAB( 30);A(0,2)
 510 PRINT
 520 PRINT "PROFITS:"; TAB( 10);P; TAB( 20);P1; TAB( 30);P2
✓530 RETURN
 900 REM ***KID ID# (1 TO 8), CANDY ID# (1 OR 2), QUANTITY
 910 DATA 4,1,3,4,2,6
 920 DATA 5,1,6,5,2,8,2,1,3,2,2,0,8,1,6,8,2,12
 930 DATA -1,-1,-1
]RUN
```

(The RUN is shown on the next page.)

KID ID	TOTAL $	CHOCOLATE	JEL.BEANS
1	0	0	0
2	3	3	0
3	0	0	0
4	6	3	6
5	10	6	8
6	0	0	0
7	0	0	0
8	12	6	12
TOTALS:	31	18	26
PROFITS:	17.7	9.9	7.8

7. Here is a good practical problem that lends itself well to using subroutines. It's a number-sorting process. We want to sort a series of numbers. For demonstration purposes, let's limit the number of values to be sorted to 25. You may want to increase the number of values to be sorted for your purposes; the exact size limit possible will depend on your computer's memory size. Our first subroutine should ask the user how many numbers are to be sorted and then initialize an array of that size (don't forget to DIMension the array). Here's a RUN of the first subroutine.

```
RUN
HOW MANY NUMBERS IN THE TEST TO BE SORTED? 8
```

The main program begins like this.

```
100 REM **NUMBER SORTING PROGRAM
110 GOSUB 400
```

Complete the subroutine below:

```
400 REM **INITIALIZING SUBROUTINE

410 _____

420 _____

430 _____
```

— — — — — — — — — — —

```
400 REM **INITIALIZING SUBROUTINE
410 INPUT "HOW MANY NUMBERS IN THE TEST TO BE SORTED? " ; N
420 DIM X(N) : FOR Z=1 TO N : LET X(Z) = 0 : NEXT Z
430 RETURN
```

8. Next, we need a subroutine to enter N numbers into array X. You may want to use INPUT, or READ from DATA statements—that's up to you. For our demonstration program, we have decided to use randomly generated integer numbers between 1 and 100. Here is the main program so far.

```
100 REM **NUMBER SORTING PROGRAM
110 GOSUB 400
120 GOSUB 500
```

Complete the next subroutine by filling in the blanks.

```
500 REM **DATA ENTRY SUBROUTINE
510 FOR Z= _____ :LET X(Z)=INT(100*RND(1)+1): _____
520 _____
```

— — — — — — — — — — —

```
500 REM **DATA ENTRY SUBROUTINE
510 FOR Z=1 TO N : LET X(Z) = INT(100*RND(1)+1) : NEXT Z
520 RETURN
```

9. Now write a subroutine to produce the printout below. You write a program segment to produce a similar RUN.

```
]RUN
HOW MANY NUMBERS IN THE TEST TO BE SORTED ?8
UNSORTED RANDOM NUMBERS:
26              34              27
21              81              32
74              29
```

Here is the main program so far.

```
100 REM **NUMBER SORTING PROGRAM
110 GOSUB 400
120 GOSUB 500
130 GOSUB 600
```

Complete the subroutine below.

```
600 REM **SUBROUTINE TO PRINT UNSORTED LIST
610 _____
620 _____
630 _____
```

— — — — — — — — — — —

```
600 REM **SUBROUTINE TO PRINT UNSORTED LIST
610 PRINT "UNSORTED RANDOM NUMBERS:",
620 FOR Z=1 TO N : PRINT X(Z), : NEXT Z : PRINT
630 RETURN
```

10. The subroutine at line 700 is the really big one. It arranges the numbers in the array into ascending order. We don't think you're ready to write this one yet, so here it is. We'll go over it together.

```
700 REM **SUBROUTINE TO SORT NUMBERS IN ASCENDING ORDER
710 FOR K=1 TO N-1
720 FOR J=K+1 TO N
730 IF X(K) <= X(J) THEN 770
740 T = X(K)
750 X(K) = X(J)
760 X(J) = T
770 NEXT J
780 NEXT K
790 RETURN
```

Fill in the blanks here. This method of sorting eventually places the smallest value in position X(1) of the array and the largest value in X(___). Between these two elements are the other numbers arranged in order. This is accomplished by comparing pairs of numbers located in contiguous array elements, one pair at a time and interchanging the two numbers wherever possible. In which statement(s) are the 2 numbers compared? _____

— — — — — — — —

X(N); 730

11. Referring to frame 10, answer the following question. If the first two array elements are compared, and if the content (value) of X(2) is less than that of X(1), then what happens? _____

— — — — — — — —

X(2) and X(1) are interchanged to that X(1) will be less than X(2).

12. What variable temporarily holds the value of X(1) so that it can later be assigned to X(2), when X(1) is larger than X(2)? _____

— — — — — — — —

T in line 740

13. Examine the two FOR-NEXT loops that begin in lines 710 and 720. Starting with the first element of the array, the computer will compare its value to all the remaining values in the array and will exchange values where needed. The first time through the loops, the value of FOR-NEXT loop control variable K is 1. The value of control variable J = K +1 = 1 + 1 = 2. So X(1) is compared to X(2) in line 730. If the value of X(1) is less than or equal to X(2), then by branching to line 770 NEXT J, the computer is ready to compare X(1) to X(3) . If the comparison X(1) <= X(3) is false, then the values of X(1) and X(3) are exchanged, and the computer continues to compare the new value of X(1) to the rest of the values in the array to see if any smaller ones are encountered that should go into the X(1) position.

Look again at line 730. How is the computer instructed to compare only the array elements with *subscripts* larger than X(K)? _____

_____

— — — — — — — — —

The second FOR-NEXT loop's control variable always starts at K + 1, so that only the elements of the array with subscripts greater than X(K) are compared.

14. Eventually, the numbers are all arranged in ascending order in array X. It's time for you to write a subroutine at line 800 to print a report like the following one.

```
          SORTED RANDOM NUMBERS:       21
          26              27           29
          32              34           74
          81

          800 REM **SUBROUTINE TO PRINT SORTED LIST
          810 _____
          820 _____
          830 _____
```

— — — — — — — — —

```
          800 REM **SUBROUTINE TO PRINT SORTED LIST
          810 PRINT "SORTED RANDOM NUMBERS:"
          820 FOR Z=1 TO N : PRINT X(Z), : NEXT Z : PRINT
          830 RETURN
```

15. Wait just a minute! Doesn't that subroutine at line 800 look *almost* exactly like the one at line 600? Why not change the program somehow so we just use the subroutine at line 600—twice. Brilliant idea. Let's look at it.

```
130 GOSUB 600

150 GOSUB 800

600 REM **SUBROUTINE TO PRINT UNSORTED LIST
610 PRINT "UNSORTED RANDOM NUMBERS:",
620 FOR Z=1 TO N : PRINT X(Z), : NEXT Z : PRINT
630 RETURN

800 REM **SUBROUTINE TO PRINT SORTED LIST
810 PRINT "SORTED RANDOM NUMBERS:",
820 FOR Z=1 TO N : PRINT X(Z), : NEXT Z : PRINT
830 RETURN
```

If we change line 130 to say

```
130 PRINT "UNSORTED ";:GOSUB 600
```

What would we do to line 150?

150 _____

— — — — — — — — — —

```
150 PRINT "SORTED ";:GOSUB 600
```

16. We can now delete the entire subroutine that starts at line 800. Show how line 610 may be changed so that the RUN will still print as shown in frames 9 and 14.

610 _____

— — — — — — — — — —

```
610 PRINT "RANDOM NUMBERS:",
```

17. You have just seen another excellent use of subroutines. Whenever you have to do the same thing more than once in a program, it can be handled in a subroutine and the RETURN will send the computer back to the statement following the GOSUB statement that called the subroutine. Here's the final program and RUN.

```
100 REM **NUMBER SORTING PROGRAM
110 GOSUB 400
120 GOSUB 500
130 PRINT "UNSORTED ";: GOSUB 600
140 GOSUB 700
150 PRINT "SORTED ";: GOSUB 600
160 END
400 REM **INITIALIZING SUBROUTINE
410 INPUT "HOW MANY NUMBERS IN THE TEST TO BE SORTED"; N
420 DIM X(N) : FOR Z=1 TO N : LET X(Z)=0 : NEXT Z
430 RETURN
500 REM **DATA ENTRY SUBROUTINE
510 FOR Z=1 TO N : LET X(Z)=INT(100*RND(1)+1) : NEXT Z
520 RETURN
600 REM **SUBROUTINE TO PRINT LIST
610 PRINT "RANDOM NUMBERS:",
620 FOR Z=1 TO N : PRINT X(Z), : NEXT Z : PRINT
630 RETURN
700 REM **SUBROUTINE TO SORT NUMBERS IN ASCENDING ORDER
710 FOR K=1 TO N-1
720 FOR J=K+1 TO N
730 IF X(K)<=X(J) THEN 770
740 T=X(K)
750 X(K)=X(J)
760 X(J)=T
770 NEXT J
780 NEXT K
790 RETURN

]RUN
```

(The RUN is shown on the next page.)

```
HOW MANY NUMBERS IN THE TEST TO BE SORTED ?25
UNSORTED RANDOM NUMBERS:
15              69              10
81              32              29
17              97              35
34              2               93
83              47              15
78              64              60
84              9               75
14              21              62
100
SORTED RANDOM NUMBERS:         2
9               10              14
15              15              17
21              29              32
34              35              47
60              62              64
69              75              78
81              83              84
93              97              100
```

Why did we add line 160 to the main program? _____

_____

— — — — — — — —

so that the computer would not attempt to execute the subroutine sections of the program after completing the main program

18. The next section of this chapter will take you through the process of assembling a program from subroutine blocks that can perform a variety of common statistical computations. Using subroutines, the program is conveniently organized according to functions performed; that is, each subroutine does a particular part of the statistical computations.

The statistical measures to be discussed are: mean, variance, and standard deviation.

If you are familiar with these statistical measures and wish to sharpen your programming skills, continue on in this section of text. Otherwise turn to frame 22.

In this section you will have the opportunity to develop the computational subroutines themselves. Perhaps more important, however, you will gain skill in using subroutines as prefabricated miniprograms (or not-so-miniprograms) by assembling previously written subroutine units into a complete program. (To learn or review statistics, we recommend Donald J. Koosis, *Statistics*, 2nd edition, from this same series of Self-Teaching Guides published by John Wiley & Sons, New York.)

The statistical measure used in previous examples in this book is the *average* or *mean* of values or scores obtained through some method of measurement or observation. The mean (referred to in statistics as "one measure of central tendency" of data) is calculated by adding all the values and dividing that sum by the total number of values. In common statistical notation, the formula for the mean is as follows.

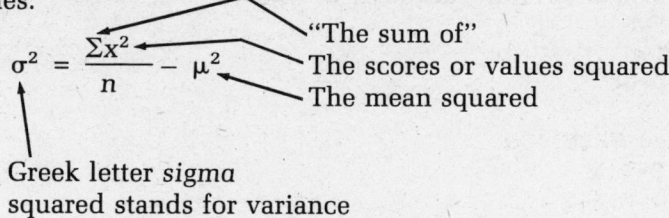

Greek capital letter *sigma*, which stands for "the sum of"

$$\mu = \frac{\Sigma x}{n}$$

← The values or scores
← The number of values or scores

Greek letter *mu*, which stands for mean

Each score in a set of scores lies some distance from the computed mean of the set; some scores may be just at the mean, some higher, some lower. The *variance* and its square root, the *standard deviation*, are measures of the "average" distance of all the scores in the set from the mean of the set. Statisticians call these "measures of variability (or dispersion)."

Following is a computational formula for finding the variance of a set of scores or values.

$$\sigma^2 = \frac{\Sigma x^2}{n} - \mu^2$$

"The sum of"
The scores or values squared
The mean squared

Greek letter *sigma* squared stands for variance

The standard deviation is the square root of the variance, and in statistical notation looks like this.

$$\sigma = \sqrt{\sigma} = \sqrt{\frac{\Sigma x^2}{n} - \mu^2}$$

We will use the following BASIC variables in the program.

N = n   (number of scores or values)
X = x   (scores or values)
M = μ   (mean)
T = Σx   (sum or total of scores)
D = Σx²   (sum or total of each score squared)
V = σ²   (variance)
S = σ   (standard deviation)

So let's get down to it. Write a subroutine to provide us with values for N, T, and D which are needed to calculate the mean and variance. The scores are provided in a DATA statement.

```
900 REM **DATA FOLLOWS. DATA LIST ENDS WITH -1.
910 DATA 75,67,38,89,23,97,75,18,56,37,-1
```

Complete the subroutine below.

```
300 REM **SUBROUTINE: COMPUTE N, SUM X, SUM X^2
```

```
300 REM **SUBROUTINE: COMPUTE N, SUM X, SUM X^2
310 LET N=0
320 LET T=0
330 LET D=0
340 READ X
350 IF X<0 THEN 399
360 LET T=T+X
370 LET D=D+X^2
380 LET N=N+1
390 GOTO 340
399 RETURN
```

19. Circle the parts of the following formulas for which subroutine 300 calculates values.

$$\mu = \frac{\Sigma x}{n} \qquad \sigma^2 = \frac{\Sigma x^2}{n} - \mu^2$$

$$\mu = \frac{\boxed{\Sigma x}}{\boxed{n}} \qquad \sigma^2 = \frac{\boxed{\Sigma x^2}}{\boxed{n}} - \mu^2$$

20. Now write a subroutine to finish the computations for the statistical measures.

```
500 REM **SUBROUTINE: COMPUTE MEAN, VARIANCE, STD. DEV.
```

```
500 REM **SUBROUTINE: COMPUTE MEAN, VARIANCE, STD. DEV.
510 LET M=T/N
520 LET V=D/N—M^2
530 LET S=SQR(V)
540 RETURN
```

21. We want a RUN of the program to look like this.

```
RUN
N = 10
MEAN = 57.5
VARIANCE = 680.85
STANDARD DEVIATION = 26.0931
```

Complete the subroutine to print the results.

```
600 REM **SUBROUTINE: PRINT RESULTS
```

```
600 REM **SUBROUTINE: PRINT RESULTS
610 PRINT "N = " ;N
620 PRINT "MEAN = ";M
630 PRINT "VARIANCE = ";V
640 PRINT "STANDARD DEVIATION = ";S
650 RETURN
```

22. All you nonstatisticians rejoin us here. We statisticians have written the following subroutines. A list of what the variables stand for is given in frame 18.

```
300 REM **SUBROUTINE: COMPUTE N, SUM X, SUM X^2
310 LET N=0
320 LET T=0
330 LET D=0
340 READ X
350 IF X <0 THEN 399
360 LET T=T+X
370 LET D=D+X^2
380 LET N=N+1
390 GOTO 340
399 RETURN

500 REM **SUBROUTINE: COMPUTE MEAN, VARIANCE, STD. DEV.
510 LET M=T/N
520 LET V=D/N-M^2
530 LET S=SQR(V)
540 RETURN

600 REM **SUBROUTINE: PRINT RESULTS
610 PRINT "N = ";N
620 PRINT "MEAN = ";M
630 PRINT "VARIANCE = ";V
640 PRINT "STANDARD DEVIATION = ";S
650 RETURN

900 REM **DATA FOLLOWS. DATA LIST ENDS WITH -1.
910 DATA 75,67,38,89,23,97,75,18,56,37,-1

RUN
N = 10
MEAN = 57.5
VARIANCE = 680.85
STANDARD DEVIATION = 26.0931
```

Complete the main program so that the program will function as indicated in the preceding RUN.

```
100 REM **MEAN, VARIANCE AND STANDARD DEVIATION
110 REM **COMPUTE N, SUM OF X, SUM OF X^2

120 _____
130 REM **COMPUTE M, V, S

140 _____
150 REM **PRINT RESULTS

160 _____

199 _____
```

― ― ― ― ― ― ― ― ― ―

```
120 GOSUB 300
140 GOSUB 500
160 GOSUB 600
199 STOP  ←――――― Or END (your choice)
```

23. Now a nice thing about subroutines is that they may easily be changed or interchanged. (Nonstatisticians can skip to frame 24.) Suppose that our data contained only two values or kinds of score. For example, we could score a voter poll using the value 1 to represent an "aye" vote and the value 2 to represent "nay" or "no opinion." The scores can then be tabulated or *grouped* by listing each kind of score (X) opposite its frequency (F) the number of times that that kind of score occurred in the data. Suppose the following are the data of two kinds.

1,1,2,1,1,2,1,1,1,2,1,1,1,2,2,2,1,2,2,1

We can set up a table showing the "frequency of appearance" of each kind of data.

	X	F	
Kind of data	1	12	
(only two pos-			} Grouped data (two groups or kinds)
sible values)	2	8	

Here are the data for the computer.

```
900 REM **GROUPED DATA FOLLOWS. DATA LIST ENDS WITH -1, -1.
910 DATA 1,12,2,8,-1,-1
```

There are 12 cases of value 1

There are 8 cases of value 2

The table following compares the formulas for mean, variance, and standard deviation for "ordinary" data versus grouped data.

Statistic	"Ordinary"	Grouped
Mean	$\mu = \dfrac{\Sigma x}{n}$	$\mu = \dfrac{\Sigma(f \cdot x)}{n}$ where $(n = \Sigma f)$
Variance	$\sigma^2 = \dfrac{\Sigma x^2}{n} - \mu^2$	$\sigma^2 = \dfrac{\Sigma(f \cdot x^2)}{n} - \mu^2$
S.D.	$\sigma = \sqrt{\sigma^2}$	$\sigma = \sqrt{\sigma^2}$

Translated into BASIC, we require values for 3 variables.

$T = \Sigma x$ or $\Sigma f \cdot x$
$D = \Sigma x^2$ or $\Sigma f \cdot x^2$
$N =$ the number of scores $(n = \Sigma f$ for grouped data)

In the DATA statement for grouped data, there are *pairs* of values: a score (X) followed by the frequency (F) of appearance of the score. There is also a double flag, which should be a programming clue for you that values are to be read in pairs. Below is a sample DATA statement.

```
900 REM ** GROUPED DATA FOLLOWS.  DATA LIST ENDS WITH -1,-1.
910 DATA 1,12,2,8,-1,-1
```

With careful reference to the formulas presented, you should be able to complete the subroutine, particularly if you worked through the earlier statistics subroutines for ordinary (ungrouped) data.

```
400 REM ** SUBROUTINE: COMPUTE N, SUM X, SUM X^2 (GROUPED DATA)
```

```
400 REM **SUBROUTINE: COMPUTE N, SUM X, SUM X^2 (GROUPED DATA)
410 LET N=0
420 LET T=0
430 LET D =0
440 READ X,F
450 IF X<0 THEN 499
460 LET T=T+F*X
470 LET D=D+F*X^2
480 LET N=N+F
490 GOTO 440
499 RETURN
```

24. Nonstatisticians rejoin us here. Look at subroutine 400 in frame 23. For which BASIC variables are values computed? _____

T, D, N (any order)

25. Look at subroutine 500 below, from our program in frame 22.

```
500 REM **SUBROUTINE: COMPUTE MEAN, VARIANCE, STD. DEV.
510 LET M=T/N
520 LET V=D/N-M^2
530 LET S=SQR(V)
540 RETURN
```

What variables must have values computed previously in order for subroutine 500 to compute M, V, and S? _____

———————————

T, D, N (any order)

26. Got the idea? Subroutine 400 for grouped data computes values for the same variables that subroutine 300 (frame 22) computes for "ordinary" (ungrouped) data. Therefore, merely by substituting subroutine 400 for subroutine 300 in the program you have a complete program for computing the statistics for grouped data.

If the DATA statement for grouped data is provided, show what modification of the main program (frame 22) is needed to RUN the complete program for grouped data. _____

———————————

Change one line in the main program: 120 GOSUB 400.

You have now finished this book. Try the following Self-Test to test your new skills. Then go on to evaluate your overall learning with the Final Self-Test. As you use BASIC on your Apple computer, you may find the summary of BASIC functions provided in the Appendix useful for quick reference.

We recommend that you review the reference manuals provided by Apple Computers Inc. for still more useful statements and functions to help complete your knowledge of programming in Applesoft BASIC. For advanced instruction, try our book *Apple Basic: Data File Programming: A Self Teaching Guide* from John Wiley and Sons.

Self-Test

This Self-Test will consist of a single long problem. Write a program that will give complete arithmetic drills to the user. You should offer the choice of addition, subtraction, multiplication, or division problems. A complete program will look something like the printed output shown below. You should prepare the following subroutines for this program.

    Addition problem generator
    Subtraction problem generator
    Multiplication problem generator
    Division problem generator
    Random number generator
    Score-keeping routine

```
RUN
ENTER YOUR NAME? LEROY
WHICH KIND OF PROBLEMS:ADD, SUBTRACT, MULTIPLY OR DIVIDE? ADD
HOW MANY PROBLEMS? 4
HOW MANY DIGITS IN EACH NUMBER IN A PROBLEM? 1

2 + 5 =? 7
RIGHT ON. GOOD

4 + 6 =? 9
SORRY, WRONG ANSWER

1 + 6 =? 7
RIGHT ON. GOOD

8 + 2 =? 10
RIGHT ON. GOOD
CONGRATULATIONS LEROY YOU HAVE COMPLETED 4 PROBLEMS
WITH A SCORE OF 3
DO YOU WANT TO DO SOME MORE? NO
```

We have allowed space for your program to be written.

Answer to Self-Test

```
10 REM **COMPLETE ARITHMETIC DRILL
20 INPUT"ENTER YOUR NAME? ";N$
30 INPUT"WHICH KIND OF PROBLEMS:ADD, SUBTRACT, MULTIPLY
   OR DIVIDE? ";C$
40 INPUT"HOW MANY PROBLEMS? ";N
50 INPUT"HOW MANY DIGITS IN EACH NUMBER IN A PROBLEM? ";D
60 LET R=0
100 REM **SUBROUTINE SELECTION ROUTINE
110 IF MID$(C$,1,1)="A"THEN GOSUB 1000
120 IF MID$(C$,1,1)="S"THEN GOSUB 2000
130 IF MID$(C$,1,1)="M"THEN GOSUB 3000
140 IF MID$(C$,1,1)="D"THEN GOSUB 4000
200 REM **PRINT RESULTS
210 PRINT"CONGRATULATIONS ";N$" YOU HAVE COMPLETED? ";N;" PROBLEMS"
220 PRINT"WITH A SCORE OF ";R
230 INPUT "DO YOU WANT TO DO SOME MORE? ";C$
240 IF C$="YES"THEN 30
250 STOP
1000 REM **SUBROUTINE FOR ADDITION
1025 FOR K=1 TO N
1010 GOSUB 5000
1020 REM **PRINT PROBLEM AND REQUEST ANSWER
1030 PRINT : PRINT A;" + ";B;" ="
1040 INPUT C
1050 REM **TEST ANSWER
1060 IF C<>A+B THEN PRINT"SORRY, WRONG ANSWER" : GOTO 1100
1070 GOSUB 6000
1080 PRINT"RIGHT ON. GOOD"
1100 NEXT K
1110 RETURN
2000 **SUBROUTINE FOR SUBTRACTION PROBLEMS
2005 FOR K=1 TO N
2010 GOSUB 5000
2020 REM PRINT PROBLEM
2030 PRINT : PRINT A;" - ";B;" =";
2040 INPUT C
2050 REM **TEST ANSWER
2060 IF C<>A-B THEN PRINT"SORRY, WRONG ANSWER" : GOTO 2100
2070 GOSUB 6000
2080 PRINT"GOOD ANSWER"
2100 NEXT K
2110 RETURN
```

(The LISTing for this program continues on the next page.)

```
3000 REM **SUBROUTINE FOR MULTIPLICATION
3005 FOR K=1 TO N
3010 GOSUB 5000
3020 REM **PRINT PROBLEM
3030 PRINT : PRINT A;" * ";B;" =";
3040 INPUT C
3050 REM **TEST ANSWER
3060 IF C<>A*B THEN PRINT"SORRY, WRONG ANSWER" : GOTO 3100
3070 GOSUB 6000
3080 PRINT"GOOD ANSWER"
3100 NEXT K
3110 RETURN
4000 REM **SUBROUTINE FOR DIVISION
4005 FOR K=1 TO N
4010 GOSUB 5000
4020 REM **PRINT PROBLEM
4030 PRINT : PRINT A;" / ";B;" =";
4040 INPUT C
4050 REM **TEST ANSWER
4060 IF C<>A/B THEN PRINT"NO GOOD" : GOTO 4100
4070 GOSUB 6000
4080 PRINT"NICE ANSWER"
4100 NEXT K
4110 RETURN
5000 REM **SUBROUTINE TO GENERATE NUMBERS
5010 LET A=INT(10^D*RND(1)) : IF A<10^D/10-1 THEN 5010
5020 LET B=INT(10^D*RND(1)) : IF B<10^D/10-1 THEN 5020
5030 RETURN
6000 REM **SUBROUTINE TO KEEP SCORE
6010 LET R=R+1
6020 RETURN
```

Final Self-Test

Now that you're done with the book, try this final examination to test all your skills. The answers follow the test. Use separate paper for your programs and calculations.

1. STARS is a number-guessing game that was first published in *People's Computer Company* magazine, now called *Recreational Computing Magazine*. It's fun to use with players of all ages and you should find it challenging to program as well.

   Here are the rules typed by the computer. You don't have to include them in your program.

   > I will think of a whole number from 1 to 100. Try to guess my number. After you guess my number, I will type one or more stars (*). The closer you are to my number, the more stars I will type. One star (*) means you are far away from my number. Seven stars (*******) means you are very, very close to my number!!

   Logic: If the guess is 64 or more away, 1 star; 32–63 away, 2 stars; 16–31 away, 3 stars; 8–15 away; 4 stars; 4–7 away, 5 stars; 2–3 away, 6 stars; 1 away, 7 stars. You will need to use the absolute value function, something new to you but easy to use.

   Clues:

   ```
   ABS(10) = 10
   ABS(-10) = 10
   IF ABS(X-Y) = 10 THEN 100
   ```

   (A sample RUN of the game is shown on the next page.)

```
RUN
ENTER YOUR GUESS? 10
**
ENTER YOUR GUESS? 25
***
ENTER YOUR GUESS? 50
******
ENTER YOUR GUESS? 60
****
ENTER YOUR GUESS? 45
******
ENTER YOUR GUESS? 42
*****
ENTER YOUR GUESS? 47
*******
ENTER YOUR GUESS? 48
WINNER!!!
```

2. You may have used matrix commands on some other computer. (*Matrix* is just another name for *array*.) Versions of BASIC for home computers generally do not include matrix commands. However, they are easy to simulate. Try it.

You have two 5-by-3 arrays called A and B, filled with small numbers that are read into the elements or boxes in the array from DATA statements. Write a program to add the contents of each element in array A to the corresponding element in array B, and place the results in the proper place in a third array, C.

A				B				C			
7	8	9		3	6	8		10	14	17
3	4	1		2	4	7		5	8	8
6	8	2		1	3	1		7	11	3
1	4	1		8	4	9		9	8	10
8	10	2		6	6	6		14	16	8

Example:

$A(1,1) + B(1,1) = C(1,1)$
$A(1,2) + B(1,2) = C(1,2)$ etc.

```
RUN
A ARRAY CONTENTS
7            8            9
3            4            1
6            8            2
1            4            1
8           10            2

B ARRAY CONTENTS

3            6            8
2            4            7
1            3            1
8            4            9
6            6            6

C ARRAY CONTENTS

10          14           17
 5           8            8
 7          11            3
 9           8           10
14          16            8
```

3. Your child plans to set up a weekend sidewalk stand selling "junk" from around the house (also known as a garage sale). Your youngster has no trouble finding merchandise and no trouble pricing it. But he or she really doesn't understand the money system and is worried about making change when people buy these "goods."

Write a program to allow the child to enter the amount of the sale and the amount of money received and have the computer then print exactly how much and what kind of change to give back. The RUN is shown below.

```
RUN
ENTER TOTAL SALES AMOUNT? .35
ENTER AMOUNT RECEIVED? 1.00
COIN CHANGE .65

1 HALF DOLLAR
1 DIME
1 NICKEL

ENTER TOTAL SALES AMOUNT? 3.45
ENTER AMOUNT RECEIVED? 20.00

BILL CHANGE IS 16
1 $10 BILL
1 $ 5 BILL
1 $1 BILL

COIN CHANGE .55
1 HALF DOLLAR
1 NICKEL
```

Warning: Applesoft BASIC will round off numbers in peculiar ways (deep inside the computer) because of the way the electronics performs arithmetic. So beware! 4.9999 pennies is no fair. Write your program to avoid this kind of problem by checking for integer values for change that include pennies.

4. Write a program to perform conversions from selected U.S. standard measures to their metric equivalents and vice versa. Set up your program so that the user can select conversions as shown in the RUN below.

```
RUN
DO YOU WANT CONVERSIONS FOR
(1) METRIC TO U.S. STANDARD MEASURES
(2) U.S. STANDARD MEASURES TO METRIC
TYPE 1 OR 2? 1
DO YOU WANT THE LIST OF CONVERSIONS (Y OR N)? Y
SELECT CONVERSION DESIRED FROM THIS LIST:
(1) CENTIMETERS TO INCHES
(2) METERS TO FEET
(3) KILOMETERS TO MILES
(4) KILOGRAMS TO POUNDS
(5) GRAMS TO OUNCES
(6) LITERS TO QUARTS
(7) DEGREES CELSIUS TO DEGREES FAHRENHEIT
ENTER THE NUMBER OF THE CONVERSION DESIRED? 5

HOW MANY GRAMS? 10
 10 GRAMS = .35 OUNCES

DO YOU WANT CONVERSIONS FOR
(1) METRIC TO U.S. STANDARD MEASURES
(2) U.S. STANDARD MEASURES TO METRIC
TYPE 1 OR 2? 2
DO YOU WANT THE LIST OF CONVERSIONS (Y OR N)? Y
SELECT CONVERSION DESIRED FROM THIS LIST:
(1) INCHES TO CENTIMETERS
(2) FEET TO METERS
(3) MILES TO KILOMETERS
(4) POUNDS TO KILOGRAMS
(5) OUNCES TO GRAMS
(6) QUARTS TO LITERS
(7) DEGREES FAHRENHEIT TO DEGREES CELSIUS
ENTER THE NUMBER OF THE CONVERSION DESIRED? 3

HOW MANY MILES? 2
 2 MILES = 3.218 KILOMETERS

DO YOU WANT CONVERSIONS FOR
(1) METRIC TO U.S. STANDARD MEASURES
(2) U.S. STANDARD MEASURES TO METRIC
TYPE 1 OR 2? 1
DO YOU WANT THE LIST OF CONVERSIONS (Y OR N)? N
ENTER THE NUMBER OF THE CONVERSION DESIRED? 1

HOW MANY CENTIMETERS? 50
 50 CENTIMETERS = 19.5 INCHES

DO YOU WANT CONVERSIONS FOR ←— And so on.
```

FINAL SELF-TEST

We suggest the following manner of organizing the program, making extensive use of subroutines. The main program is shown at the top; here the user selects which type of conversion is to be made. The program then branches to subroutines which list the specific conversions. From these subroutines, the program GOSUBs again, to one of 14 sub-routines (7 for each "direction" of conversion).

```
DO YOU WANT CONVERSIONS FOR
(1) METRIC TO U.S. STANDARD MEASURES
(2) U.S. STANDARD MEASURES TO METRIC
TYPE 1 OR 2? 2
```

To selected subroutine

```
DO YOU WANT THE LIST OF COVERSIONS (Y OR N)? Y
SELECT CONVERSION DESIRED FROM THIS LIST:
(1) CENTIMETERS TO INCHES
(2) METERS TO FEET
(3) KILOMETERS TO MILES
(4) KILOGRAMS TO POUNDS
(5) GRAMS TO OUNCES
(6) LITERS TO QUARTS
(7) DEGREES CELSIUS TO DEGREES FARENHEIT
ENTER THE NUMBER OF THE CONVERSION DESIRED? 5
```

To selected subroutine

```
DO YOU WANT THE LIST OF CONVERSIONS (Y OR N)? Y
SELECT CONVERSION DESIRED FROM THIS LIST:
(1) INCHES TO CENTIMETERS
(2) FEET TO METERS
(3) MILES TO KILOMETERS
(4) POUNDS TO KILOGRAMS
(5) OUNCES TO GRAMS
(6) QUARTS TO LITERS
(7) DEGREES FARENHEIT TO DEGREES CELSIUS
ENTER THE NUMBER OF THE CONVERSION DESIRED? 3
```

To selected subroutine

From any one of these subroutines, return to the subroutine that sent it, and from there return immediately to the main program to start over again.

Here are the conversion values to include in the program.

Metric to U.S. standard	U.S. standard to metric
1 centimeter = .39	1 inch = 2.54 centimeters
1 meter = 3.28 feet	1 ft. = .3048 meter
1 kilometer = .62 mile	1 mile = 1.609 kilometers
1 kilogram = 2.2 pounds	1 pound = .45 kilogram
1 gram = .035 ounce	1 quart = .946 liter
1 liter = 1.0567 quarts	°F = (9/5)°C + 32
°C = (5/9)(°F − 32)	

Answers to Final Self-Test

1.  ```
    10 REM **STARS GAME
    20 LET N=INT(100*RND(1))+1
    30 INPUT "ENTER YOUR GUESS? "; G
    35 IF G=N THEN PRINT "WINNER!!!" : GOTO 20
    40 LET D=ABS(G-N)
    50 IF D>=64 THEN 170
    60 IF D>=32 THEN 160
    70 IF D>=16 THEN 150
    80 IF D>=8 THEN 140
    90 IF D>=4 THEN 130
    100 IF D>=2 THEN 120
    110 PRINT "*";
    120 PRINT "*";
    130 PRINT "*";
    140 PRINT "*";
    150 PRINT "*";
    160 PRINT "*";
    170 PRINT "*" : GOTO 30
    ```

2.  ```
    10 REM **SIMULATION OF MATRIX ADDITION
    15 REM **INITIALIZE
    20 DIM A(5,3), B(5,3), C(5,3)
    25 REM **LOAD A AND B ARRAY FROM DATA STATEMENTS. PRINT ARRAYS
    27 PRINT "A ARRAY CONTENTS" ; PRINT
    30 FOR X=1 TO 5
    35 FOR Y=1 TO 3
    40 READ A(X,Y) : PRINT A(X,Y),
    45 NEXT Y
    55 NEXT X: PRINT
    57 PRINT "B ARRAY CONTENTS" : PRINT
    60 FOR X=1 TO 5
    65 FOR Y=1 TO 3
    70 READ B(X,Y) : PRINT B(X,Y),
    75 NEXT Y
    85 NEXT X : PRINT
    90 REM **ADD A + B INTO C
    92 PRINT "C ARRAY CONTENTS" : PRINT
    95 FOR X=1 TO 5
    100 FOR Y=1 TO 3
    105 LET C(X,Y)=A(X,Y)+B(X,Y) : PRINT C(X,Y),
    110 NEXT Y
    120 NEXT X
    130 REM **DATA FOR A ARRAY
    135 DATA 7,8,9,3,4,1,6,8,2,1,4,1,8,10,2
    140 REM **DATA FOR B ARRAY
    145 DATA 3,6,8,2,4,7,1,3,1,8,4,9,6,6,6
    ```

3.
```
10 REM **COIN CHANGER
20 INPUT "ENTER TOTAL SALES AMOUNT? "; T
30 INPUT "ENTER AMOUNT RECEIVED? "; M
40 IF M<T THEN PRINT "NOT ENOUGH MONEY RECEIVED":GOTO 20
50 IF M=T THEN PRINT "EXACT CHANGE, NO CHANGE REQUIRED":PRINT:GOTO 20
60 LET C=M-T:IF C<1.00 THEN 150
65 PRINT
70 LET B=C-(C-INT(C)):PRINT "BILL CHANGE IS"; B
75 LET C=C-B
80 LET B1=INT(B/20):IF B1=0 THEN 100
85 PRINT B1; "$20 BILL"
90 LET B=B-(B1*20)
100 LET B2=INT(B/10):IF B2=0 THEN 120
105 PRINT B2; "$10 BILL"
110 LET B=B-(B2*10)
120 LET B3=INT(B/5):IF B3=0 THEN 140
125 PRINT B3; "$5 BILL"
130 LET B=B-(B3*5)
140 IF B<1 THEN 150
145 PRINT B; "$1 BILL":PRINT
150 LET C=INT((C+.005)*100)
152 LET C=INT(C)
155 PRINT "COIN CHANGE"; C/100:PRINT
160 IF C<50 THEN 180
170 PRINT "1 HALF DOLLAR":LET C=C-50
180 IF C<25 THEN 200
190 PRINT "1 QUARTER":LET C=C-25
200 LET D=INT(C/10):IF D=0 THEN 220
210 PRINT D; "DIME":LET C=C-(D*10)
220 LET N=INT(C/5):IF N=0 THEN 240
230 PRINT N; "NICKEL":LET C=C-(N*5)
240 IF C<1 THEN PRINT:GOTO 20
250 PRINT INT(C); "PENNY":PRINT:GOTO 20
```

4.  ```
    100 REM **SELECTED MEASUREMENT CONVERSIONS
    110 PRINT "DO YOU WANT CONVERSIONS FOR"
    120 PRINT "(1) METRIC TO U.S. STANDARD MEASURES"
    130 PRINT "(2) U.S. STANDARD MEASURES TO METRIC"
    140 INPUT "TYPE 1 OR 2? "; N
    150 ON N GOSUB 1000, 1100
    160 GOTO 110

    1000 REM **USER SELECTS DESIRED METRIC TO U.S. CONVERSION
    1010 INPUT "DO YOU WANT THE LIST OF CONVERSIONS (Y OR N)? "; A$
    1020 IF A$="N" THEN 1040
    1030 PRINT "SELECT CONVERSION DESIRED FROM THIS LIST:"
    1031 PRINT "(1) CENTIMETERS TO INCHES"
    1032 PRINT "(2) METERS TO FEET"
    1033 PRINT "(3) KILOMETERS TO MILES"
    1034 PRINT "(4) KILOGRAMS TO POUNDS"
    1035 PRINT "(5) GRAMS TO OUNCES"
    1036 PRINT "(6) LITERS TO QUARTS"
    1037 PRINT "(7) DEGREES CELSIUS TO DEGREES FARENHEIT"
    1040 INPUT "ENTER THE NUMBER OF THE CONVERSION DESIRED? " ;
         M : PRINT
    1050 ON M GOSUB 2100,2200,2300,2400,2500,2600,2700
    1060 RETURN

    1100 REM **USER SELECTS DESIRED U.S. TO METRIC CONVERSION
    1110 INPUT "DO YOU WANT THE LIST OF CONVERSIONS (Y OR N)? "; A$
    1120 IF A$="N" THEN 1140
    1130 PRINT "SELECT CONVERSION DESIRED FROM THIS LIST:"
    1131 PRINT "(1) INCHES TO CENTIMETERS"
    1132 PRINT "(2) FEET TO METERS"
    1133 PRINT "(3) MILES TO KILOMETERS"
    1134 PRINT "(4) POUNDS TO KILOGRAMS"
    1135 PRINT "(5) OUNCES TO GRAMS"
    1136 PRINT "(6) QUARTS TO LITERS"
    1137 PRINT "(7) DEGREES FARENHEIT TO DEGREES CELSIUS"
    1140 INPUT "ENTER THE NUMBER OF THE CONVERSION DESIRED? "; S : PRINT
    1150 ON S GOSUB 3100,3200,3300,3400,3500,3600,3700
    1160 RETURN

    2100 REM **CM TO INCHES
    2110 INPUT "HOW MANY CENTIMETERS? "; C
    2120 PRINT C; "CENTIMETERS = "; C*.39; " INCHES"
    2130 PRINT : RETURN

    2200 REM **METERS TO FEET
    2210 INPUT "HOW MANY METERS? "; M
    2220 PRINT M; "METERS = "; M*3.28; " FEET"
    2230 PRINT : RETURN
    ```
    ```

```
2300 REM **KM TO MILES
2310 INPUT "HOW MANY KILOMETERS? "; K
2320 PRINT K; "KILOMETERS = "; K*.62; " MILES"
2330 PRINT : RETURN

2400 REM **KG TO POUNDS
2410 INPUT "HOW MANY KILOGRAMS? "; K
2420 PRINT K; "KILOGRAMS = "; K*2.2; " POUNDS"
2430 PRINT : RETURN

2500 REM **GRAMS TO OUNCES
2510 INPUT "HOW MANY GRAMS? "; G
2520 PRINT G; "GRAMS = "; G*.035; " OUNCES"
2530 PRINT : RETURN

2600 **LITERS TO QUARTS
2610 "HOW MANY LITERS? "; L
2620 PRINT L; "LITERS = "; L*1.0567; " QUARTS"
2630 PRINT : RETURN

2700 REM **DEGREES C TO DEGREES F
2710 INPUT "HOW MANY DEGREES CELSIUS? "; D
2720 PRINT D; "DEGREES CELSIUS = "; 9*D/5+32;
     " DEGREES FARENHEIT"
2730 PRINT : RETURN

3100 REM **INCHES TO CM
3110 INPUT "HOW MANY INCHES? "; I
3120 PRINT I; "INCHES = "; I*2.54; " CENTIMETERS"
3130 PRINT : RETURN

3200 REM **FEET TO METERS
3210 INPUT "HOW MANY FEET? "; F
3220 PRINT F; "FEET = "; F*.3048; " METERS"
3230 PRINT : RETURN

3300 REM **MILES TO KM
3310 INPUT "HOW MANY MILES? "; M
3320 PRINT M; "MILES = "; M*1.609; " KILOMETERS"
3330 PRINT : RETURN

3400 REM **POUNDS TO KG
3410 INPUT "HOW MANY POUNDS? "; P
3420 PRINT P; "POUNDS = "; P*.45; " KILOGRAMS"
3430 PRINT : RETURN
```

```
3500 REM **OUNCES TO GRAMS
3510 INPUT "HOW MANY OUNCES? "; O
3520 PRINT O; "OUNCES = "; O*28.35; " GRAMS"
3530 PRINT : RETURN

3600 REM **QUARTS TO LITERS
3610 INPUT "HOW MANY QUARTS? "; Q
3620 PRINT Q; "QUARTS = "; Q*.946; " LITERS"
3630 PRINT : RETURN

3700 REM **DEGREES F TO DEGREES C
3710 INPUT "HOW MANY DEGREES FARENHEIT? "; D
3720 PRINT D; "DEGREES FARENHEIT = "; 5/9*(D-32);
     " DEGREES CELSIUS"
3730 PRINT : RETURN
```

BASIC Functions

This appendix describes some of the more common and useful Applesoft BASIC functions you will use when programming. It is not meant to be a complete list but a reference list for you to use as you write programs, in case you forget how something works! For a complete list of Applesoft statements and functions, see the following materials from Apple Computer Inc.: *BASIC Programming Reference Manual*; *Applesoft: The Applesoft Tutorial*; *The DOS Manual*.

ARITHMETIC FUNCTIONS

(In the following, "exp" stands for any BASIC expression, variable, or number.)

ABS(exp): Gives the absolute value of the expression, i.e., ABS(A) = A if A >= 0, ABS(A) = −A if A < 0.
Example:

```
IF ABS(X-G) >= 64 THEN PRINT "*"
```

EXP(exp): Computes the exponential function, base e, where e = 2.71828.... Usually there is an upper limit on the value of the variable. In Applesoft BASIC, the value in the parentheses must be less than 87.0296.
Examples:

```
B = EXP(X)
Y = C*EXP(-A*T)
```

FRE(0): Used to determine how much space is left in the computer's memory that is not being used by BASIC or the program stored in memory. Enter it in a print statement, with zero in the parentheses, and the number of unused bytes is given.
Example:

```
PRINT FRE(0)
```

See also FRE(string variable) under "String Functions."

INT(exp): Computes the greatest integer less than or equal to exp. Notice that INT(3.14) = 3, but INT(−3.14) = −4. You may wish to check the reference manual for your version of BASIC for the similar function FIX.

LOG(exp): Gives the natural logarithm, base e, of exp.
Example:

```
D = LOG(1 + X^2)
```

RND(parameter): Generates a random number between 0 and 1 with control by the parameter value. For example, in Applesoft BASIC, any positive value in the parentheses gives a new random number each time. A zero in the parentheses gives the same random number as was last generated by a RND function. Each different negative number (including fractions) gives a different random number, but the same random number is always given for the same negative value in the parentheses.

SGN(exp): Gives a 1 if the expression evaluates to a positive value (>0); gives a 0 if the expression evaluates to zero (=0); gives a −1 if the expression evaluates to a negative value (<0).
Example:

```
ON SGN(X) +2 GOTO 100, 200, 300
```

If X is negative, the above statement will branch to line 100; If X = 0, it will branch to line 200; if X is positive, it will branch to line 300.

SQR(exp):Gives the positive square root of exp. Expression in parentheses must be zero or a positive value (no negative values).

TRIGONOMETRIC FUNCTIONS

SIN(exp), COS(exp), TAN(exp), ATN(exp): The SIN, COS, and TAN functions give the sine, cosine, or tangent of exp, where exp is assumed to be given in radians. ATN computes the principal value of the arctangent, in radians. The value of ATN(exp) will be in the range $-\pi/2.086 <$ ATN(exp) $< \pi/2$.

OUTPUT POSITIONING FUNCTIONS

HTAB(exp): Horizontal tab moves the cursor across the screen to the column indicated by the expression (1–40).

VTAB(exp): Vertical tab moves the cursor to the vertical line on the screen indicated by the expression (1–24).

SPC(exp): Used in print statements to space over the number of spaces indicated by the expression, variable, or value in the parentheses.
Example:

```
PRINT X;SPC(5); Y; SPC(5); 2
```

STRING FUNCTIONS

ASC(string): Gives the ASCII code numeric value for the first character in a string.
Example:

```
PRINT ASC(B$)
```

CHR$(exp): Converts a number to the corresponding ASCII character.
Example: The ASCII code number 7 rings the bell on a teletypewriter or causes a beep on many video terminals. To ring the bell, use CHR$(7) in a PRINT statement, like this: PRINT CHR$(7)

FRE(string variable): Gives the number of free (unused) bytes in the memory's reserved string space. See also FRE function under "Arithmetic Functions."

LEFT$(string, length): Gives the leftmost characters in a string, including the number of characters indicated by the value given for length.
Example:

```
B$ = LEFT$(X$,3)
```

RIGHT$(string, length): Gives the rightmost characters in a string, including the number of characters indicated by the value given for the length.
Example:

```
C$ = RIGHT$(Y$,4)
```

MID$(string, start position)

MID$(string, start position, length): First form gives the portion of the string from the character at the start position to the right end of the string. Second form gives the portion of the string from the character at the start position and including as many more characters toward the right end of the string as indicated by the length value.
Examples:

```
PRINT MID$ (X$,3)
PRINT MID$ (X$,3,5)
```

LEN(string): Gives the number of characters included in the string; spaces are always counted as characters.
Example:

```
FOR K - 1 TO LEN(X$)
```

STR$(exp): Converts a numeric expression to a string. The minus sign in a negative value is included in the string, and the leading space for the assumed "+" in a positive value is included in the string.
Example:

```
B$ = STR$(X*Y)
```

VAL(string): Converts a string representation of a number to a numeric value. String must be numeric character.
Example:

```
X$ = "33.3"
X = VAL(X$)
```

GRAPHICS FUNCTIONS

COLOR= : In low-resolution graphics, COLOR is used to set the color to be plotted by subsequent commands.

GR: Places the Apple into low-resolution graphics mode. The screen is cleared to black (TEXT returns the Apple to text mode).

HLIN: Used to draw horizontal lines in low-resolution graphics mode using the color most recently indicated by a COLOR statement. HLIN 15,30 at 20 will draw a horizontal line at row 20 connecting points 15 and 30.

PLOT x,y: Places a color dot at the screen location specified by x,y.

VLIN: Used to draw vertical lines in low-resolution graphics mode using the color most recently specified by a COLOR statement. VLIN 10,30 at 15 will draw a vertical line in column 15 connecting points 10 through 30.

APPENDIX

ASCII Character Codes

DEC = ASCII decimal code
CHAR = ASCII character name
n/a = not accessible directly from the APPLE II keyboard

DEC	CHAR	WHAT TO TYPE	DEC	CHAR	WHAT TO TYPE
0	NULL	ctrl @	33	!	!
1	SOH	ctrl A	34	"	"
2	STX	ctrl B	35	#	#
3	ETX	ctrl C	36	$	$
4	ET	ctrl D	37	%	%
5	ENQ	ctrl E	38	&	&
6	ACK	ctrl F	39	'	'
7	BEL	ctrl G	40	(	(
8	BS	ctrl H or ←	41	)	)
9	HT	ctrl I	42	*	*
10	LF	ctrl J	43	+	+
11	VT	ctrl K	44	,	,
12	FF	ctrl L	45	−	−
13	CR	ctrl M or RETURN	46	.	.
14	SO	ctrl N	47	/	/
15	SI	ctrl O	48	0	0
16	DLE	ctrl P	49	1	1
17	DC1	ctrl Q	50	2	2
18	DC2	ctrl R	51	3	3
19	DC3	ctrl S	52	4	4
20	DC4	ctrl T	53	5	5
21	NAK	ctrl U or →	54	6	6
22	SYN	ctrl V	55	7	7
23	ETB	ctrl W	56	8	8
24	CAN	ctrl X	57	9	9
25	EM	ctrl Y	58	:	:
26	SUB	ctrl Z	59	;	;
27	ESCAPE	ESC	60	<	<
28	FS	n/a	61	=	=
29	GS	ctrl shift-M	62	>	>
30	RS	ctrl ^	63	?	?
31	US	n/a	64	@	@
32	SPACE	space	65	A	A

DEC	CHAR	WHAT TO TYPE	DEC	CHAR	WHAT TO TYPE
66	B	B	81	Q	Q
67	C	C	82	R	R
68	D	D	83	S	S
69	E	E	84	T	T
70	F	F	85	U	U
71	G	G	86	V	V
72	H	H	87	W	W
73	I	I	88	X	X
74	J	J	89	Y	Y
75	K	K	90	Z	Z
76	L	L	91	[	n/a
77	M	M	92	\	n/a
78	N	N	93	]	] (shift-M)
79	O	O	94	^	^
80	P	P	95	_	n/a

Personal Computing Periodicals of Interest to Apple Users

Applesauce
Box 598
Venice, CA 90291

Apple Orchard
PO Box 1493
Beaverton, OR 97075

BYTE
70 Main Street
Peterborough, NH 03458

Call–A.P.P.L.E
Apple Pugetsound Program Library Exchange
304 Main Ave. S., Suite 300
Renton, WA 98055

Classroom Computer News
P.O. Box 266
Cambridge, MA 02138

Compute Magazine
PO Box 5406
Greensboro, NC 27403

The Computing Teacher
Computing Center
Eastern Oregon State College
La Grande, OR 97850

Courseware Magazine
4919 N. Millbrook, #222
Fresno, CA 93726

Creative Computing
Box 789-M
Morristown, NJ 07960

Electronic Learning
902 Sylvan Ave.
Englewood Cliffs, NJ 07632

Infoworld
375 Cochituate Rd., Rte. 30
Framingham, MA 01701

Interface Age
PO Box 1234
Cerritos, CA 90701

Microcomputing
80 Pine St.
Peterborough, NH 03458

Nibble Magazine
PO Box 325
Lincoln, MA 01773

Peelings II
PO Box 188
Las Cruces, NM 88004

Popular Computing
70 Main St.
Peterborough, NH 03458

Purser's Magazine
Box 466
El Dorado, CA 95623

Recreational Computing
P.O. Box E
Menlo Park, CA 95472

Softalk Magazine
11021 Magnolia Blvd.
No. Hollywood, CA 91601

Softside Magazine
PO Box 68
Milford, NH 03055

Program Index

This Program Index is to help you locate programs that use techniques you want to review. Short demonstration programs are not included in this Index. Programs are listed in the order of first appearance in the text—that is, where a version of the program first appears or starts to be developed, with page numbers indicated for other versions or modifications of the program.

Number Guessing Game, 4–5, 128–31, 211–12 (see also Letter Guessing Game)

Bicycle Wheel Circumference Programs, 51–53, 65–71, 174, 180

Interest on Money Calculations, 54–55, 81, 137, 199

Change of Address Programs, 64, 74–75, 192–93

World's Most Expensive Adding Machine, 76–78, 104–05, 146, 194, 210, 212, 269–276

Temperature Conversion Programs, 88, 94 (see also Metric or U.S. Measurement Conversions)

Simple Checkbook Balancing Program, 90, 94

Metric Measurement Conversions, 91, 95, 144, 145, 164 (see also Metric or U.S. Measurement Conversions)

Addition Practice Programs, 111, 119–27 (see also Complete Arithmetic Drill)

A Friendly "Mean" Program (calculates averages), 106–07, 147, 190–92

Compassionate Multiplication Practice, 134 (see also Complete Arithmetic Drill)

Questionnaire Analysis/Vote Counting Programs, 153–55, 173, 180, 279–85, 302, 306, 313–28, 351–52, 355

Die Roller, 170–71 (see also Dice Roll Counting Program)

Coin Flipper, 175, 176, 180, 181

DATA Statement Item Counter, 177, 181
Pattern Printing Program, 178, 181–82
Multiplication Worksheet, 204–06
Population Growth, 209–10, 212
Theater Marquee (graphics), 224
Ode to the Maya (graphics), 228–30
Block Letters (graphics), 230–34
Red Cross (graphics), 235, 237
American Flag (graphics), 236, 238
Blank Bar Graph 0–100 (graphics), 237–38
String READ/DATA Course List, 241, 250–51
String DATA Home Library List, 242–43
String Telephone Retrieval System, 252, 257–58
Letter Guessing Game, 255–56
Candy Sales Analysis Programs, 258–96, 328–340, 361–63
"Computer Dating" Program, 296–300
"United Collection" Record Keeping, 303, 306
Test Correcting Program, 304, 307
Dice Roll Counting Program, 305, 307
Quiz Answer Analysis Programs, 340–49
Sales Analysis by Style, 352–53, 356
Store Price Comparisons, 354, 356
Random Number Sorting Program, 364–70
Statistical Analysis Programs, 370–88
Complete Arithmetic Drill, 379–82
Stars, A Number Guessing Game, 383–84, 390
Simulation of Matrix Addition, 384–85, 390
Coin Changer Program, 386, 391
Metric or U.S. Measurement Conversions, 387–89, 394–96

Index

Note: Please consult the reference materials from Apple Computer Inc. described on page 9 for information not covered in this text.

ABS, 397
Accumulating statements (*see* Tallying statements)
Accuracy in calculations, 26, 386
Addition, 16, 20–24
Alphanumeric, 239 (*see also* Character)
Apple Reference Manuals, 9
Applesoft BASIC
  described, vii, ix, 1–3
  prompt character (*see* Bracket)
  Reference Manual, 9
Argument, 320
Arithmetic expressions, 16–39, 115, 155–57, 268–69
Arrays (*see also* Variables, subscripted):
  example programs, 272–307, 313–82
  initialization, 280, 287, 291, 316
  one dimensional, 267–72
  two dimensional, 309–13
  string, 292–95
Art, 88, 93, 181–82, 207, 230 (*see also* Graphics, GR, TAB)
ASC, 247–48, 399
ASCII Code Chart, 401–02
Assignment statements, 43–53, 71, 189 (*see also* LET, INPUT, READ, Subscripted variables)
Asterisk (*) 17, 22, 34, 54 (*see also* Multiplication)
ATN, 398
Average, calculation of, 106–07, 147

Back-arrow key (*see* Left arrow key)
Backslash (\\), 15 (*see also* CTRL/X)
Back-space key (*see* Left arrow key)
BASIC (*see* Applesoft BASIC)
Blank PRINT statement, 59, 65–6, 73, 104, 196
Blank spaces, 69, 119, 126, 166–69, 180–81, 185 (*see also* Output positioning techniques)
Block letters, 230–33
Bracket, 9–11, 15, 48–51 omitted, 12, 54
Branching (*see* GOTO, IF . . . THEN)
BREAK message, 62, 70, 72, 75, 116–17, 135, 359
Bugs (*see* ERROR conditions)
Business programs (*see* Program Index)

Calculations (*see* Evaluating expressions)
Calculator mode (*see* Direct mode)
Cancel (*see* CTRL/X)
Carriage return, 65, 119, 126, 171–72, 188–89, 196 (*see also* RETURN key supressing)
Cassette recorder, 2
CATALOG, 79
Celsius, 88, 94, 387–89, 394–96
Character
  ASCII codes, 247–49, 401–02
  count, 240 (*see also* LEN)
  defined, 12
  positions, 157–67, 253 (*see also* MID$, LEFT$, RIGHT$)
CHR$, 247–49, 399
Clear memory (*see* NEW)
Colon (:), 97, 126–27
Command (*see* LIST, NEW, RUN)
Comma separators
  for DATA items, 143
  for INPUT entries, 59, 72–5
  for INPUT variables, 73–4
  in PRINT statements, 72, 75, 262
  for READ variables, 150–51

Comma spacing, 155–66 (*see also* PRINT, Output format techniques)
Commas imbedded in strings, 72, 75, 262
Comparison symbols, 97, 101, 130 (*see also* IF . . . THEN)
Computation (*see* Evaluating expressions)
Computer language (*see* Applesoft BASIC)
Conditional branching (*see* IF . . . THEN)
Constants, numeric, 42–5, 83–5 (*see also* Strings)
CONTROL/C(*see* CTRL/C)
Control variable, 186–89, 191, 195–97, 209, 367 (*see also* FOR)
Coordinates (*see* Grid, PLOT, HLIN, VLIN)
Corrections (*see* Error corrections)
COS, 398
Counting statements (*see* Tallying statements)
CTRL/C, 62–5, 75, 109
CTRL/X, 15, 35
Cursor, 9, 10, 213 (*see also* Bracket)

Data, 57, 250
DATA, 142–52
  with mixed items, 250–51
  with numeric values, 142–55
  with string items, 167–69
Dataname (*see* Variables)
Debugging (*see* Error conditions)
Delayed execution (*see* Statement, Line number)
Deleting characters, 13 (*see also* Left arrow key)
Deleting program lines, 82, 125–27, 155 (*see also* CTRL/X)
Delimiters (*see* Commas as separators, Quotation marks, FOR)

407

DIM (Dimension), 272–74, 315–16, 331, 341, 345–46
Direct assignment statement, 43–5 (see also LET)
Direct mode, 9, 11, 188
Directory (see CATALOG)
Direct statements, 11–35, 42–55 (see also Line number)
Disk, 4, 78–9
Disk drive, vii, 2–4, 78–9
Display, 2–4, 6, 8, 9, 82–83, 156–66
Division, 18–24
Documentation, 64, 120, 147 (see also REM)
Dollar sign ($) (see Variables, string)
DOS, 78–9
Doubly subscripted variables (see Two-dimensional arrays)
E+ (see Floating point notation)
Editing
  deleting program lines, 82, 125–27, 155
  erasing mistakes 13–15, 52
Empty PRINT statement (see Blank PRINT statement)
Empty string (see Null string)
END, 135, 359
End of data flag (see Flag)
Entry errors (see Error corrections)
Erase memory (see NEW)
Erasing mistakes (see Error corrections)
Error
  corrections, 11, 13–15, 52–53
  messages, 10, 15, 72, 117, 142, 147, 217, 282, 286 (see also The Applesoft Reference Manual)
Error conditions, 52, 84–5, 93, 117, 219, 272 (see also Error messages)
Evaluating expressions, 16–27, 115, 155–57, 268–69
Execute (see RUN)
EXP, 397
Exponent, 24–7 (see also Floating point notation)

Exponentiation, 24–7, 35–6, 54–5, 205
Expressions, 115, 155 (see also Evaluating expressions)

Fahrenheit, 88, 94, 387–89, 394–96
False (see IF . . . THEN)
Filter, 108, 130, 132 (see also IF . . . THEN)
Flag, 104–07, 147, 152, 177, 250–51, 286, 344
Flashing cursor (see Cursor)
Floating point BASIC (see Applesoft BASIC)
Floating point notation, 28–33, 36, 42, 143
FOR, 184–211, 222, 270 (see also Loops)
FP BASIC (see Applesoft BASIC)
FRE, 397, 399
Function Reference List, 397
Functions
  definition, 109, 115

GOSUB, 359–63
GOTO, 61–70, 79–80, 102–03, 129, 184
GR, 213, 400
Graph, 214, 238
Graphics
  high resolution, 234
  low resolution, 213–37
  text window, 217–18, 233
Graphics tablet, 234
Grid for lo-res graphics, 214

Headings, 162, 165–66, 173, 208–12, 289–90, 318, 322–28, 349
Hi-res graphics, 234
HLIN, 226–34, 400
HOME, 218, 221, 340, 356
HTAB, 398
IF . . . GOTO (see IF . . . THEN)
IF . . . THEN, 97–108, 120, 129–30, 135, 148–49, 243–52
  condition or comparison symbols, 97, 101, 245
Immediate mode (see Direct mode)
Inclusive, 116–17
Index to Programs, 405

Indirect statement, 47–9, (see also Program, Line number)
Infinite loops (see Loops)
Initializing
  arrays, 280, 287, 291, 316 (see DIM)
  disks, 78
  variables, 76, 80, 275
INPUT, 56–60, 119, 126, 135
  entry tests, 135, 243, 261
  in loops, 76, 104, 191–92, 194
  multiple INPUT variables, 58–60, 73–5, 240–44
  prompt (message) string, 67–8
  question marks, 56–61, 68, 82
  variables, 82
Input/Output device (see Display, Keyboard, Printer)
Instruction (see also Statement, Program, Direct mode)
INT, 7, 114–19, 122–27, 211, 306, 398
Integer BASIC, vii
Interest calculations (see Program Index)
Invisible string (see Null string)
Iteration, (see Loops, FOR)

Keyboard, 2–4, 9
  diagrams, 10, 25

Label (see Variable)
Left arrow key, 13–15, 52
LEFT$, 257, 399
LEN, 259–61, 102–03
Length of a string (see LEN)
LET, 42–55, 60, 102–03, 131
  omitted or implied, 44–45, 103
Line feed, 65, 119 (see also RETURN key, ASCII Code Chart)
Line length (see also Character positions, Displays)
Line number, 6, 47–49 (see also GOTO, GOSUB, ON . . . GOTO, IF . . . THEN)

INDEX

LIST, 49–53, 66, 217–18, 221
List (see One-dimensional array)
LOAD, 4, 78–79, 223
Lo-res (see GR)
Logical operators (see Operators, IF . . . THEN)
Loops (see also FOR, Tallying statements):
   FOR-NEXT, 183–212, 270–71, 277–78, 287, 367
   GOTO, 62–64, 76–77, 80–81, 99–100, 104, 135, 142, 183, 222–25
   infinite, 63–64 (see also GOTO, CTRL/C)
   nested, 200–203, 266–67 (see also FOR, Two-dimensional array)
Low-resolution graphics, 213–38

Main program (see GOSUB)
Magazines, 403–04
Mantissa, 28–33 (see also Floating point notation)
Matrix, 311 (see also Two-dimensional arrays)
Memory, vii, 2, 48–50, 234
Message string (see INPUT prompt string)
Metric conversions, 389 (see also Program Index)
Microsoft BASIC, vii, 2
MID$, 253–61, 399
Minus sign, 16–17
Mistakes (see Error corrections)
Monitor, 2–3, 215 (see also Display)
Multiple READ variables, 150–52
Multiple statement program lines, 126–27, 184, 284
Multiplication, 17, 20–24

Nested loops, 200–01, 203, 220–21, 316 (see also FOR, Arrays)
NEW, 48–49, 54, 56
NEXT, 184–87, 198, 202, 271 (see also FOR)
Non-entries (see INPUT)

Null string, 59–60, 73–74, 82
Numeric value (see Value)
Numeric variable (see Variable)

ON . . . GOSUB (see GOSUB, ON . . . GOTO)
ON . . . GOTO, 124–27, 170–71
One-dimensional arrays, 267–72
Operators
   arithmetic, 20–26
   precedence of, 20–26
   relational, 97, 101
   string, 245–46
Order of evaluation in arithmetic, 20–26
Out of data error message, 142, 147, 250
Output format techniques (see PRINT, Commas, Semicolons, Blank PRINT statements, TAB, HTAB, VTAB, SPC, PRINT USING

Parentheses, 22–27, 114–17, 266
Periodicals, 403–04
Peripheral devices, 2
PLOT, 216–25, 400
Power (see Exponentiation)
PR #, 64
Precedence, Rules of, 20–26 (see also Parentheses)
Press RETURN To Continue, 82–3
Prettyprinting (see Output format techniques)
PRINT statement, 11–28, 33, 43, 45 (see also Output format techniques):
   ? (abbreviation for PRINT), 27–28, 33, 43, 45
   blank lines, 65–66, 104
   commas in, 72, 75, 155–66, 262
   numeric expressions, 16–27
   numeric values as strings (see CHR$, STR$, VAL, ASC)
   semicolons in, 119
   strings (see Strings)
Printer, 2–4, 8, 64, 83 (see also Display)

Printing a heading (see Headings)
Print positions and zones, 156–66, (see also Output format techniques)
PRINT USING (see Applesoft Reference Manual)
Problems (see Self-tests, Program Index)
Program, 4–8, 47–49 (see also Line numbers)
Program examples (see Program Index)
Program Index, 405
Program loading (see LOAD)
Prompt character, 56 (see also Bracket, INPUT question mark)
Prompt string or message, 5, 67–68 (see also INPUT)

Question mark, 9, 27–28, 56–61, 68, 82, 119 (see also PRINT, INPUT)
Quotation marks, 6, 12, 67–72, 119, 169, 262 (see also DATA, INPUT, Strings)

Random digits, 111–19
Random integers, 111–19, 122, 128, 131, 205, 212, 229
Random numbers (see RND)
READ, 142–55, 294 (see also DATA, RESTORE)
Recursion, 198 (see also FOR, GOSUB)
Relational expressions (see IF . . . THEN)
Relational operators (see Operators, IF . . . THEN)
Replacing program lines, 52–53, 55
Replacing variable values, 42–43, 55
Reserved words, 84–85
RESTORE, 239, 250–52 (see also READ, DATA)
RETURN, 357–59 (see also GOSUB)
RETURN key, 10–11, 47–51, 54, 56, 61
RIGHT$, 257, 399
RND (Pseudo-random number generator), 109–19, 122, 398
RUN, 4–5, 7–8, 50–53

SAVE, 78–79, 127, 222, 230
Scientific notation (see Floating point notation)
Scratch (see NEW)
Screen (see Display)
Screen formatting (see Output format techniques)
Scroll, 217
Self-tests
  Ch. 1, 8
  Ch. 2, 34–9
  Ch. 3, 85–95
  Ch. 4, 136–40
  Ch. 5, 171–82
  Ch. 6, 206–12
  Ch. 7, 235–38
  Ch. 8, 261–64
  Ch. 9, 301–07
  Ch. 10, 350–56
  Ch. 11, 379–82
  Final, 383–96
Semicolon
  in INPUT statements, 67
  spacing in PRINT statements, 119, 166–69, 321
  to suppress carriage return/line feed, 119, 126, 171–72, 189, 196, 368
SGN, 398
Simulation, 138, 170–71, 175–76, 180–81, 384–85, 390
SIN, 398
Singly subscripted variables (see One-dimensional arrays)
Slash (/) (see Division)
Slowing rate of display, 82–83, 109
Sorting, 364–69
Spaces
  in DATA string, 169
  in LISTings, 126
  in strings, 69, 119, 126, 166–69, 180–81, 185
SPC, 399 (see also TAB, Output format techniques)
SPEED=, 83, 109
SQR (Square root), 398
Statement (see also Direct mode, Line numbers):

defined, 6, 10–11, 47–49
direct or immediate mode, 11–33, 43–48
Statistics, 370–81
STEP, 196–99
STOP, 135, 359
Stored program, 47–51
Strings, 12 (see also Substrings):
  in arrays, 292–95
  comparisons, 243–46, 249–51
  commas included in, 72, 75, 262
  constants, 12, 115, 119
  length (character count) (see LEN)
  maximum length, 69
  null string,
  spaces in, 69, 119, 245, 249
  variables, 45–46, 239–40
STR$, 244–45, 400
Subroutines (see GOSUB)
Subscripted variables, 265–69, 309–14
Substrings, 253 (see also LEFT$, RIGHT$, MID$)
Subtraction, 16–17, 34
Superscript, 24–25
Suppressed carriage return/line feed, 119, 126, 171–72, 188–89, 196
Suppressed INPUT question marks, 82
Symbols (see Operators)
Syntax, 10–11
Syntax error message, 10–11
System prompt (see Prompt character, Bracket)

TAB, 319–28, 339–40 (see also Output format techniques)
Table (see Two-dimensional Array, Output format techniques)
Tallying statements 76–81, 104–06, 146–47, 153–54, 183–84, 191, 269–71, 280–81, 288, 290, 316–17, 332
TAN, 398
Television, 2–3 (see also Display)

Terminal (see Display, Keyboard, Printer)
TEXT, 213, 218
Text window, 217–18, 233
Time delay (see also SPEED=, Press RETURN to Continue using FOR-NEXT, 222–23)
Trap (see Flag, IF . . . THEN)
True (see IF . . . THEN)
Truncation (see INT)
TV, 2–3 (see also Display)
Two-dimensional arrays, 309–49
Typing errors (see Error corrections)

Up arrow, 25 (see also Exponentiation)
User friendly, 120, 133
User's groups, 234

VAL, 244–45, 400
Values, 42–45, 115
Variable (see also Values, INPUT, READ, LET):
  assigning values, 43–45, 56–60
  defined, 42–46, 83–85, 115, 255–56
  initial value (see Initializing)
  integer (see Apple's Reference Manuals)
  names, 83–85
  numeric, 42–45, 83–85
  string, 45–46, 60, 83–85, 239–41
  subscripted, 265–69, 301, 309 (see also Arrays)
Vector (see One-dimensional arrays)
Video black, 215
Video display (see Display)
VLIN, 226–38, 400
Vote Counting Programs (see Program Index)
VTAB, 398

Wash, 220–21, 227
Wraparound, 69

Note: Please consult the reference materials from Apple Computer Inc. described on page 9 for information not covered in this text.